INSIGHT GUIDES

Malta

Edited by Geoffrey Aquilina Ross
Principal Photography: Lyle Lawson

Editorial Director: Brian Bell

APA PUBLICATIONS
Part of the Langenscheidt Publishing Group

ABOUT THIS BOOK

The Maltese Islands are not quite like any others. These are islands where contrasts are made all the more visible because they are contained in so small an area. Considerable new wealth rubs shoulders with a simple, hardworking rural lifestyle; crowded town development threatens unspoiled countryside; and everywhere there appears to be building or rebuilding. It is a familiar scenario for any nation determined to succeed in the modern world.

The editor of the book, **Geoffrey Aquilina Ross**, is a prominent Maltese journalist who, dividing his time between Malta and London, has edited magazines, written countless travel articles and authored several books. The son of Malta's best known composer of band marches, Major Anthony Aquilina, he is also a fan of Maltese music. It was his editorial talents, however, perfectly attuned to the photojournalism approach pioneered by Apa Publications, which led to his appointment as editor of this book.

Ross maintains a watchful eye on the book and keeps the current edition upto date.

Like all Insight Guides, this book owes much to superb photography. The images here are mostly the work of inveterate world traveller **Lyle Lawson**. An American who lives in England, she was editor and photographer of Apa's *Waterways of Europe*, and has contributed to many Insight Guides. To see as much of the islands as possible, she took helicopter rides, climbed towering cranes in the dockyards and worked exceedingly unsocial hours. The Maltese, she soon discovered, are an exceptionally obliging people.

Rowlinson Carter, another Apa regular, is a journalist with his roots in philosophy and history. For this book, he was carried along by the islands' history, charting the sweeps and changes of power in the Mediterranean as each conqering nation arrived.

At home in Gozo is **Ann Monsarrat**, who contributed the Gozo section. Trained as a journalist in the UK on a Kent newspaper, she graduated to London's *Daily Mail*. In 1961 she married the writer Nicholas Monsarrat and lived with him in Canada, Barbados and Guernsey before arriving in Gozo in 1969, intending to stay only long enough for him to finish his novel *The Kapillan of Malta*. She has been resident ever since and is, she says, addicted to the island and its people. She has written two books, a history of wedding customs and a biography of the Victorian novelist William Makepeace Thackeray, and is working on another.

Maud Ruston also came visiting only to find she had settled in Attard with her husband a short distance from the pealing bells of the parish church. Discovering *Malti* to be impenetrable and nothing like the languages she already spoke, she decided to study the tongue and planned to speak it with the Maltese rather than English. "After much study," she began translating from *Malti* into English and is the translator of two books and a number of short stories by the eminent Maltese writer Guzi Chetcuti.

Deborah Wald, who helped compile the Travel Tips section, is a London magazine journalist. Although much travelled through Europe, the Middle East and America, she made her first visit to the islands for this book and now claims, having braved the eccentric driving habits on the roads, to know the islands better than any other place. Yes, she admits, she found the peo-

Aquilina Ross

Lawson

Carter

Monsarrat

Ruston

Wald

Montanaro

Ellul

ple charming; never be afraid to ask for help. The Maltese, she writes, have given the islands a warmth and genuine honesty quite unexpected.

Reflecting on World War II, the British period and the islands' future is **Anthony Montanaro**. Having given up reading law to join *Il-Berqa*, a Maltese language daily, he became its editor and, from 1966 to 1991 he edited the English-language *Sunday Times*.

Michael Ellul contributes information on the incomparable architectural treasures contained in the Palace of the Grand Masters and the cathedrals of Valletta and Mdina, about which he is passionate in his enthusiasm. An architect and architectural historian, he is advisor to the Prime Minister on Conservation and the National Archives with offices at Auberge de Castille. Among his books is *History of St Elmo.*

Another expert contributor to the architectural assessment was **Leonard Mahoney**. Now deceased, he was the author of the *History of Maltese Architecture*, published in Malta. An architect and engineer, Mahoney brought enormous authority to a discussion of Maltese architecture.

Writing about Comino is **Eric Gerada-Azzopardi**, managing director in London of one of Air Malta's tour operating companies. After a brief career as an officer with the Royal Malta Artillery, he entered Malta's diplomatic service and then, changing course, moved first to Air Malta, then became an author. He has written two books: *Malta – An Island Republic* and *Malta Revisited.*

Nicholas de Piro was born in Malta but educated in England by Benedictine monks and had his interests in art stimulated by regular visits to Florence at an early age. His roots, however, remain in Malta. Among his published books is *The International Dictionary of Artists Who Painted Malta.* He has opened Casa Roca, an historic, patrician house in Valletta for visitors.

Analysing religion in Malta – where Catholicism still plays an important if, in common with many other Catholic countries, less dominating part in everyday life – is **Peter Serracino Inglott**, the former Pro-Rector of the University of Malta. An outspoken figure known simply as Father Peter, he is involved with many international institutions and journals.

Writing about daily life is **Daphne Caruana Galizia** who combines raising three boisterous sons with contributing a weekly column to *The Malta Independent* and writing features for the other English language newspapers.

A strong contribution to the book's photography content was made by **Bob Krist,** an American photographer known for his work with *National Geographic* magazine. Also contributing were two Maltese photographers: **Eddie Aquilina**, whose local company handles some of Malta's premier advertising accounts as well as publishing books and magazines, and **Daniel Cilia**, a young award-winning photographer born in Gozo but currently based in Florence. Cilia has made home-life in Gozo his study.

Mahoney

The editor wishes to thank officials of the Malta National Tourist Office in London and Malta for their help, in particular **Leslie Agius** and **Connie Grech**. The original book's production was supervised by **Jill Anderson** and proof-reading and indexing were handled by **Christopher Catling**.

CONTENTS

Preceding pages: bow of a traditional Luzzu fishing boat with eyes to see and ward off evil; a watchtower; Ta' Pinu National Shrine, Gozo.

TRAVEL TIPS

It hardly seems credible that in the long and chequered history of the islands the Maltese should have remained so steadfastly themselves, a proud nation distinct from any other. But they have, and they would have it no other way.

In spite of being conquered, subjugated and led over the centuries by the powerful nations of the times – and with faces that even now reflect some of that past with features recalling the Romans, Arabs and Phoenicians – the Maltese have doggedly clung to insular individuality. With roots planted firmly in a group of tiny islands, whose total area adds up to no more than 316 sq. km (122 sq. miles), there is a strong sense of identity born out of a mixture of self-preservation and stubbornness, qualities the Maltese have in abundance. The same applies to Maltese emigrants settled abroad.

An estimated 350,000 Maltese live in Malta and Gozo, with about an equal number in Australia, Canada, the United Kingdom and the United States. These are the emigrants and families of emigrants who set sail for the lands of golden promise in the expansive days of migration at the end of World War II when hope was offered to poorer communities. Many, homesick after making their fortunes in a modest manner, return to build modern villas that are named in fond memory of chances given: Villa Wallaby, Melbourne Court, Brentford House, Casa Orlando and, simply, Bondi. The islands have that kind of draw.

Greener land: The term Maltese embraces the people of both Malta and Gozo, although Gozitans are always quick to point out that they come from a far sweeter and greener land. Comino, the only other inhabited island in this archipelago, has nothing but its sporty hotel complex.

To their surprise, many outsiders who

Preceding pages: Birzebbuga in the evening; Fort St Angelo and Senglea across the Grand Harbour from Valletta; St Paul's Island and a statue of St Paul; Ghajn Tuffieha ridge in springtime; Mdina school break; morning of the band parade at Hamrun *festa*. **Left,** a grandmother's love. **Right,** Baron Trapani Galea Ferriol and family outside their home.

have married a Maltese have found that it is they who adapt to a Maltese way of life, wherever they live, rarely the other way round. Man or woman, they accommodate; they find they quickly become part of the extended Maltese family and adapt to its customs. Even when living abroad, they return with their new families whenever they can to their adoptive homes. Undoubtedly the subconscious spirit behind this urge is another facet of the Maltese sense of self-preservation.

Of course, this may be helped by the fact that the Maltese, almost without exception, are gregarious, friendly and welcoming to foreigners – if not to each other. Ask any tourist what first appeals to them about the islands and the answer will always be the people. The Maltese love the opportunity to be generous, especially if it is during the parish *festa* when the patron saint is celebrated. Even in the simplest rural community they enjoy being hospitable and sharing what they have, a whisky, a cold drink, a cup of tea, their friendship.

The Maltese are proud of their homes. These are spotlessly clean inside, with patterned marble tiled floors gleaming, everything in its prescribed place. Almost everyone, whatever their social level, maintains a formal sitting room, to be used only when guests are invited to the house. It is here that wealth and social achievement can be demonstrated. Even in the most unsophisticated villages, these rooms will have furniture made to order, sofas and armchairs and wall units to hold pieces of whimsical china figurines and framed pictures. Close by will be drinks to offer guests – most likely Johnnie Walker or Chivas Regal, Martini and Aperol, the least alcoholic of aperitifs. It is acceptable for a visitor to request a soft drink, although it gives far greater pleasure

ing returned to its former architectural glory.

But other equally important aesthetic considerations are regarded as of lesser consequence. Beauty spots and sweeping panoramas are under threat. Perhaps it is because the Maltese see new building, or rebuilding, as an object of envy, as putting money to conspicuous use. Elegant turn-of-the-century seafront villas are flattened to make way for faceless blocks of apartments, housing estates or factories are built on valuable arable land, and villas or holiday compounds appear where the landscape is picturesque and unspoiled. No land is sacred. Like all Latin countries, it is who you know that matters if you want to bend the rules.

to the hosts if a man accepts whisky. That a guest accepts hospitality is what matters.

But if the houses are clean, often the streets are not. Although there is an efficient daily refuse collection, and special services for removing household items like old mattresses or rusting refrigerators, old habits die hard. Refuse tipping still occurs. However, the government has been trying, through television campaigns, to create pride in the environment and, thanks to better organised teams of sweepers, the streets, after years of neglect, are rapidly becoming among the cleanest in Europe. Money is being spent on the infrastructure and Valletta is finally be-

The landscape of the islands is characterised by low hills and terraced fields and it is a pleasing, if surprising, fact that even in built-up Malta (as opposed to greener Gozo) there is so much greenery outside the major conurbations. In spring wild flowers run riot, a mixture of yellow, red and crimson, a beautiful backdrop to the historical splendour and to the coastline with its bays, creeks and rocky coves.

Yet trees lining the roads are ruthlessly pruned, stone pavements are replaced with concrete, and roads are driven through open countryside so that ribbon housing development can be built shamelessly along them. It is as if a wicked genie lacking any aesthetic sense were roaming the land.

When the Nationalist government decided to erect a new electricity generating station, they chose to site it at a pretty waterside section of Marsaxlokk Bay adjacent to some excellent rock beaches. No one can claim it enhances what was once a beauty spot. The fact that the site is also outside the windows of the previous (opposition) prime minister's summer house may be relevant.

It is no secret that politics play an important part in daily life. All Maltese are politically aware and, because party allegiances are known and rewarded, business people expect to do better when their side is in

the faithful, and a change of government can usually be attributed to a significant shift in the numbers of new first-time voters, to deaths in the ranks of the old faithful and to the movement of the district boundaries (a favourite manoeuvre of both parties at election time). The Maltese system of voting is proportional representation.

For many years the Church had played a key role in life, both secular and political, making its views known on all key issues as well as running many of the better schools. In election years parish priests often exhorted congregations during Sunday homilies to place their votes with the Nationalist party.

But, as has happened elsewhere in Europe,

power. As the parties change, so do the people in key positions in the civil service and in government-run organisations. Bureaucratic power changes hands; new ropes are oiled. On a more human level it is not unusual either in some neighbourhoods for a particular shop to be boycotted by some because its owner supports the other party. (There are only two to choose from, Nationalist or Labour.) Maltese are born to a party and no amount of rhetoric will change that allegiance. Politicians, therefore, preach to

the sway of the Church has become less important. Although the parish *festa* (a religious celebration wrapped into a social occasion) can still be the most important event on the annual calendar, and although Pope John Paul paid a memorable visit in 1990, many of the faithful no longer attend Mass.

Topless bathing: However, there may be an opportunity for spiritual rebirth. No longer can all the clergy be charged with being narrow-minded or bigoted. Contraception and abortion are accepted subjects for discussion and, while the clergy may insist on decorum in dress, on the streets as well as when visiting churches, topless bathing is

<u>Left</u>, time now for reminiscence at Xewkija.
<u>Above</u>, just married and time for champagne.

tolerated on some beaches. However, nude bathing is strictly against the law and may well lead to prosecution. Still, the islands have come a long way since the days when girls were whisked away by police for wearing bikinis.

Life moves with the times, too, the good coming with the bad. Since the increase of tourism and the arrival of the widest variety of visitors, so the drug problem has surfaced in the young set. Cases of Aids have been registered.

But the Maltese, although industrious, seem determined to enjoy life to the full. Almost without exception, they delight in a party or wedding and seize any opportunity

to gossip, to tell jokes, to laugh. There is a ribald sense of humour devoted, for the most part, to *double entendre*. *Malti* may be an unsophisticated language but it gives ample opportunity for double meanings.

On the minus side, the Maltese, in true Latin tradition, can be hard on each other, prone to jealousy and quick to take advantage or pick a quarrel. A crossed Maltese stays crossed and, although thrifty by nature, the Maltese also enjoy gambling. The weekly government lottery succeeds because of thousands of small stakes. There are often neighbourhood raffles in the smaller towns and villages at weekends where a few cents will buy a ticket that could win the Saturday prize of a pair of rabbits or a brace of cockerels.

Conspicuous wealth has its place, too, especially in clothes and jewellery. Wealth in the home, however, is kept concealed behind doors, away from prying eyes and the temptation of burglars. In many patrician houses there are reputed to be collections of paintings and silver that would fetch stupendous prices at any international auction. This wealth sometimes leads to problems with inheritance and provokes inter-family quarrels. Many a grand house is falling to ruin because sons cannot agree about its disposal and many a daughter tells of receiving nothing in settlement.

As for cars, these are a Maltese passion – whatever their age. On the roads are revered, expensive roadsters too fast for any country and cars that belch enveloping clouds of black fumes, cars that would fail any roadworthiness test. Family saloons from the 1950s and '60s, patched and rusting, can find buyers as long as they move. What all have in common is the style in which they are driven: erratically. Driving here is an adventure – even for the Maltese.

Dodgem cars: There *is* a highway code, which indicates, *inter alia*, that traffic is to be driven on the left, in the British manner. Quite often this rule is adhered to, but you are just as likely to find cars, vans and trucks in the centre of the road, or simply where the shade is, or where there are no potholes. As of habit, drivers overtake on the inside and reverse into main roads. If they judge the route to be shorter, some may choose to drive on the wrong side of a dual carriageway or even the wrong way around a roundabout. As a consolation to the visitor, however, the cost of participating in this excitement is low: car hire rates are among the most competitive in Europe.

What of the future? Business is booming and the number of tourists arriving in any one year now exceeds the local population. The nation's airline, Air Malta, is buying more planes and flying to further destinations. To the Maltese, prospects have seldom looked rosier.

<u>Above</u>, Mosta parish priest in social conversation. <u>Right</u>, hot and crusty, Maltese bread straight from the baker's oven.

The knights of the Order of St John of Jerusalem were once the most fabulous figures in Christendom, heroes who at heart deplored violence but were more than capable, as a last resort against unspeakable evil, to climb into suits of armour and prove their worth. Although the Order later became almost synonymous with Malta, it was actually formed in about 1085 as the Hospitallers, a community of monks set up to nurse Christians who fell ill while on pilgrimage in the Holy Land; in that capacity they survive in Britain as the St John Ambulance Brigade, the selfless volunteers who drive ambulances and provide first-aid at sporting events and in theatres.

As pilgrims came under attack in the 11th century, however, they needed physical protection rather than cures for minor ailments, and young knights were recruited specifically to provide that protection.

The fighting knights were drawn from aristocratic families in France, Italy, Spain, Portugal and England. Nobility was an essential qualification for knighthood, and even the lesser ranks and servants had to prove that their family background was "respectable". This was not considered to be ordinary, mercenary work. "To volunteer in a Crusade against the Infidels with the Muslims in possession of the Holy Land", says E.W. Schermerhorn in her masterful history of the Order, *Malta of the Knights*, "aside from the great service rendered to Christianity, and the safe and sure place it promised in the world to come, was the sport *par excellence* of the Middle Ages".

Bending the rules: Ambitious parents put a son's name forward for the Order as soon as he was born and paid the hefty registration fees while he was still an infant. Popes tried to bend the rules of membership to get their sons in; one of the rules was that an applicant's pedigree on both sides of the family should not have been blemished by illegitimacy for several generations, a problematic

condition for some popes at that time.

The vows of celibacy, poverty and obedience required of the knights on acceptance were also problematical, especially, it seems, celibacy. Some knights begged for a formal release from the vow to rescue their noble names from threatened extinction. Others simply took matters into their own hands – quietly at first, blatantly later – whether or not there was any shortage of heirs in the family pipeline. The lax interpretation of vows evoked one of Edward Gib-

bon's celebrated epigrams. The knights, he wrote, "neglected to live, but were prepared to die, in the service of Christ".

The rising tide of Islam eventually drove the knights out of the Holy Land. They regrouped on the island of Rhodes, turned it into a stronghold and from there sailed in their fleet of resplendent galleys to harry the Infidel. Leadership of the Islamic world, however, had passed to the Ottoman Turks and Rhodes, just off the Turkish coast, was for them an intolerable provocation. "That abode of the Sons of Satan" was one of numerous unflattering terms of Turkish reference for Rhodes. Ottoman forces seized

Preceding pages: armour in the Palace of the Grand Masters, Valletta. **Left**, the Palace Corridor. **Above**, Grand Master Manoel de Vilhena (1722–36), patron of Manoel Theatre.

Constantinople in 1453 and Belgrade in 1520. The whole of Europe knew Rhodes would be next, but when the assault came "no Christian King lifted a finger; all were too busy killing each other."

The opposing commanders in the battle for Rhodes, which raged for six months, were Suleiman the Magnificent, greatest of all the sultans, and, for the knights, Philippe Villiers de L'Isle-Adam, "tall, lithe, graceful, alert, with delicately sensitive face, high cheek-bones, an aristocratic aquiline nose, soft, flowing white beard and hair... the embodiment of the soldier and gentleman." Rhodes fell. The distraught Grand Master was in his seventies. "It is not without some

who, as Charles V, was also Holy Roman Emperor and therefore the symbol of almost everything the knights stood for. Nor could he bear the thought of having to accept the disbandment of Christendom's most prestigious fighting force in such ignominious circumstances. A new home had to be found for them. He had, as it were, a couple of surplus properties in his inheritance. One was Tripoli, capital of what is now Libya, the other consisted of the islands of Malta.

The knights were familiar with Tripoli as a beleaguered Christian outpost among notoriously hostile natives and the worst kind of Barbary Coast pirate. Needing more information about the comparatively unknown

degree of pain", the victorious Sultan sighed, "that I force this Christian, at his time of life, to leave his dwelling".

The defeated knights were allowed a dignified departure with all their possessions, not least St John the Baptist's hand, a cherished relic. The Greek inhabitants had misgivings about remaining on Rhodes under Turkish rule, so 100 families were given places in the Christian galleys. As Suleiman suspected, however, the knights had no idea where they were going.

The prospect of these illustrious veterans adrift in the Mediterranean was more than could be countenanced by the King of Spain

Malta, the knights sent commissioners to look into what was on offer.

Malta, they reported disdainfully, was "merely a rock of a soft sandstone... scarcely covered with more than three or four feet of earth... no running water, nor even wells... wood was so scarce as to be sold by the pound... about 12,000 inhabitants, of both sexes; the greatest part of whom were poor and miserable." In short, "a residence in Malta appeared extremely disagreeable – indeed, almost insupportable – particularly in summer".

Tripoli, however, was even worse. Malta it would be. But the arrangements were not finalised for seven years, by which time the shiploads of knights with their servants and their Greek passengers were understandably "battling with pestilence, poverty and discouragement."

Human detritus: The arrival of the knights and hapless Greeks put Malta under the spotlight of Europe for the first time. The 12,000 poor inhabitants of the islands were regarded, in so far as they were given any consideration at all, as the human detritus of a vaguely perceived concoction of Phoenicians, Arabs, Norman princes and diverse vagabonds.

One of the results, according to the knights' commissioners, was that the inhabi-

to learn the language, dismissing it as a "perfidious idiom" offensive to the ear.

Charles V was not inclined to waste much time over the Maltese either. A document preserved in the National Library in Valletta records his gift of Malta to the knights. "In order that they may perform in peace the duties of their Religion for the benefit of the Christian community, and employ their forces and arms against the perfidious enemies of the Holy Faith, we have voluntarily determined on granting them a fixed home out of the particular affection we bear the Order, that they may no longer by necessity be compelled to wander about the world..."

As for the inhabitants, "all who may now

Vèrdala essendo Governatore dell'Artiglieria accresce e risarcisce gli strumenti di guerra, e si diporta in que sta carica con universale soddisfazione l'anno 1561.

Vèrdala amministrando in convento molte e principali cariche, con somma diligenza e intiera fedeltà,viene eletto ricevitore e procuratore,del comun tesoro per Tolosa

tants had been left speaking "a sort of Moorish". The true nature of the language was later to provoke intense academic speculation. Until that happened, a typical assessment of the language was that it made the islanders sound "more rough than they really are, it being much akin to Turkish". The Italian knight who passed this opinion was no scholar: he believed, for example, that Arabs and Turks were one and the same people. Like most knights, he made no effort

Left, a superb collection of armour in the Palace Armoury. **Above**, fresco scene of a Grand Master's life, Verdala Palace.

be dwelling or shall hereafter dwell in said islands... shall receive and consider the said Grand Master as their true and feudal lord... and shall perform and obey his behests as good and faithful vassals should always obey their lord".

The barefooted fishermen and peasants of Malta welcomed the influx of knights as prospective employers and customers and as protectors against Barbary Coast corsairs who routinely raided the islands as an easy source of slave labour, but the local nobility were not at all keen on being displaced by a superior force enjoying a special relationship with the Pope and Holy Roman Emperor. Moreover, they had secured from one of Charles's predecessors a guarantee that Malta would not be passed around the Crowns and Dukedoms like a parcel, a guarantee that was now being ignored.

In spite of the sullen reservations of the indigenous ruling class, the face of Malta was transformed. Before, it had been little more than a small fishing village, the Borgo, an old fort called St Angelo and an "old deserted town" in the interior, a description which did not flatter the local notables, who happened to live there. Accommodation had to be found or built immediately for several thousand newcomers, with no less urgency attached to the construction of defences ca-

graphical extent, the number of the population or its material sources".

Napoleon rated Malta's importance no less highly. During the lull in Anglo-French hostilities after the Treaty of Amiens, Britain offered to leave Malta if France evacuated the Netherlands and Switzerland. Napoleon replied that the Netherlands and Switzerland were "mere trifles" in comparison with Malta. "I would put you in possession of the Faubourg Saint Antoine [an abbey on the outskirts of Paris] rather than of Malta." It was in fact largely over Malta that the war was resumed and not settled until Waterloo.

The apparent suddenness, historically speaking, of Malta's rise from obscurity

pable of withstanding a repeat of the attack by the shadowing Ottoman troops.

The onslaught of the Ottoman Turks when it came accelerated Malta's new-found fame as the bastion of religious knights who had "the chivalric duty of helping mankind", so much so that Voltaire remarked that "nothing is better known than the siege of Malta."

Some of the fame might have worn off in the two centuries that followed the siege, but Malta's military importance was, if anything, enhanced. British strategists, when contemplating the threat posed by Napoleon, concluded that Malta had "a significance to the Empire out of proportion to its geo-

turned out to be misleading. Perhaps almost nothing of note had happened on the island during 1,000 years or so of Roman rule, and then the normally industrious Arabs left little to show for their subsequent occupation. The truth, when eventually uncovered, painted an entirely different picture of a fascinating but still largely enigmatic culture considerably earlier than the conventional date (around 3000 BC) attached to the birth of Western civilisation in the Aegean.

Above, Latin inscription from Roman period, Gozo Museum. **Right**, the eight-pointed cross that would become known as the Maltese Cross

DECISIVE DATES

Malta's history spans more than 6,000 years. The islands are believed to have formed part of the land mass that once joined Europe to the North African coast.

Before 5000 BC: First settlers arrive in Malta, probably from the north.

circa **3400 BC:** The Copper Age.

circa **3200 BC:** Megalithic temples of Hagar Qim, Ggantija and Mnajdra are built, the oldest free-standing edifices in the world.

circa **2000 BC:** The Bronze Age.

circa **900 BC:** The Iron Age.

circa **700 BC:** Hellenic influence begins.

circa **800–480 BC:** Phoenician colonisation.

circa **480–218 BC:** Period of Carthaginian domination.

218 BC: Malta is incorporated into the Republic of Rome.

AD 60: St Paul is shipwrecked. First converts to Christianity, including Publius, Chief Man of the island, whose house was where Mdina Cathedral now stands.

AD 117–138: Declared a Municipality during Hadrian's reign.

AD 395–870: Byzantine domination.

AD 870: The Aghlobite Arabs arrive bringing with them a language that would help *Malti* evolve.

1090: Normans invade under Count Roger and Christianity returns.

1194–1266: Swabian domination (German).

1266–1283: Angevin domination (French).

1283–1530: Aragonese domination (Spanish).

1350: King Ludwig of Sicily establishes the Maltese nobility.

1530: The Order of St John arrives to take formal possession of the islands, a gift from Charles V of Spain. They select Birgu, where Vittoriosa is now established, as their base.

1561: The Inquisition is established in Malta.

1565: The Great Siege.

1566: Founding of Valletta, a new fortified city prepared for the return of the Ottoman Turk.

1798: Napoleon takes Malta. The Order of St John is despatched. The Inquisition is abolished.

1799: The Maltese rise against French domination. Britain decides to intercede, offering the

islands its protection in the name of King of the Two Sicilies.

1800: French force capitulates. Malta comes under the protection of the British Crown.

1802: Peace of Amiens decides that Malta should be returned to Order of St John. It is not returned. Declaration of Rights in Malta.

1814: Treaty of Paris: Malta becomes a British Crown Colony.

1914–18: World War I. Malta provides care for the wounded and becomes known as "Nurse of the Mediterranean".

1919: The Sette Giugno riots. As the war ends the Maltese economy fails, resulting in considerable poverty and unemployment. An angry crowd riots in Valletta causing the troops to be called in. Four Maltese in the crowd are shot.

1921: Self-government is granted at last. The first Malta Parliament is opened; domestic affairs are finally in Maltese hands.

1930: The Constitution is suspended because the Church tells people to vote Nationalist.

1932: The Constitution is again restored.

1933: The Constitution is withdrawn. Malta reverts to Crown Colony status it held before 1814.

1936: The Constitution is repaired: members of Executive Council are to be nominated.

1939–45: Pivotal role in World War II.

1940: First air raids. Second Great Siege two years later. George Cross is awarded for bravery.

1947: Self-government restored. Governor assumes administration.

1964: Malta becomes an independent state within the Commonwealth.

1971: The first Maltese Governor-General is appointed.

1972: An agreement is signed with Britain and NATO to use islands as military base.

1974: Malta becomes a Republic, with a President whose duties are nominal and ceremonial, but remains within the Commonwealth.

1979: Military agreements are terminated. British forces leave.

1989: The Malta Summit, when US President George Bush and Soviet leader Mikhail Gorbachev used the islands as a meeting-place..

1990: Malta seeks membership of the European Community.

It is widely imagined that the Maltese islands once formed part of a causeway which joined Europe to Africa but, until 1801, it was not generally agreed to which continent they properly belonged. A British Act of Parliament later decided the matter: "the said Island of Malta and dependencies thereof shall be deemed, taken and construed to be part of Europe for all purposes, and as to all matters and things whatever; any law or laws, usage or custom, or act or acts, to the contrary thereof notwithstanding".

As a bridge between the continents, the causeway was evidently a thoroughfare for animals escaping from the encroaching ice of Northern Europe. Many died en route or were perhaps trapped by a rising sea which turned the causeway into a necklace of island stepping stones. In any event, the cave of Ghar Dalam, the so-called Cave of Darkness near Birzebbuga, is only one of several which contain the bones of 36 prehistoric and extinct animals, including dwarf elephants and hippo from around 100,000 BC. The elephants used by Hannibal on his epic crossing of the Alps, a journey which began in North Africa, were rather smaller than the African variety, so it is not inconceivable that they were related to the luckless examples that got no farther than Ghar Dalam.

Human teeth: Of the people who were stranded or otherwise chose to live on the Maltese islands, very little is known. Among the animal bones at Ghar Dalam were a couple of Neanderthal human teeth from about 40,000 BC, and it seems that there was a fairly sizeable human population which lived in caves along the coastal cliffs or, taking advantage of the soft stone, dug themselves in and existed as troglodytes. They eventually emerged from their caves to live in settlements of tiny huts; the Skorba people are so named after the remains of such huts discovered in the west of Malta.

In about the fourth millennium BC, before the Egyptians turned their hands to pyramids

but still a thousand years before Minoan civilisation began at Knossos, the Maltese were engaged in the construction of great megalithic temples. Ggantija temples on Gozo were probably the first, but they were soon joined by the temples of Mgarr Mnajdra and Hagar Qim on Malta proper.

The temples were an assembly of massive slabs of rock, with alcoves for altars and statues associated with ancient religious rituals. The temple at Hagar Qim incorporates a single stone which is 22 ft (6 metres) long, a testament to the considerable engineering skills of those who manoeuvred it into position. At Tarxien three temples were embellished with carvings which are remarkably sophisticated for their time.

The circumstances in which the Tarxien temple was discovered in 1914 are fairly typical of what archaeologists are up against in Malta where, as the knightly commissioners reported, bare rock is topped by the thinnest layer of earth. The earth is rich in phosphates, but there is so little of it that ordinary trees, which is to say those whose roots would not seek fissures in the rock, would impoverish the soil around them. The hoe and the mule-drawn wooden plough tipped by a hard ploughshare are primitive methods of cultivation but as good as any to eke the best out of this thin crust.

Farmers working thus equipped were not inclined to toy with any impediment, and in 1914 a farmer complained that his ploughs were constantly striking blocks of stone at a certain depth. The formidably named but much-loved Maltese archaeologist Sir Themistocles Zammit excavated the site to uncover the Stone Age temples which, in the following Bronze Age, were evidently converted into places of burial.

Big woman: One of the courts of Tarxien produced the quintessential Stone Age art of Malta: a statue of a woman whose arms and feet are normal but with all the bits in between swollen to elephantine proportions. The style is known, commendably, with no beating about the bush, as "Fat".

Malta's most remarkable Neolithic remains came to light only a few years before the Tarxien discovery, on this occasion re-

Preceding pages: massive stone entrance to the Neolithic temples of Hagar Qim. **Left,** prehistoric peoples created the first known free-standing statue of a deity.

vealed by a builder who was digging down to the limestone to lay foundations for a house.

The Hypogeum of Hal Saflieni (the last part of the name refers not to some ancient deity but to the area in Paola where the builder was proposing to put up the house) is a vast, three-storeyed underground chamber carved by human hands out of solid rock. It is supposed that the chambers once housed an oracle and were used for "initiation into the mysteries of priestcraft". Only later did they become, like Tarxien, burial chambers. So huge is the Hypogeum that it is estimated to have held no fewer than 7,000 bodies. Apart from the fact that they lived about 5,000 years ago, practically nothing is

As to the purpose of the tracks, Sir Themistocles Zammit surmises that "the material handled must have been abundant, cheap, and of the greatest value to those who carted it". In Malta that could have meant soil. "When the increasing population required as much land as possible under cultivation on which to grow food-stuffs, they could only do this by carrying earth from the valleys up on the sides and tops of hills where terraces were built and the soil spread." Later experts believe the cart tracks are evidence of a more elaborate transport and communications system involving the use of slide-carts.

Malta edges into recorded history on the fringes of the momentous, three-cornered

known about these temple people.

The islands' "cart tracks", too, are an enigma. These are what the name implies, parallel ruts in hard rock usually 54 inches (135 cm) apart, which corresponds with the axle still used on the "modern" Maltese country cart. The more obvious questions concerned the use to which these tracks were put, especially as some apparently led pointlessly up hills or indeed with lemming implications to the edges of cliffs. Were the ruts, V-shaped and generally between 6 and 20 inches (15 to 50 cm) wide, first cut with tools or simply worn away haphazardly by constant use?

power struggle for the then-known world between Phoenicians, Greeks and Persians. The Phoenicians set the ball rolling by sailing the breadth of the Mediterranean from the cities of Tyre and Sidon, in what is now Lebanon, to semi-secret copper and tin deposits in Spain. The Phoenicians were intrepid sailors, but they preferred to remain within sight of land and furthermore to break the journey into comfortable stages. Staging-posts were therefore needed at regular intervals along the route which, because of hostile Greek expansion along the European shores of the Mediterranean, increasingly followed the North African coast.

The story of Dido, born Elissa, daughter of King Mutton I of Tyre and sister of the subsequent King Pygmalion, is an allegorical reflection of Phoenician expansion westwards. Fleeing her brother's murderous intent, she and a group of sympathisers reached Tunisia and founded Carthage.

In reality, this newly established colony was soon almost as prosperous and powerful as the Phoenician homeland, but the connection between the two was severed after a bungled attempt by Phoenicians and Persians acting in concert to crush the Greeks. The Greeks beat both enemies in surprise victories that are reputed to have taken place on the same day in 470 BC. The Persians lost base for their galley crews and began to cultivate olives and carobs. The excellent quality of the local clay for pottery purposes was also recognised and exploited. These innovations must have improved the islands' economy, but the terrible price paid by the local inhabitants was to see many of their number carried off as slaves to Carthage.

The priceless exceptions to the generally poor Carthaginian legacy, almost exclusively cave tombs, are a pair of marble *cippi* discovered in 1697. The gist of the inscriptions on these columns was of no great interest (a dedication by two brothers to the god Melqarth). An astounding fact, however, was that next to the cursive Phoenician

their fleet, commanded by Xerxes, at Salamis; the Phoenicians were defeated at Himera in Sicily. The Mediterranean was effectively cut in half: Greeks supreme in the east; Phoenicians (now more properly called "Carthaginians") in the west. Planted in the middle of the dividing line was little Malta.

The rise of Carthaginian power displaced the Greeks who had been inspired to name the islands Melita (i.e. "honey") by the rich, sweet variety produced by the local bees. The Carthaginians used Malta as a training

Left, entrance to chambers at Mnajdra temples.
Above, the Roman public toilets at the baths.

script, the progenitor of the European alphabet, was a Greek translation. These *cippi* – one in Malta's Museum of Archaeology, the other in the Louvre – were the key to deciphering Phoenician in exactly the same way as the Rosetta Stone unlocked the secrets of hieroglyphics.

On modern analysis, *Malti*, the language of the Maltese, appears to be a living legacy (subject of course to 2,000 years of natural evolution and later additions) of spoken Phoenician, which helps to explain the outlandish appearance, at least to European eyes, of the Maltese translation of Longfellow's *Psalm of Life*, courtesy of Sir

Augustus Bartolo and quoted in Sir Harry Luke's entertaining and informative *Malta*. The first line of Longfellow is "Tell me not, in mournful numbers"; the rest hardly matters for present purposes.

Tghidulix li id-dinja hi holma,
Mhiex hlief frugha, u niket, u hemm;
Dak li jidher fil-wicc hu qarrieqi,
Ujekk torqod ir-ruh taghna tintemm.

As Sir Harry remarked in the context of Mussolini's campaign to persuade the world that the Maltese spoke a form of Italian (and Malta ought, therefore, to be handed over to him): "It doesn't really look much like a dialect of Italian, does it?" Sir Harry also draws attention to a popular Maltese name,

Nibblu, which is the diminutive form of Hannibal, who was, of course, Carthage's most famous general.

Hannibal's crossing of the Alps with 59,000 men and 37 elephants, of which only one survived, is the most famous event of the three Punic Wars which raged between Rome and Carthage between 264 and 146 BC. It was a glorious but ultimately futile attempt to attack Rome from the north. On the rampage in Northern Italy for 16 years, he defied every Roman attempt to dislodge him until a bright young general, Scipio, hit on the simple expedient of launching a direct counterattack on Carthage itself. Hannibal

hurried across the Mediterranean to its defence, but too late. The final act of the third war was to carry out to the letter the message with which Cato had been in the habit of ending every speech to the Roman senate: "*Delenda est Cartago*" ("Carthage must be destroyed"). The city, and with it the Carthaginian empire, was obliterated.

Malta was tossed about in this struggle to the death between the current superpowers, although there are few specific references to it in Roman accounts of the war. Great Harbour, as it came to be known, served as a Carthaginian naval base and was therefore subject to attack, especially as Rome realised that the Carthaginian threat would have to be met at sea as well as on land. Malta was ceded to Rome as part of Carthage's indemnity after the first war.

According to Livy, Hannibal's father, Hamilcar, was in Malta when he surrendered with 2,000 men. The Carthaginians must somehow have regained Malta because it was ceded again after the second war. In any event, the islands were firmly in Rome's orbit for a good millennium after the Punic Wars. Although Malta had a certain degree of autonomy in Roman times, it was generally lumped together with Sicily for administrative purposes. Verres, a Roman governor in Sicily, never visited but he sent over agents to see if there was anything worth stealing. Two enormous elephant tusks in the most sacred Temple of Juno were the first to go, followed by a mountain of goods.

Corrupt official: Verres was equally rapacious in Sicily and is judged, against stiff competition, to have been one of the worst officials in Roman Republican history. He was impeached in 70 BC, and, at the beginning of what were expected to be lengthy proceedings in Rome, Cicero mocked him: "I don't need to be told where you obtained 400 jars of Maltese honey and a huge quantity of Maltese cloth, or for that matter 50 sofa cushions and 50 candelabra, but I am curious about what you proposed to do with so much stuff unless, of course, you merely intended to make presents of it to the wives of all your friends." Cicero was still warming to the task when Verres, on counsel's advice, fled the country, never to return.

With the appalling Verres out of the way, Malta prospered under unobtrusive Roman rule. Diodorus of Sicily, one of the very few

Latin historians who so much as mentions Malta, describes the inhabitants as "Phoenicians". The Maltese coins of the period bore Phoenician symbols with Latin or Greek inscriptions, and the tradition of cremation and burial in pit tombs was maintained. In general, therefore, it would seem that the Roman presence was confined to a garrison which had no impact either on the local culture or on the language.

The greatest single upheaval in Maltese culture occurred in AD 60 when a ship bound for Rome with 275 passengers, including a famous prisoner, was caught in a dreadful storm off the northeastern coast. "They knew not the land but they discovered a

remained on the island for three months, St Paul living most of the time in a grotto at Rabat but also, for three days, as the guest of Publius, "the chief man of the island," whose father he also cured "of a fever and of a bloody flux". According to tradition, St Paul not only converted Publius to Christianity but made him bishop, his house being nominated as Malta's first church. The present cathedral is said to stand on the very site.

If, as is surmised, the Maltese were still speaking a fairly pristine form of Phoenician with its Canaanite origins, St Paul's preaching would have been greatly facilitated by the fact that he, as a native of Tartus, also spoke a Canaanite dialect. In any case, Malta

certain creek with a shore, into which they were minded, if it were possible, to thrust in the ship... And when they were escaped, then they knew that the island was called Mel-i-ta. And the barbarous people shewed us no little kindness: for they kindled a fire, and received us every one, because of the present rain, and because of the cold."

The author of the quotation was St Luke (Acts of the Apostles: XXVIII) and the prisoner was St Paul. The shipwreck victims

Left, inscription in stone from the island's Arabic period, Gozo Museum. **Above**, the burial chambers of St Paul's Catacombs, Rabat.

was one of the first Roman colonies to become Christian, which is reflected in the existence of catacombs from the 2nd century onwards. One of the characteristics of these is tables cut into the rock walls of the vestibule, on which mourners reclined for a ceremonial feast in honour of the deceased.

Malta seems to have escaped the attentions of the Vandals and Goths, who between them first destroyed the Roman provinces in North Africa and then Rome itself. Life continued in what must have been blessed obscurity; history records simply that Belisarius, the Byzantine conqueror of the northern scourges, called in at Malta between campaigns which, in 533, won Carthage for Constantinople.

The islands seem to have been relatively unaffected, too, by the Islamic tide which swept westwards across North Africa in the 7th century. Malta was not in fact occupied by Arabs until 870 and even then probably only as an adjunct to their wider ambitions in Sicily and on the European mainland. No doubt influenced by the same military considerations, the Arabs took over the old Roman fortifications, including what was later to become Fort St Angelo, and added to the walls around Mdina. A number of Arab graves have been found, but the greatest legacy of their 200-year rule undoubtedly lies in the Arabic words and phrases added to what must have been, to begin with, a mutually comprehensible language.

The Arab hold on Malta was challenged in 1090 by Roger I, Count of Sicily, who fooled the garrison with a mock attack on St Paul's Bay while other troops scaled the perilous western cliffs. Roger was probably less interested in taking over the island than in making sure that the Arabs living there were not in a position to trouble him in Sicily. Malta was thus, for centuries, in the shadow of the higher priorities of whoever ruled Sicily, a good enough reason for concise histories of Malta (not excluding this one) to skip lightly over Normans with names like William the Bad and his offspring William the Good, and a succession of Angevins, Aragonese and Castilians. By marriage, inheritance or war, the islands passed from hand to hand, the Maltese themselves having little say in the matter, although a rebellion in 1428 managed to exact certain rights under a Royal Charter. Eventually the islands reached the hands of Ferdinand of Aragon and Isabel of Castile.

Ferdinand and Isabel's determination to rid Europe, particularly Spain, of the "Moors" – a catch-all term for Arabs and North African Berbers – who had migrated across the Mediterranean under the protection of Islam had unforeseen consequences. The full implications would be realised when their grandson, the Emperor Charles V, made a gift of the islands to the homeless knights of the Order of St John of Jerusalem.

Right, below ground, a temple for worship and burial; the Hal Saflieni Hypogeum at Paola.

44

There can never have been more natural enemies. The Barbary Corsairs, as the pirates of North Africa were generally known, did not wait for the arrival of the knights before forcing their attentions on Malta. They raided and sacked the islands constantly, three times in the space of only 10 years. In 1525, for example, the fact that many of the population were infected with an outbreak of plague did not deter those who landed at St Paul's Bay and plundered the surrounding countryside from carrying off 400 prisoners. The captives were either enslaved or put up for ransom, the latter arrangement being run like a well-regulated business with recognised prices on the heads of various ranks and nationalities. A single Corsair expedition to Italy netted no fewer than 11,000 captives, a lucrative haul.

The Barbarossa band: The profits from piracy enabled the Ottoman *deys* and *beys* in control of the Barbary ports to employ the finest fighting commanders and crews available. The best, at the beginning of the 16th century, were the brothers Barbarossa, from the Greek island of Lesbos, and their protégé Dragut, a peasant's son who had special cause to know all about the knights.

Born on the Caramanian coast opposite Rhodes, he joined the Turkish navy as a boy and was recognised as "a good pilot and a most excellent gunner." He joined the Barbarossa band based at Algiers and quickly rose to the rank of lieutenant with the command of 12 galleys.

"From thenceforward this redoubtable Corsair passed not one summer without ravaging the coasts of Naples and Sicily: nor durst any Christian vessels attempt to pass between Spain and Italy; for if they offered it, he infallibly snapped them up: and when he missed any of his prey at sea, he made himself amends by making descents along the coasts, plundering villages and towns, and dragging away multitudes of inhabitants into captivity."

Preceding pages: The Turkish invasion begins. Detail from a fresco in the Palace of the Grand Masters. **Left**, the Christian garrison beseiged. **Right**, Grand Master Jean Parisot de la Valette.

In 1540, Dragut was captured and put to work as a galley slave in a ship belonging to the famed Andrea Doria: "officially an admiral [in the Genoese navy], he was at the same time personally a Corsair, and used his private galleys to increase his wealth". Ironically, one of Doria's officers, who had himself once been captured by Turks and done a spell as a galley slave, knew Dragut of old. He spotted him straining at the oars and cried: "*Señor Dragut, usanza de guerra!*" ('tis the custom of war). To which the pris-

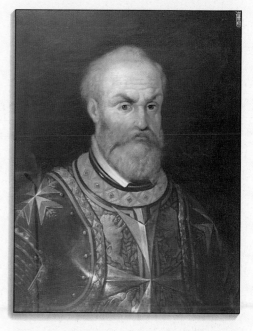

oner, recognising the officer, replied cheerfully, "*Y mudanza de fortuna*" (A change of luck!). The officer in question was Jean Parisot de la Valette, the future Grand Master.

Barbarossa recovered Dragut soon afterwards for 3,000 crowns and restored him to his old job. "Imprisonment had sharpened his appetite for Christians, and he harried the Italian coasts with more than his ancient zeal." According to a Turkish chronicle, he had become "the drawn sword of Islam". The Duke of Bourbon, the Viceroy of Naples and the Pope all financed unsuccessful expeditions to eliminate Dragut. At last Doria believed he had his former galley slave cornered in an inlet at Jerba, the Tunisian island, "and sent joyous messages to Europe, announcing his triumph".

He spoke too soon. During the night Dragut had a canal dug and escaped to open water. "Never did Doria curse the nimble Corsair with greater vehemence or better cause." Tiring of solitary roving, which he found "almost too exciting", Dragut joined the Ottoman navy and in 1551 sailed out of the Dardanelles in second command (under Sinan Pasha) of a fleet of nearly 150 galleys and 10,000 soldiers – "witherbound no Christian could tell".

They found out soon enough. The knights had, by then, been on Malta for 20 years,

surrender on what he believed were the same generous terms which had allowed the knights to remove themselves from Rhodes with 100 Greek families. "But Sinan… was in a furious rage with the whole Order" and all but a handful of the garrison were carried off in chains. The insult was compounded soon afterwards by a Turkish attack, also involving Dragut, on the Christian fortress at Jerba which had been established following Dragut's escape.

The Christians were routed. They lost 56 ships to the Turks and "eighteen thousand Christians bowed down before their scimitars". Surveying the mountain of Christian heads on Jerba beach on 11 May 1560,

steadily improving the defences although the Fort of St Elmo had not yet been built. The Turks, landing on the tongue of the promontory between the two great harbours, were intimidated by the sight of Fort St Angelo so they redirected their assault and plundered the interior and Gozo instead. Sinan's head "sat uneasily upon his neck" because of the failure to take the knights head-on and he thought it prudent, before returning to Istanbul, to dislodge them from their unwanted outpost at Tripoli.

The task was made easier by a French renegade who pointed out the weak spots in the wall. Gaspard de Villiers was forced to

Andrea Doria, by now an old man, could only say: "Take me to the church." The scene was set for the Siege five years hence.

La Valette, approaching 70 years of age, did not expect to wait long (or to die) before his venerable adversary Dragut came looking for him. He had been in action at Rhodes 43 years earlier, a tall, handsome man, devoutly religious and an inspirational leader of men, albeit "cold and even cruel in his severity". He had learned Turkish during his spell as a galley slave, but his sufferings "had increased his hatred of the Infidel".

To face the impending invasion, the fortification of Malta was accelerated in the great harbour to include the fortress of St Michael that protected the approach to the Senglea peninsula. Fort St Angelo was further strengthened and Fort St Elmo, facing the sea on the point of Mount Scebberas (where Valletta would one day stand), was also fortified. The entrances to the harbour and the sheltered creeks of the Borgo were guarded by a ferocious chain of stakes and metal. La Valette ordered the granaries filled and the cisterns kept topped up with water. A chain of warning beacons was erected around the coast. He asked the Viceroy of Sicily to be ready to help and appealed to all absent knights to return to Malta at once. In the meantime, 700 knights and 3,000 Mal-

senior army officer, and the admiral Piali had little choice but to begin without him.

The beacons along the coast flared with the warning. Peasants rushed into the fortresses with the last of the food and their livestock. Mdina, where the cavalry was quartered, closed its gates. Poison was dropped into the wells on the flat ground of Marsa, where the enemy were expected to make their camp.

The Turks took their time, building earthworks ready for an attack on the relatively small garrison of St Elmo before moving on to the main targets, Birgu and St Michael. Arriving at last, Dragut disagreed with these tactics but the preparations were too far

LA PRESA DI S. ELMO. A DI 23 GIUG. 1565

tese troops, supplemented by about 5,000 mercenaries, waited.

On 18 May 1565 the huge Ottoman fleet hove into view. It consisted of 180 ships carrying more than 30,000 of the best troops the Sultan could muster: Janissaries, reared from infancy for fighting, Thracian horsemen, Anatolians and volunteers from all parts of the dominions. Dragut was delayed and word was received that it would be two weeks before he could assume overall command of the operation. Mustafa Pasha, the

Fresco scenes from the Palace depicting the enemies as they faced each other.

advanced to be abandoned. Mustafa professed himself confident that St Elmo would fall within five days.

The sheer weight of the attack, when it was launched, put the Turks within three hours in possession of the ravine in front of the gate. The defenders, no more than 60 knights and a few hundred men, doubted that they could withstand a second assault and sent a message to that effect to the Grand Master. La Valette replied that he, if necessary, would come and take over St Elmo's defence. Dragut threw a bridge across the ravine and ordered his men in.

A battle raged on the bridge for five hours,

in the course of which the Turkish losses were heavy. Having been denied a quick victory, Dragut encircled St Elmo with his heaviest guns and poured in 7,000 rounds a day while the Janissaries repeatedly charged the walls.

The story of the siege of Malta has been told countless times, horror piled upon horror with almost every retelling: the ravine beneath Dragut's bridge overflowed with putrefying corpses; Christian defenders on the wall, their flowing white robes set aflame by fire hoops, plunged into the ravine like comets, and so on. The one incontrovertible fact is that during the action Dragut himself was mortally wounded – according to Mal-

tese legend, by the shrapnel of a shot fired from Mount Scebberas. Mustafa is said to have thrown his cloak over the prostrate Dragut until he could be carried to the safety of his tent.

The battle continued. La Valette gave up asking for the promised help from Sicily and the St Elmo defenders in turn asked no more for reinforcements. Having committed their souls to God, they "made ready to devote their bodies in the cause of His Blessed Son". On 21 June La Valette insisted that the as yet untested knights in Birgu hold the traditional Corpus Christi festival. The next day the St Elmo knights were in hand-to-hand combat

with the Turks and on 23 June a Turkish flag was run up over the fort.

It is said that word reached the dying Dragut in his tent that St Elmo had at last fallen without a single survivor, whereupon he lay back dead. There may have been some survivors – nine knights, who were never heard of again, and five Maltese, who swam to safety across Grand Harbour. The Turks lost 8,000 men. "If the child has cost us so dear", said Mustafa, contemplating what lay ahead at St Angelo and St Michael, "what will the parent cost". He sent five wooden crosses floating across the harbour in the direction of St Angelo, each bearing the headless body of a knight. La Valette's riposte was to order the execution of all Turkish prisoners and to fire their heads back at the Turkish lines as cannon balls.

Mustafa proposed terms of capitulation to La Valette. His reply was to point at the depth of the ditch around the two as yet untouched forts with the remark: "Let your Janissaries come and take that."

Bizarre battle: Turkish guns were manoeuvred into position to bombard the forts, but the rock-hard ground provided little cover for crews who were therefore exposed to brisk counterfire. Engineers were brought in under cover of darkness to cut trenches, but the sound of their picks gave the Christian gunners something to aim at. Mustafa would have liked to bring the Turkish ships to lend fire support to his infantry and gunners; La Valette's spiked barrier, however, blocked the entrance. An attempt by Turkish swimmers to cut the chain with axes led to a bizarre battle with Maltese troops who, knowing the water, dived in with knives between their teeth to see them off.

The Turks threw 10 assaults at St Michael supported by fire from ships dragged across the lower slopes of Mount Scebberas to circumvent the defences laid at the harbour entrance. Janissaries swarmed up scaling ladders but were hurled back, "a huddled mass of mangled flesh". Knights defended by dropping huge blocks of masonry on to the heads of their assailants.

"The scimitar", we are told, "was no match for the long two-handed swords of the Christians" and the water was red with Turkish blood and "mottled with standards and drums and floating robes". The Christians spared only two prisoners, although their respite was brief; they were "delivered over to the mob to be torn in pieces".

Still no help came from Don Garcia de Toledo, the Viceroy in Sicily, although it seems that messages passed freely backwards and forwards during the long weeks. On 7 August Mustafa threw 20,000 men at the two bastions. A mine brought down a long line of battlements with a gigantic roar and the Turks poured through the breach into the town of Birgu itself. "At that supreme moment even the aged Grand Master... came down to the front of battle and used his sword and pike like a common soldier."

The Turks seem to have been distracted at the very moment of their victory by the sight amid growing concern about the prospect of being stranded in Malta during the approaching winter. Mustafa's concern was increased on 7 September by reports of the arrival of 28 enemy ships and some 8,000 men. This time the rumours of reinforcements were true; the exhausted Turks marched to engage them at Naxxar. Realising that he must withdraw, Mustafa formed a rearguard with Dragut's son, Hassan, to protect a retreat which nevertheless left St Paul's Bay choked with Turkish bodies.

At nightfall on 8 September, the battered gates of Senglea and Birgu were opened and the knights' Cross again flew over St Elmo. The survivors emerged blinkingly on to the

and sound of cavalry riding down from the Old Town, Mdina. Assuming that they were the long anticipated reinforcements from Sicily, the soldiers turned tail, retreating over the 2,000 dead who lay after eight hours of fighting and ignoring their commander's entreaties that this cavalry was merely the 200 members of the Old Town garrison.

Mustafa managed to regroup but his men had lost the stomach for a fight. The Turkish offensive thereafter was left to the gunners

Left, the knights as Hospitallers tending the sick in the Great Ward. **Above**, Valletta and the Three Cities, their fortifications completed.

ruined battlefields outside their fortifications. "The Grand Master and his few surviving knights (the entire force was reduced to some 600 men) looked like phantoms, so pale and grisly were they, faint from their wounds, their hair and beard unkempt, their armour stained and neglected... men who had hardly slept without their weapons for more than three memorable months."

The anniversary of the ending of the siege on 8 September has, ever since, been the most important holiday on the Maltese calendar. It was thought that no moment of pain or glory could equal it – until Malta's second Great Siege, in 1940.

Grand Master Jean Parisot de la Valette was the hero of Europe. Even Queen Elizabeth of England, whose father Henry VIII had withdrawn the English knights from the papist Order, remarked that a Turkish victory would have imperilled the rest of Christendom. La Valette declined a cardinal's hat but accepted a magnificent sword with a gold hilt and an enamelled and jewelled dagger from Philip II. Other monarchs vied to lavish honours and money on the Grand Master and the Order.

The first task in devastated Malta was to build a city fortified against any future attack. With the Order's coffers overflowing, expense was no object. The site chosen was Mount Scibberas, the high ground from which the Christian enclaves had taken so much Turkish fire.

The Grand Master, after whom "The Most Humble City of Valletta" was named, did not see the city completed. He suffered a stroke, after a day's hawking, and earned the distinction of being the first person buried in the city. His body was placed in the crypt of the Cathedral of St John as soon as that was ready, the inscription reading: "Here lies La Valette, worthy of eternal honour. Once the scourge of Africa and Asia from whence he expelled the barbarians by his Holy Arms, he is the first to be buried in this, the beloved city which he founded."

Artists, sculptors, jewellers and craftsmen were eager to be associated with such a prestigious project. Levelling the site on Mount Scebberas proved more difficult than expected and was abandoned prematurely; this accounts for the number of streets that end in a steep dive down a flight of stairs to the sea. In general, though, Valletta was laid out as a pure example of Renaissance symmetry, a homogeneous blend of large and small, public and private buildings.

Visiting in 1830, the young Benjamin Disraeli put a "complete stop to all business"

with his appearance – "long, hyacinthine curls, rings on his fingers, gold chains, and velvet dresses of the most gorgeous description" – while enjoying a city which "equals in its noble architecture, if it even does not excel, any capital in Europe".

The forts of St Angelo and St Michael were rebuilt and enlarged, as were the fortifications around Birgu – renamed Vittoriosa to commemorate the victory – and Senglea, which resisted attempts to impose on it the pompous name "Invitta" (Invincible). Ever

mindful of the possibility of another attack, engineers were worried that loose earth and stones around the new city might be used by some resourceful enemy to improvise breast-works and trenches. The Order therefore bought all fields between Valletta and the plain of the Marsa and had the soil scraped away down to bare rock. Although the Turks made sporadic raids on Malta well into the 17th century, any real threat from that quarter evaporated with the defeat of the Turkish fleet at Lepanto in 1571, an action in which the knights' resident fleet of galleys played an enthusiastic part.

Three years later, almost as a symbol of

intended reversion to its less belligerent function in the Holy Land, the Order built a hospital outside St Elmo, the most advanced in Europe. Boiling surgical instruments in water was meant to reduce the agony but was of course an important step in the as yet unrecognised matter of sterilisation. The hospital could accommodate 746 patients, and the principal ward was, at 502 ft (153 metres), the longest room in Europe. Lunatics and galley slaves were treated on a lower floor. Patients were well fed – 200 chickens went daily into broth alone – off silver plate which, when melted down (in controversial circumstances, as we shall see) weighed 3,500 lb (1,600 kg).

than another, but the general standard seems to have been high. "I never failed", wrote an enthusiastic visitor to one of the French establishments, "to admire the quantity of the viands that are served and to wonder how so dry and barren a rock can produce such refreshment and so much game. Every day the market is full of vegetables and of almost every kind of fruit; the bread is excellent; beef and mutton of a marvellous taste. Veal and poultry are eaten at all seasons, notwithstanding the fact that there is little pasture. Partridges, pigeons, rabbits, thrushes and other game are fatter than anywhere else in Europe…" etc, etc.

While excitement was in the air, the vari-

Conjugal arguments: The knights themselves were divided into "langues", and each lived in their particular auberge, which was not unlike an Oxford or Cambridge college or, perhaps, an American fraternity house. The langues represented eight "nationalities" on the political map of Christian Europe as then existed: Auvergne, Provence, France, Aragon, Castile, Italy, Germany and England, although the last was withdrawn following Henry VIII's conjugal disagreements with the papacy. The Order as a whole was often referred to as the "Religion" and its base as the "Convent".

The food in one auberge might be better

ous nationalities got along well enough. "No nobler sight can be imagined", exclaimed one traveller, "than to behold the Grand Master and the Grand Crosses at their devotions". Another observed that "Mortal enemies are dearest friends here and leave to their countries the ennui of sustaining their masters' quarrels. The French skip, the Germans stru, the Spanish stalk, but nevertheless all are so well amalgamated that, while national peculiarities are retained, like national dress, none are striking."

If the same travellers had returned at other times they may have formed different impressions. It took four years of patient papal diplomacy to settle a state of near civil war between the respective langues when a Spanish knight was murdered by an Italian soldier, and the Spanish were in deadlock with the French for several months over who was entitled to service first in the meat market. There were terrible arguments about the order of precedence in church processions, and even one between two officers over who should open the city gates when there were reports that Turks had landed and the battalion within was itching to get at them.

The archives of Valletta contain 14 folios of procedures against members of the Order for various offences, ranging from libel, turning Muslim, running away, theft and

Grand Master Lascaris, an austere figure who lived to 97, believed temptation was best frustrated by a programme of constant exercise. "Wine, women and song sap virility", he warned. Knights were expected to neutralise their libidos by endlessly playing a kind of football in the "Maglio".

"Who can answer for the just indignation of a high-spirited company of warriors of illustrious birth, against the usurpation of their liberties and privileges by a stranger sent here solely for jurisdiction over heresy?" The objectionable stranger was the Inquisitor, a key figure in a power struggle as interminable as the Religion's energy-sapping sporting activities.

forging the Grand Master's name. The majority of offences seem to have been violations of the vow of celibacy, either straightforward "adulterous association with loose or public women" or, in the case of two Italian knights, dressing as women in order to infiltrate the females attending midnight mass. Another convicted of sneaking into a nunnery at night was banished to Gozo, where there were no nuns at all.

Left, the City Gate entrance to Valletta with its drawbridge and narrow bridge over the dry moat. **Right**, the Auberge de Provence, now the National Museum of Archaeology.

The Grand Master was officially on a par with the monarchs of Christendom and could, for example, strike his own coins. But, as Sir Harry Luke wrote, "he had to endure two rival authorities, the Bishop and the Inquisitor, who in their several ways sought to make his life a burden and often succeeded in their purpose".

In granting Malta to the Order, the Emperor had reserved the right to nominate the local bishop who, moreover, had to be Spanish and be given a say, if not a vote, in the Order's affairs. The bishop therefore came to be regarded as a semi-secret agent reporting to the King of Spain. The Inquisitor, originally invited to Malta by the bishop to look into "pestilential heresies", stayed on to emerge as the papal agent. They thereupon schemed to maximise their influence within the Order.

The simple expedient employed by the bishop was to "confer the tonsure" which, apart from the unusual hairstyle, signified that the persons concerned (many of whom had absolutely no intention of abandoning the lay life) were "clerks" in his service and therefore technically beyond the jurisdiction of the Grand Master. The Inquisitor dispensed with such subtleties: he offered potential informers the unattractive alternative of being thrown into the commodious dun-

the curtain between the antechamber and the adjoining room ought to be fully drawn, as it would be for the bishop, or merely raised a few inches by the hand of a chamberlain in the case of the Inquisitor.

Unforeseen encounters in the street between any two or, heaven forbid, all three of these worthies were tricky. If, for example, Grand Master and Inquisitor both happened to be in their coaches, the Inquisitor was expected to stop to allow the former to pass. If the Grand Master happened to be on foot, the Inquisitor was required to descend from his coach and compliment the Grand Master, who was equally obliged to stop to receive the compliment. If the Grand Master hap-

geon of his palace in Vittoriosa on suspicion of heresy. When Bishop Cagliares decided to build a new palace for himself, the Pope refused to allow him to include a dungeon.

The three-cornered struggle between an independent-minded Grand Master and two alien agents was likely to show itself in occasional issues like the right to shoot rabbits or in daily rules of precedence and protocol. "Each dignitary conceded to the hated rival the absolute minimum of deference while observing that outward appearance of formal courtesy which was regarded as all-important in those days." It mattered greatly at audiences with the Grand Master whether

pened to be in his coach and the Inquisitor on foot, the latter was supposed to salute but not to advance towards the coach.

Protocol was no less stringent when the time came for the three of them to wish each other a happy Christmas. The tension built up over several days, the end result being apparently "the least convivial series of Christmas dinners on record".

One of the most severe challenges to the Inquisitor came in the improbable shape of two middle-aged English Quaker ladies, Katherine Evans and Sarah Chevers, who proposed nothing less than to save Malta from Catholicism. They went straight into his dungeon but found a window from which they kept up an uninterrupted flow of theology, necessarily but unfortunately in English, which no one understood. This continued for three years and was only brought to an end in 1662 by a direct papal order for their release.

In this kind of climate, the Religion lost its sense of purpose. Knights drank, brawled and duelled over honour as well as for the favours of local women. Petition and counter-petition, edict and counter-edict flew between Valletta and Rome. The knights could only support their extravagant style of life by indulging in piracy every bit as rank as that of the Barbary Corsairs whom they

putting into the mouths of the wretched rowers pieces of bread soaked in wine to prevent them from fainting". If someone did faint, "he is flogged until he appears to be dead and is then flung overboard without ceremony". De Bergerac not only survived but contrived to live to the age of 95.

Adopted son: In 1644 some Maltese galleys, thus propelled, intercepted a Turkish convoy in the Aegean and, after a tremendous fight (a painting of which now hangs in the Palace) took off with the *Sultana*, a magnificent galleon belonging to the Chief of the Black Eunuchs, the third dignitary of State of the Ottoman Empire. The passengers included a heavily bejewelled beauty

were theoretically there to contain.

The oars of their galleys were manned by whomever came to hand: prisoners-of-war, convicts, even the odd Huguenot. One of these, a Frenchman named Jean Marteille de Bergerac, described conditions in the galleys: totally naked men chained six to a bench, officers flogging them with whips – "ten, twelve, even twenty hours at a stretch, without the slightest relapse or rests, and on these occasions the officer will go round

Left, the slaves' prison, in caves beneath the *Bagno*, by the Grand Harbour. **Above**, inside St John's Cathedral, Valletta.

named Zafire, one of the Sultan's favourites, whose little boy of two was assumed (probably wrongly) to be the Sultan's son. Whatever his true parentage, he and his mother were deposited in Malta. She died soon afterwards, and the little fellow was adopted by the knights as a kind of pet.

Osman, as he was known, appears to have developed a rather obnoxious personality under all this attention, but he turned Christian and trained for the priesthood. With his exotic background, the young priest was sent for by the pope in Rome and later given a regal tour of the courts of northern Italy, arriving next at the court of Louis XIV in

France. As "Padre Ottomano" he was a sensation in Paris, the subject of "innumerable flattering if indifferent poems". Following the fashion of the day, he affected shyness and a love of solitude.

Osman's glory as a delicate, retiring young priest thrust him helplessly into the notoriously bloody siege of Candia by which his putative father, Sultan Ibrahim, was trying to wrest control of Crete from the Venetians. The plan was to smuggle Osman into Crete and spring a surprise on the Turkish troops; Osman was to announce himself as the Sultan's son and urge them to follow his example by converting to Christianity.

The wilder ambition of the plan was that

the apparition of young Osman might act as the catalyst which would bring about nothing less than the unification of the Byzantine and Ottoman Empires. Osman did his best but, as history records, the plan was not practical. He returned to Rome and, after six years in a convent, was sent back to Malta as Vicar-General. He lived modestly in a small house in Senglea but was dead within the year. Having lived for 34 eventful years, he fell victim to a plague which, between 1675 and 1676, killed nearly 12,000 people.

As if to compensate for a decline in their real power and importance, the Grand Masters adoped ever more ostentatious uni-

forms, not to mention redundant suits of armour. Some pursued eccentric interests, such as Emanuel Pinto, one of the rare Portuguese Grand Masters, who had in his Palace "a man who claims to be a chemist".

The man in question was a notorious scoundrel known as Cagliostro, who later became involved in the curious business of Queen Marie Antoinette, the diamond necklace, and the cardinal who was duped into believing that the Queen loved him. In Pinto's service, however, he had been given a laboratory and was carrying out experiments "to concoct a certain elixir of life designed to keep a man sound in health and strength". Whether or not Cagliostro deserves the credit, Pinto lasted until he was 92.

The once-dreaded fleet similarly sacrificed efficiency for show, as noted by a traveller in the late 18th century: the ships "are defended, or rather embarrassed, by an incredible number of hands; the flagship had eight hundred men on board. They were superbly ornamented, gold blazed on their numerous bas-reliefs and carvings on the stern; enormous sails, striped blue and red, carried in the centre a great cross of Malta painted red. Their gorgeous flags floated majestically. In a word, everything rendered them a magnificent spectacle.

"Their construction, however, was little adapted either for fighting or foul weather. The Order kept them as an emblem of ancient splendour rather than for practical purposes. The navy was one of those institutions which had once served to render the brotherhood illustrious but which now only attested its selfishness and decay."

The knights were soon to be looked down on as "a corrupt, fanatical and hypocritical lot, as cruel as the Turk they fought, and as morally loose as the Popes and Cardinals they catered to. That they should have taken vows of poverty, chastity and obedience, and then built palaces and kept mistresses and defied authority generally [was] an offence not to be extenuated by any argument based on the standards or practices of the age."

The Order was usually dominated by the French contingent, and it was to be expected that when the French Revolution came along they were firmly on the side of the monarchy, even to the extent of sending money to Louis XVI. The victorious revolutionaries, no more surprisingly, exacted revenge. A large part of the Order's income was derived from property and investments in France. These were sequestered and the French Langue stripped of its nationality.

Napoleon felt he needed Malta to pursue his designs on British influence in the Mediterranean in general and Egypt in particular. The Grand Master, the German Ferdinand von Hompesch, could see trouble coming and opened negotiations to bring the Order under the protection of Tsar Paul of Russia. These were in progress when 300 French warships appeared off the island demanding the supply of water. Von Hompesch insisted on not more than four ships entering at a time; Napoleon demurred. Within two days

of families whose titles of nobility antedated the occupation of Rhodes, and after boasting that its Standard had never been lowered to any foe, surrendered the island to the French warships without a struggle, is simply not to be defended".

On Napoleon's orders, French troops looted the various auberges and palaces of paintings and tapestries. Napoleon personally helped himself to the jewelled sword presented to La Valette by Philip II of Spain. The magnificent silver service in the hospital was melted down and used to pay for Napoleon's troops in Egypt. Although the majority of Grand Masters had been French, the language of the Order was traditionally Ital-

the islands were in French hands.

The feeble surrender to the French cost the knights the last vestiges of Maltese respect. "To the educated and the aristocratic Maltese, well-informed on local history," says Miss Schermerhorn, "the memory of the imperious Order that took away their parliament and free institutions, interfered with the sacred privileges of their Bishopric, snobbishly refused membership to the sons

Left, French General Marmond and troops land to take Malta. <u>Above</u>, 1798, the Order of St John's surrender complete, Napoleon is rowed ashore in a longboat.

ian. French became the official language of Malta overnight.

Napoleon stayed only a week before launching himself on Egypt. He left behind a garrison of 1,000 men under General Claude Vaubois. The Royal Navy under Nelson, however, caught up with him at Alexandria and, at the ensuing Battle of the Nile, the French fleet was annihilated. One of the notable casualties was the *Orient*, which exploded and sank. It took to the bottom much of the treasure so recently looted from Malta. The French garrison left behind was not deterred by these setbacks from plundering Maltese churches further; the crowning insult was a public auction held in Mdina of the contents of the Church of Our Lady of Mount Carmel.

Furious Maltese slaughtered the small garrison in Mdina and set off in pursuit of Vaubois, who speedily locked himself in the safety of Valletta. A siege was laid by a popular force under the distinguished command of the Canon of Mdina Cathedral, Saverio Caruana, and Vincenzo Borg ("Braret"), armed with 1,000 muskets provided by the British ship *Orion*.

The King of Naples responded to a call for assistance by providing mostly Portuguese ships to tighten the blockade of Valletta, and when Nelson arrived in Naples fresh from

some of these and, on one occasion, executed 43, including their ringleaders, Don Michele Scerri and a Corsican pirate named Guglielmo Lorenzi.

As the 19th century dawned, Britain decided to turn the screw with additional forces under Brigadier General Thomas Graham, who quickly set about raising a local regiment. The mass of volunteers who came forward thereby became the Maltese Light Infantry, part of the British Army, a new departure in Maltese military history. The French hung on in Valletta for two months, eventually giving themselves up when their bread was reduced to three days' supply.

In spite of their substantial contribution to

his victory he was pleased to contribute a British squadron. Vaubois was not to be intimidated, however, and he led his men out of the city against the 10,000 rebels who had declared themselves to be subjects of the King of Naples.

Having lost Gozo, Vaubois proved remarkably resilient where he was. Captain Alexander Ball, the British commanding officer on the scene, was not inclined to do more than patrol the coastline to prevent French reinforcements from slipping in. It was left to the Maltese to sustain the pressure on the ground with the help of fifth columnists within the walls. The French unmasked

the outcome, the Maltese were given no say in the final negotiations and were outraged when the French, like the Knights of St John in Rhodes, were given leave to depart with their possessions, a large proportion of which the Maltese recognised as belonging to them. The British flag was run up over Malta on 5 September 1800. The departing French took with them, too, the ghost, if not the corpse, of the Religion.

Above, de Brocktorff watercolour of the Business Room (the State Drawing Room) in the Palace. **Right**, in ceremonial dress, knights of the Sovereign Order of St John today.

64

THE KNIGHTS TODAY

From the top of a massive stone tower close to the main gate entrance to Valletta, the flag of the "Religion", a white cross on a red field, flutters proudly. It is the centuries-old emblem of the Order of St John, whose title now is the Sovereign Military and Hospitaller Order of St John of Jerusalem, Rhodes and Malta. The tower is St John's Cavalier, an isolated fortified work, higher than any of the city's embattlements which, together with its twin counterpart of St James' Cavalier alongside the imposing Auberge de Castille, dominate and guard Valletta's landward approach.

For close on four centuries their embrasures bristled with cannon. Beautifully restored, the Cavalier is now the residence of the ambassador of the Order accredited to Malta – a perfect example of the suitable re-use of a historical building, and a valuable link in the continuity of history.

When the Order was ousted by Napoleon most knights returned to their native soils and the proud Brotherhood found itself in disarray. After numerous attempts at regaining territorial possession of Malta, the Order settled in Rome in 1834.

The Order thus lost its cohesion and military character, but from its new base continued the humanitarian works for which it was constituted. After repairing its lost income by re-establishing several of the suppressed priories in Europe, the Order opened hospitals in Rome and Naples and in Palestine.

The Order's ambulances and military hospitals did sterling work among the wounded of the Italian Risorgimento and the Central European conflicts of the 1860s and 1870s. Medical help was also supplied during the Boxer Rebellion in China and the Boer War in South Africa.

In 1872, as a move to the international scene the Order promoted the grouping of knights into national associations and established diplomatic relations with various countries. That same year a Maltese Association of the knights was set up. Similar associations were subsequently established in Europe, the United States and Australia.

The old hospitaller spirit was thus rekindled and in World War I, when Malta earned the title Nurse of the Mediterranean, the Order was accorded international gratitude for its work.

From its headquarters in Rome, the Order directs a complex organisation which, at a moment's notice, can send help wherever required. It responds to natural disasters such as floods or earthquakes. A small flight of aircraft is on hand to transport patients and supplies.

At the head of the Order since 1988 is His Eminent Highness Fra' Andrew Bertie, a Scotsman and descendant of Mary Stuart, who, before his election, lived in Malta for more than 20 years.

The Maltese Association is wholly dedicated to charitable and philanthropic work. Annual pilgrimages are organised to the Sanctuary of Ta' Pinu in Gozo and to Lourdes in France. Wives of members, some of them Dames of the Order, have a voluntary group whose main work is visiting the terminally ill. A number of young calling themselves Volunteers of the Order look after the elderly in a home while others care for the Physically Handicapped.

A blood bank, originally set up in conjunction with the Metropolitan Chapter of the Cathedral of St John, is financed by the Order's Magistracy in Rome. On Gozo, the St John Foundation assists the sick and destitute, the elderly and – today's problem – the drug addict.

In the cultural field, new activity has been generated by a handsome donation from the Australian Association for the cataloguing and indexing of a section of the Order's archives preserved in Malta. Donations made by the German Association to Mdina's Cathedral Museum are used to sponsor exhibitions and publications perpetuating the links between the Order and the islands.

On 8 September each year, the anniversary of the raising of the Great Siege of 1565, the knights of the Malta Association in full regalia, gather in the Conventual Cathedral of St John to hear mass and pay homage to the dead. The sculptured walls, the paintings of the vault, the memorials to knightly predecessors, all provide a marvellous setting for the remembrance of a glorious episode in the joint history of the Maltese and the Order in an unforgettable moment in time. ∎

The negotiation of the Peace of Amiens between France and Britain in 1802 took an alarming turn, in Maltese eyes, with talk of Britain, after two years of occupation, handing back all the French colonies. A brief taste of French rule made the prospect of its return to France as unsavoury as the resurrection of the discredited knights. Malta stated its case unequivocally in a Declaration of Rights: Malta must come "under the protection and sovereignty of the King of the free people, His Majesty the King of the United Kingdom of Great Britain and Ireland".

Ancient experience of the islands being passed around as chattels necessitated the proviso that "his said Majesty has no right to cede these Islands to any power... if he chooses to withdraw his protection, and abandon his sovereignty, the right of electing another sovereign, or of governing these islands, belongs to us, the inhabitants and aborigines alone, and without control".

Lowly language: Malta's political institutions and law were gradually anglicised, but it was probably in the matter of language that the nuances showed through most clearly. While spoken by all sections of the Maltese people, *Malti* had never acquired status and it remained, as far as most foreigners were concerned, "a kind of Moorish". As the language of the nearest country in Europe, Italian was the language of the Church and the law and was generally used by society in Maltese drawing-rooms.

The commercial community in Valletta had picked up some English because of contact with English men-of-war and merchantmen which had been regular callers at Grand Harbour from the 17th century, but the language was not more widely known than that. Lord Bathurst's instructions to Sir Thomas Maitland on his appointment as the first British governor in 1813 contained a note significant in the light of later events: "You will be pleased to issue all Proclamations in

English as well as Italian, and in a few years the latter may be gradually disused." He added that, as yet, "no permanent or definite system had been laid down for their Government".

The people of Malta and Gozo were not formally made "subjects of the British Crown and entitled to its fullest protection" until Russia officially removed a Maltese nightmare. Russia let it be known that, having broken with Napoleon, it no longer wished to pursue the restoration of the

knights of the Order of St John to Malta!

As Sir Harry Luke, a British Lieutenant-Governor of Malta (1930–38), observed, the history of Malta under British rule, at least until World War II, lacks "the glamour, the international ramifications, the world-wide appeal of the epopee of the Knights". It concerns the beginnings and development of modern Maltese politics, education, the liberation of the Maltese church from Sicilian domination and the regulation of the rights of the Maltese nobility.

In various government proclamations, for example, those nominating His Majesty's Judges, the switch from the earlier routine

Preceding pages: carved in stone, Britain's royal emblem that once indicated garrison presence. **Left,** a statue of Queen Victoria erected to mark her jubilee. **Right,** a painting of a British ship in harbour by the brothers Schranz.

could hardly have been more simple: the words "Grand Master" were crossed out and "The King" substituted.

The history of the British period includes, in one of the smaller footnotes, the implications of having a Queen on the throne. In Victoria's reign a Maltese marchioness became entitled to kiss her cheek (like an English peeress) instead of kissing only her hand. A similar footnote shows Victoria doing her bit for the Maltese lace-making industry with an order for "eight dozen pairs long and eight dozen pairs short mits, besides a scarf".

An inscription found on Manoel Island in Marsamxett harbour is an indication of weightier issues than the Queen's mits. While rather longwinded as inscriptions on gallows normally go, it is a pithy reminder of the vulnerability of a small island community to epidemics, especially in view of the apparently precipitous disappearance of the population in prehistory.

"THESE GALLOWS WERE ERECTED
ON THE 26TH DAY OF MARCH OF THE
YEAR 1814
FOR THE EXECUTION OF
FELIX CAMILLERI
ONE OF THE GUARDS OF THE
LAZZARETTO
WHO HAD BEEN CONDEMNED TO
DEATH
FOR HAVING OPENLY BROKEN
QUARANTINE
BUT RECEIVED A FREE PARDON
FROM HIS MAJESTY'S GOVERNOR
AS HAVING BEEN THE FIRST
INDIVIDUAL
SENTENCED TO SUFFER DEATH
AFTER THE SOVEREIGNTY OF THESE
ISLANDS
HAD BEEN ASSUMED
BY HIS ROYAL HIGHNESS THE PRINCE
REGENT
IN THE NAME AND ON BEHALF OF
THE KING"

One may wonder whether, during the remainder of his reprieved life, Camilleri proudly showed friends this unusual claim to fame, the hidden significance of which lies in the worst plague Malta had endured since the 17th century. Nearly 5,000 died, all foreign trade was suspended and the government was all but bankrupted. In the circumstances, the death penalty for "openly" breaking the quarantine was considered perfectly reasonable – and Camilleri's reprieve exceptionally lucky.

The Civil Commissioner who guided Malta into the British way of doing things was Rear Admiral Sir Alexander Ball, the naval officer who had been involved from the start. His first task had been to let the Order know that it would definitely not be returning. Grand Master Tommasi was waiting in Sicily fully expecting the call to return; when it didn't come, he sent his plenipotentiary, the Bailiff Buzi, to investigate the reasons for the delay. Buzi assumed he could move into the Palace in Valletta; instead he was politely advised that Sir Alexander was in residence and found it "absolutely necessary" to remain so. Buzi was told to wait – in vain as it transpired.

Poetic justice: Ball was rather more hospitable towards Samuel Taylor Coleridge and indeed appointed him Private Secretary after the poet arrived in Malta in 1804 for health reasons. Having found other accommodation, Ball left Coleridge to live alone in the vast Palace feeling, he said, like "a mouse in a Cathedral on a fair market day".

The poet-cum-civil-servant seems to have liked the Maltese people as much as he scorned the recently departed knights. "Every respectable family had some one knight for their patron, as a matter of course; and to him the honour of a sister or a daughter was sacrificed, equally as a matter of course. But why should I thus disguise the truth? Alas! in nine instances out of ten, this patron was the common paramour of every female in the family."

Sir Harry Luke – who was also the "Bailiff Grand Cross and Registrar of the Order of St John of Jerusalem in the British Realm; Cross of Merit, First Class with Crown, of the Sovereign Order of Malta" – thought Coleridge was being "fantastic" in this respect, "quite apart from the circumstance that they were entirely at variance with the strict family life of the Maltese". He also thought the poet harsh in judging the knights "little better than a perpetual influenza, relaxing and diseasing the heart".

Grand Tourists were close in the wake of the British takeover, including another famous poet. Lord Byron, just turned 21, was offended by the paucity of the reception laid on by Ball for his arrival in 1809. He was pleased, though, with the accommodation in Old Bakery Street, Valletta. He began to take Arabic lessons but was distracted by what was to become a notorious weakness. The woman concerned was appropriately special. Still in her mid-twenties, she was the Austrian-born daughter of the Austrian Internuncio in Constantinople and married to Charles Spencer Smith, the British representative at the same court.

Their affair lasted a furious three weeks, during which Byron had to be restrained from fighting a duel on her behalf with an aide-de-camp. She appears in his poetry as "Florence" and they talked about running away together to Friuli. Almost inevitably,

Adieu, ye cursed streets of stairs!
(How surely he who mounts you swears!)
Adieu...

Lady Hester Stanhope's long-suffering travelling physician, Dr Charles Meryon, faithfully logged in his diary during their short visit in 1810 an interesting description of Maltese life and manners in this period.

"The upper classes of the inhabitants dress like the French; but the common people wear a dress resembling that which is given to Figaro in the opera, with this difference, that they have trousers instead of tight breeches.

"The women are small and have beautiful hands and feet... They are fond to excess of gold ornaments which they estimate by

Byron let her down badly and knew it. But he was probably not so diffident about the collapse of the affair because he was moved to write a farewell to Malta which is generally regarded as his very worst work, his despair evidently exacerbated by his club foot.

Adieu, ye joys of La Valette!
Adieu, scirocco, sun, and sweat!
Adieu, thou Palace rarely entered!
Adieu, ye mansions where
I've ventured!

Lower Barracca gardens with the statue of Sir Alexander Ball, the first British Governor, given Grecian embellishment.

value more than taste; their ears, necks and arms are stiff with rings, chains and bracelets. They wear shoe-buckles of gold or silver. Although very brown, they are often handsome – I think generally so; and when I say that they are in figure like English maidservants, I do not mean to disparage them by comparison, but rather mark the plumpness of their flesh and roundness of their limbs...

"The repasts of the Maltese are plentiful; they dine at twelve and sup in the evening. When an entertainment is given, it is common to have three complete courses, and from five to ten different sorts of wine. They rise from table after dinner, taking coffee and liquers like the French. Both rich and poor indulge themselves with a siesta after dinner... (when) one would suppose that the island was deserted."

Malta played host to many celebrities of the day. Sir Walter Scott, paralysed and apoplectic by strokes brought on by his literary efforts to buy off creditors, spent three weeks of the last year of his life in Malta. He attended a ball given in his honour, and noted privately that it was "an odd kind of honour to bestow on a man of letters suffering from paralytic illness".

William Makepeace Thackeray's visit started inauspiciously in quarantine on Manoel Island, where Felix Camilleri had

ties". Young Disraeli was too clever by half for the taste of the British officer corps. "What rendered matters worse was his great knowledge and memory, which enabled him to make short work of any bold soldier who encountered his argument."

If Disraeli knew what people thought of him, he didn't care. "You should see me in the costume of a Greek pirate," he wrote home to his father.

On another occasion: "Here I am sitting in an easy chair, with a Turkish pipe six feet long, an amber mouthpiece and a porcelain bowl. What a revolution! But if I tell you that I have not only become a smoker, but the greatest smoker in Malta! The fact is I find it

escaped the gallows. On being released he was enchanted by "beggars, boatmen, barrels of pickled herrings and maccaroni; the shovel-hatted priests and bearded Capuchins; the tobacco, grapes, onions and sunshine; the signboards, bottled-porter stores, the statues of saints and little chapels which jostle the stranger's eyes as he goes up the famous stairs from the Water-gate..."

Dizzy's debates: Of all these visitors, the one whose impressions probably had a profound influence on Britain's political and diplomatic stance in the latter half of the 19th century was "highly unpopular and unwanted at the regimental messes and par-

relieves my mind."

Disraeli never forgot his enjoyment of Malta when it was relevant to the diplomatic tangles which ground towards World War I. Britain and France had of course patched up their differences by then and Winston Churchill, then First Lord of the Admiralty, invited his French counterpart "to use Malta as if it were Toulon". It was then that Malta became "the Nurse of the Mediterranean", providing more than 25,000 beds for the care of the wounded.

Malta's first self-governing constitution came into being after the war in 1921. The constitution separated responsibilities pertaining to the island's role as an imperial fortress – e.g. defence and foreign relations – which remained with Britain, from domestic affairs, which were put into the hands of a Senate and Legislative Assembly. Political activity was fused into the Nationalist Party until, in 1927, it was defeated by the Constitutional Party under Sir Gerald (later Lord) Strickland, who had been Chief Secretary of Malta and was Maltese through his mother, the Contessa della Catena.

Lord Strickland and the Church did not get along, and he was none too pleased when the bishop circulated a pre-election pastoral letter to his flock which stated: "You may not, without committing a grave sin, vote for sistently injurious to religion, since it discredits Bishops and clergy, upsets ecclesiastical discipline and tends to destroy the religious traditions of a people so deeply attached to the Church". The British government promptly suspended the General Election while it tried to find out what was going on.

The Governor General, Sir David Campbell, oversaw new elections, which resulted in the return to office of Sir Ugo Mifsud and the Nationalists, who thereupon took the curious course (for Nationalists) of reversing the previous encouragement given to the use of the Maltese language by imposing Italian. The Secretary of State for the Colonies looked into the situation and, having

Lord Strickland and his candidates." A postscript to priests reminded them that they were "strictly forbidden to administer the Sacraments to the obstinate who refuse to obey these our instructions".

The British government sent a protest note to the Pope over this ecclesiastical intrusion into the freedom of voters in a British colony, only to be told that Lord Strickland and his party's attitude was "undoubtedly and con-

Left, Valletta seen from the Grand Harbour, lithograph by the Schranz brothers, 1840. **Above**, watercolour of the Palace and ceremonial by de Brocktorff, 1822.

discovered that "only about 15 per cent of the population can speak Italian" and that English was "far more widely used and understood" the suspicion arose that Italian Fascists were at work.

And so it turned out. Mussolini's propaganda machine was determined to persuade Italians that the Maltese were a branch of the Italian race, their speech was an Italian dialect and that they, the Italians, ought to be ready to back his plan to sieze Malta – plus other choice bits of the Roman Empire – when he gave the word. The Maltese reaction to Mussolini's version of history was explicit when World War II was declared.

On 10 June 1940, Italy's dictator Benito Mussolini cast his lot with Adolf Hitler. Italy was at war with Britain and France. That night Malta heard Il Duce broadcast to jubilant crowds from his balcony overlooking Piazza Venezia in Rome. His "million bayonets", he shouted, would be on the march as from midnight. What they did not know, nor did Hitler, was that Mussolini's first action would be against Malta, the following morning, 11 June.

Hitler, records Ernle Bradford (who had served as a naval officer in the Malta convoys) in his book *Siege: Malta 1940–1943*, was at that moment "at his temporary headquarters in a deserted village in southern Belgium and the second half of his campaign against France, Operation Red, was proceeding as smoothly as was the whole German war machine. France, weak within and without, was collapsing according to plan and almost to schedule… These were the golden hours of Hitler's life."

Hitler, he continued, "tried to persuade the Duce to withhold his entry into the war but eager to lay his hands upon the spoils, the other partner in the Axis had determined to rush in as soon as it was clear that France was falling". It was, as Winston Churchill described Mussolini's move, "the behaviour of a jackal" seeking to gorge itself on smaller meats while backs were turned.

Secret bid: What the Maltese did not know as Mussolini spoke to the mob below, many of whom were waving placards demanding the occupation of Gibraltar, Suez, Tunisia and Malta, was that the islands' destiny with Italy had already been discussed. In order to keep Italy from joining Germany in the war, Britain's War Cabinet had some days earlier received a proposal from the French Prime Minister, Paul Reynaud, suggesting the Allies offered Italy "belligerent status" and so

give Italy the right to a seat at an eventual peace conference. There her territorial claims to Malta could be put on the agenda.

The proposal was rejected by the five-man War Cabinet by one vote. Neville Chamberlain and pacifist-minded Lord Halifax voted for the proposal; Churchill, Clement Attlee and Arthur Greenwood against.

Whether the islands were defensible had been a matter of contention. Both the Army and the Royal Air Force had considered Malta too vulnerable to attack from enemy

planes based on neighbouring Sicily and favoured evacuation. The Royal Navy had thought otherwise and its voice carried. It was to be proved right – though at high cost.

On the night of the broadcast the Maltese went to bed knowing they would be first in Mussolini's line of fire. By 7 a.m. they were. Air raid sirens wailed and, for the first time, a voice on Redifussion's cable radio, found then in almost every home, cried: "Air raid warning, air raid warning, *sinjal ta' hbit mill-ajru*." (The Maltese equivalent never caught on; air raid warning became part of the Maltese language instead.) Minutes later, the whistle of falling bombs could be heard

Preceding pages: Grand Harbour today with tanker concealing Fort St Angelo and *dghajsa* promising loyalty; soldiers assembled in blitzed dockyard for the ceremonial unveiling of a regimental badge carved in the rock wall. **Left**, July 1942, Valletta after the "raiders passed" signal. **Right**, heading for shelter during a raid.

around Valletta and the Grand Harbour as ten high-flying Savoia Marchetti bombers escorted by Macchi fighters droned overhead. A barrage of rapid fire came from the anti-aircraft guns of Malta's artillery batteries accompanied by the staccato of the 4-inch guns of *HMS Terror*, a survivor from World War I berthed in Pieta creek. It was the first of what were to be eight raids that day.

To face the enemy aircraft Malta had but three old Gladiators, planes apparently left behind accidentally at the RAF base at Kalafrana when the carrier *Glorious*, to which they belonged, set sail for the North Sea at the time of the German invasion of Norway. They had become known as *Faith*,

the war. Wartime restrictions were in force, blackout introduced and deep shelters were dug deeper into the limestone rock. The sirens sounded their warnings and their all-clears. The 30,000 troops divided into equal numbers of British and Maltese. The civilian population stood at 255,500.

As new allied planes arrived Malta began to take an offensive role. On November 11, an airborne torpedo attack by planes from the carrier *Illustrious* hit the Italian fleet sheltering in Taranto harbour, accounting for three battleships and two cruisers. They had been located with the help of reconnaissance planes flying from Malta. Three warships were rendered unservicable.

Hope and *Charity* and on that first raid one was lost. Folklore has it that it was *Charity* because "Malta never lost Hope or Faith in the final victory." (Heroic *Faith* is at the National War Museum for all to see.)

The Governor of Malta, Lieutenant General Sir William Dobbie, issued an Order of the Day: "The decision of His Majesty's Government to fight until our enemies are defeated will be heard with the greatest satisfaction by all ranks of the Garrison of Malta... I call on all Officers and other ranks humbly to seek God's help, and in reliance on Him to do their duty unflinchingly."

The islands were soon fully embroiled in

By December more than 200 Italian air raids had been logged but Malta seemed impregnable. Operation Hercules – Italy's codename for the planned invasion and occupation of the islands – was proving too herculean a task for them to complete.

Churchill was convinced of the islands' strategic importance. Malta, he insisted, must be held, whatever the cost. And the strength of Malta's strategic position was not lost on the German forces either. As the Allies made advances in North Africa, and Italy suffered setbacks with her disastrous venture into Greece, so Hitler turned his attention to the Mediterranean arena.

Rommel's Afrika Korps was attempting to advance along the North African coast to Egypt but sitting astride his key supply lines from Europe was Malta, a solid military base with both airfields and a dockyard. Malta would have to be disarmed.

To achieve this it was decided that the full might of the German Luftwaffe would be thrown against the islands and against the warships and the convoys of merchant ships they escorted. Cut the supply lifeline and the islands would be lost.

Their greatest success, however, was in January 1941 against the carrier *Illustrious* while she was escorting a convoy bound from Alexandria. The flight deck was put out

88s filled the sky. They would sink the *Illustrious* before she too could reach the shelter of shore-based guns.

In spite of a relentless onslaught the *Illustrious* bravely sailed on with fires raging and her steering gear out of order. On the night of 10 January, one year after Mussolini's speech, she limped in to harbour and berthed in Dockyard Creek. Here she was sheltered by the heights of Kordin on one side but was otherwise exposed to full view. Every hand in the area was called out. Casualties were evacuated and men from the dockyard swarmed the carrier. Working around the clock they carried out repairs.

It was six days before the enemy returned

of commission, putting the carrier's own airborne planes in the predicament of needing somewhere to land. They made for Malta; their mother ship limping towards the Grand Harbour with the remnants of the convoy that evening.

On reaching Malta, as the first two merchantmen passed safely through the defensive nets at the breakwater entrance into the comparative calm of the Grand Harbour, so waves of Stuka dive-bombers and Junker

Left, 1942, merchant ship under attack in a convoy heading for Malta. Above, after an air raid, fire rages deep in the Grand Harbour.

to their attack, time enough for them to re-arm themselves for the final kill. But it was six days not wasted in Malta; the Allies had planned their defence.

The Gunners proposed the best their guns could offer, a "box barrage", an umbrella of exploding shells, above the carrier. To achieve this every gun around the harbour – like those in the forts St Elmo, St Angelo and Tigne – as well as those within range of the harbour, would be coordinated so that they threw up a theoretically impenetrable curtain of fire around the prize target. No pilot would choose to fly through it.

On the afternoon of 16 January the attack

came. In Valletta the resilient community went about its business and sailors on shore leave joined the crowds to see Laurel and Hardy in *Fra Diavolo*. But as the film commenced, so did the attack. Buildings shook as bombs exploded and the barrage of anti-aircraft fire opened up. There had been no noise like it before. Patrons ran to nearby air-raid shelters only to see dive bombers flying at roof-top level, screaming down to where the carrier was berthed. Shrapnel rained down from the bursting barrage above.

One RAF fighter pilot pursued a bomber right through it. Having dropped his bomb, the German pilot tried to make his escape so low over the harbour that he had to lift the

the *Illustrious* but did little damage.

Undaunted, the enemy returned on the 18th. This time their objective was to put the land-based planes out of action by making the runways unusable. They succeeded, but only briefly. As they always did, teams of willing hands soon filled in the craters again.

In a lull a few days later the *Illustrious* set sail for Alexandria en route for the United States and major repair. The Luftwaffe had lost 30 aircraft in two days and, for a while, Malta enjoyed a respite. The Mediterranean fleet was without its carrier and Malta without the combined air-sea fire power needed to escort essential convoys through the gauntlet now known as Bomb Alley.

plane's nose to clear the breakwater. As the plane rose, the fighter got it. Its pilot was heard to remark afterwards that he was not impressed by the barrage box; in fact, his plane was so badly damaged by it that it never flew again.

It was a massive raid. Ten enemy planes were destroyed; five by the few fighters Malta could deploy, five by the ground artillery. And the damage to buildings on both sides of the Grand Harbour was the heaviest recorded in any one raid. Casualties were so high it was decided to evacuate the Three Cities bordering the dockyard area, Senglea, Cospicua and Vittoriosa. Only one bomb hit

Constant threat: The battle for Malta, which had begun almost as a personal crusade on Mussolini's part, took on a different complexion with growing German involvement. Rommel's Afrika Korps had joined battle in North Africa, and Malta was pivotal in the North African theatre because its aircraft, ships and submarines were a constant threat to Rommel's exposed supply line between Naples and Tripoli. Massed Panzers engaged over the expanse of the desert consumed enormous quantities of fuel, every drop of which had to be imported.

German convoys were careful to pass by only at night and never closer than about 150 miles (240 km). If Malta-based aircraft missed the supplies as they crossed the sea, they were given a second chance as the supplies trundled east along the North African coast. There was no practical port in the hundreds of miles that separated Tripoli and Tobruk, hence the determination by both Allies and Axis to win and hold the latter.

Field Marshal Albert Kesselring repeatedly reminded Rommel of this vulnerability, and on one occasion was overheard to say: "You risk everything if you try to reach the Nile while the British still hold Malta." Wing Commander Laddie Lucas, the highly decorated RAF ace, compared the island to "some wounded and enraged beast of prey", a men-

blockade. Many ships were sunk before they reached sight of harbour, others as soon as they anchored.

But morale was high. In spite of the hardship and danger, many of the population watched the aerial dogfights and learned to distinguish the types of planes. They could guage exactly where the bombs were falling by the reverberating sounds. There were shortages of everything; stocks of staple foods had run gravely low. In February 1941 food rationing was introduced. Kerosene, the fuel then used in many kitchens, was also rationed. The black market thrived. Many families moved to rural Gozo where the only enemy target was a small runway. Anti-

ace not only to Rommel but a hindrance to Hitler's strategy in the Middle East and, by tying down 600 German bombers and fighters in Sicily and Southern Italy, a relief valve for the Western Front.

Malta got off more lightly in the first half of 1941 than would have been the case if Rommel had not gone against Kesselring's advice with a decision to secure Tobruk first and worry about Malta afterwards. In fact, fewer convoys were getting through the

Left, reinforcements, soldiers in winter kit disembarking in Valletta. **Above**, air raid alert as a fighter pilot scrambles into action at Luqa.

aircraft gunners were given hours when they were to hold their fire, no matter how tempting the target, in the interest of conserving ammunition.

But while few convoys were getting through, Malta's submarines and bombers armed with torpedoes could, and did, still inflict heavy losses on ships carrying supplies destined for the Afrika Korps. The good news was that, with the German invasion of Russia, planes that would have been deployed in Sicily were now serving at the Russian front. The odds in getting a convoy through were improving.

In July, running the gauntlet, another convoy destined for Malta headed out from Gibraltar with an escort that included aircraft carrier *Ark Royal* and battleship *Nelson*. But although within range of the Italian navy, the enemy fleet made no attempt to engage. Soon the reason became clear.

High level bombers and planes armed with aerial torpedoes swung into action. A cruiser was crippled, a destroyer sunk. On the 24th, six of the large merchantmen reached harbour but these, the Italians knew, they could kill off as they sat, sitting ducks, in the Grand Harbour. They had in reserve a secret force they had not called on yet, a special unit of fast E-boats and manned torpedoes.

According to Prince Valerio Borghese,

who took over command of this unit later, these small deadly craft were designed with a Malta campaign in mind when the sovereignty of Malta and the claims of territorial rights by Italy first surfaced. In *Decima Flottiglia Mas*, his book titled after this unit, he wrote: "The idea of forcing Valletta, the harbour of Malta, the chief stronghold of the British navy in the Mediterranean, the possession of which is a constant threat to Italy, had been considered as long ago as 1935, when the human torpedo was taking shape. Malta was the objective for which this weapon was planned."

They required the utmost courage on the

part of the wet-suited pilot crouching behind a nose packed with high explosives and a mid-mounted engine. The theory was that the pilot drove his craft at the target, waited until the last moment to throw a lever which activated the charge, and then abandoned ship. The craft would explode on impact and the pilot, if the shockwaves did not incapacitate him and he was lucky, would be picked up by an attendant E-boat.

These manned torpedoes had already been used with some success in Gibraltar and Crete. Soon they would be used in Alexandria where they would damage the battleships *Valiant* and *Queen Elizabeth*.

In the event, their pluck counted for nothing. The Italians had reckoned without the islands' radar system – or the coastal defenses. For, soon after leaving the port of Augusta in Sicily under cover of darkness on the 25th, the small craft and their mothership *Diana* were picked up on the island's radar screens. As, slowly, the enemy sailed into range the coastal batteries of the Royal Malta Artillery took their bearings. Breaking the silence a wailing siren woke the residents as an air raid, designed as a diversionary tactic, was signalled.

Within minutes, lit by a spectacular concentration of searchlights, each one of the small craft was pinpointed and sunk by the concentration of fire from the defences. Thousands of spectators in Sliema and other vantage points had a grandstand view. Three pilots survived to be taken prisoner; none returned to *Diana*.

The abortive invasion added another great boost to morale. Malta's only damage was a small gap in the breakwater. Unknown to them, however, the islands were about to enter the second Great Siege of their history. The Germans could not allow this strategic outpost to remain in Allied hands any longer. Rommel pressed Berlin for action with urgent messages. In one he wrote: "without Malta the Axis will end by losing control of North Africa".

The objective now was to neutralise Malta. The islands would be besieged until they surrendered. It was the new year, 1942. The first waves of bombing came in mid-January and then continued with such brutal force that air superiority seemed to be firmly in the hands of the Axis powers. In March and April twice as many tons of bombs rained down on Malta as in a whole year at the height of London's Blitz.

To crush the population's will to fight on, there were 154 days of continuous day and night raids (London had 57), and 6,700 tons of bombs were dropped on the Grand Harbour area (by comparison, the worst night of destruction in Coventry was achieved with 260 tons). Buildings were flattened, 40,000 homes destroyed, casualties were high. "Victory Kitchens" were set up to feed the population who were suffering acute malnutrition. Ammunition was rationed.

The blockade was complete; nothing could reach the islands. Churchill signalled: "The eyes of Britain are watching Malta in islands the George Cross. The citation read: "To honour her brave people I award the George Cross to the island fortress of Malta to bear witness to a heroism and devotion that will long be famous in history."

Danger periods: It was an emotional time. Remote villages of no conceivable military significance suffered like everywhere else. Although houses built of stone did not burn, the confined blast of a bomb landing in a narrow alley was lethal. A low-flying plane could drop a bomb and be gone before an unsuspecting pedestrian knew what was happening, so during the worst of the bombing offensives the villagers took shelter underground. Many passed the danger periods

her struggle day by day. We are sure success as well as glory will reward your efforts."

He also signalled President Roosevelt: "Air attack on Malta is very heavy." With the *Ark Royal* recently sunk, could Roosevelt allow the United States aircraft carrier *Wasp* to airlift essential Spitfires to Malta. "*Wasp* at your disposal", came the reply. On April 14 she set course from Britain for Gibraltar. On her decks were 47 vital fighters. Perhaps Malta's luck was changing.

The next day King George VI awarded the

Left, carrier with relief planes. **Above**, the Royal Opera House reduced to rubble, Kingsway.

reciting their rosaries, a bucket of water always at hand to wet a handkerchief which went over the nose as a filter against choking dust mixed with the smell of cordite.

If the meal in the "Victory Kitchen" included a morsel of meat, it was goat. Church bells, whose peal was the inescapable concomitant of normal life in Malta, were silent. They were reserved for use as a warning of imminent invasion. As reaction to each and every air raid warning would have prevented any work from being done, the degree of probable danger was denoted by a system of signals, a red flag when bombers were expected, a red and white one for fighters or mere reconnaissance flights. The flags were run up on the Governor's Palace and on the Auberge de Castile, but as these were invisible from certain places, Boy Scouts took it on themselves to relay the appropriate signal with miniature flags on hand-held poles. Nearly 1,000 Scouts were awarded the Scouts' Bronze Cross for their efforts during the war.

Douglas Bader, then a Squadron Leader helping with Spitfires for Malta records a touching episode as told by another ace pilot, Wing Commander Laddie Lucas: "I recall, soon after reinforcements had landed, being hit ignominiously in the glycol tank by a cannon shell from a (Messerschmidt) 109 in

the aircraft and then on my arm. As she made the sign of the cross, devoutly and deliberately, a smile of benign dignity spread over that kindly, ageing face. For a moment, in a blessed Malta field, the Roman and the Anglican churches were as one."

For nearly two years there had been raids at the rate of about three a day, but a chink of hope interrupted this gloomy milestone. The American carrier *Wasp* was on its way with 74 more Spitfires. They took off unarmed (to save weight) but with extra disposable fuel tanks which enabled them to reach Malta at 1am with barely 20 gallons (90 litres) to spare. The Germans had previously been aware of the arrival of new aircraft and had

circumstances which are best left unsaid. Aided by fortune rather than skill I contrived to coax the Spitfire back across the coast, and with a dead stick and a fair quantity of smoke emerging from the coolant tank, landed the aircraft, wheels up, in a small cornfield in the south-west of the island. Three old Maltese women in long dresses with black scarves over the heads were working in the field. As I climbed out of the cockpit into the dusty heat of the day, one of them came stumbling over the rough ground towards me. She stared anxiously into my face. Tears, not words, spelled out her relief. With simple dignity she laid her hand first on the wing of

timed raids to catch them en masse on the ground during the day or so it took to make them fully serviceable. On this occasion, two soldiers and two airmen were waiting for each Spitfire, which was led to a pen as soon as it landed, refuelled, armed and loaded – all within the space of six minutes.

The new arrivals were already in the air and waiting when the Luftwaffe made its customary call. The German pilots were evidently caught completely off guard, their radio channels suddenly clogged with cries of "*Achtung! Achtung! Schpitfeurer.*" They lost 30 aircraft that first day under the new rules. The Luftwaffe returned in even greater force the following day – and lost another 63.

The Stukas, especially, were extremely vulnerable to modern fighters when carrying their bomb loads and even more so as they came out of their vertical dives with pilots reeling under the effect of the G-forces. The rubber dinghies of so many downed Stuka crews were bobbing in the sea between Malta and Sicily that one of the Spitfire pilots was moved to remark that the scene reminded him of "Henley on Regatta Day".

Spectacular dogfights: Between August 1940 and October 1942, 718 fighters were flown to Malta, 367 of them Spitfires. On 10 May, the month that logged the 2,000th air raid, it appeared as if the tide of fortune had

But prayers were being answered. Slowly working its way to Malta was a convoy of 14 supply ships with an enormous escort consisting of three aircraft carriers, two battleships, seven cruisers and 24 destroyers. This convoy had to get through.

"The garrison and people of Malta," read a signal from the flagship, *Nelson*, "who have been defending their island so gallantly against incessant attacks by the German and Italian air forces, are in urgent need of replenishments of food and military supplies. These we are taking to them… Every one of us must give of his best. Malta looks to us for help. We shall not fail them."

Day and night, a moving target, the con-

turned. The Spitfires that day seemed to be clawing the enemy out of the sky in spectacular dogfights that were watched excitedly by Maltese leaving the safety of the shelters. But the truth was different. Malta was only two months away from the date the authorities had decided would have to be the day of surrender if supplies did not get through. Conditions had now become so dire they would have no other choice.

Left, anti-aircraft battery in action across the harbour from Senglea. **Above**, survivor of the Santa Marija convoy, the damaged tanker *Ohio* reaches harbour.

voy was attacked by sea and air taking heavy losses as it sailed through a corridor of fire. Of the carriers, the *Eagle* was ripped open and sunk by torpedoes and the *Indomitable* put out of action. A merchantman was lost. Nearing Sicily the heavier warships turned back to the task force in Gibraltar; the convoy's protection was reduced to four cruisers and 12 destroyers. Now the enemy concentrated the attack, but somehow the remnants continued to progress. Two cruisers were put out of action, five merchantmen sunk.

On 13 August word spread in Malta as the first ships were sighted. Crowds gathered. First to reach harbour were the supply ships

Port Chalmers, *Melbourne Star* and *Rochester Castle*. Two days later, on 15 August – which was an important day on the Catholic calendar, the feast day of Santa Marija (the Virgin Mary) – in came the *Brisbane Star* and the battered, charred hulk of the tanker *Ohio*, which was barely above water and was being towed by two minesweepers and a destroyer. Lining the battlements, crowds cheered and waved; tears were wept for joy.

But for the arrival of the Santa Marija convoy the islanders would have had to surrender in two weeks. The courageous *Ohio* symbolised the islands' determination to hold out.

Of this event that was so crucial to survival, Churchill recorded: "Thus in the end five gallant merchant ships out of 14 got through with their precious cargoes. The loss of 350 officers and men and of so many of the finest ships in the Merchant Navy and in the escorting fleet of the Royal Navy was grievous. The reward justified the price exacted. Revictualed and replenished with ammunition and essential stores, the strength of Malta revived."

Thereafter the Afrika Korps was primarily concerned with defending its retreat to Tobruk and from there to Benghazi, Tripoli and ultimately to Tunisia. The changing tide

manifested itself to the Maltese when four merchant ships bobbed into Grand Harbour having made the run from Alexandria unscathed. At Christmas it was even possible to announce a special treat in the rations: about half a pound per head each of beans and sugar and a quarter of currants!

Glad tidings: There was better news to come on 23 January 1943 with the announcement that the Allies had taken Tripoli – or, as the Maltese preferred to think of it, the Italians had lost it.

General Eisenhower sent a message: "The epic of Malta is symbolic of the experience of the United Nations in this war; Malta has passed successively through the stages of woeful unpreparedness, tenacious endurance, intensive preparation and the initiation of a fierce intensive."

On 12 May the Afrika Korps capitulated, Malta having barred the way to the evacuation of 291,000 Germans and Italians who might otherwise have fought another day. The following month it was possible for King George VI to visit the island while Montgomery and Eisenhower planned the invasion of Sicily. The Maltese people got a hint of the invasion plans when the Msida Creek was filled in. It was assumed, at first, that this was simply part of a cleaning-up exercise, but one morning they woke to discover that it was a kind of slipway for numerous landing craft that had suddenly materialised.

Equally mysterious – though not for long – was the arrival of Scottish troops, tough-looking men who bristled with equipment and kept to themselves. The landing craft, the Scots and all the rest of a vast invasion force were gone on 9 July.

The islands became the Allied springboard for the invasion of Sicily. On 8 September the Italian fleet surrendered, as Commander-in-Chief, Admiral Cunningham notified Admiralty in London: "under the guns of the fortress of Malta". By coincidence, that momentous day was also a feast day of the Virgin Mary. It was also the anniversary of Malta's victory over the Turks in the Great Siege of 1565.

<u>Above</u>, citation with George Cross awarded to the Maltese for outstanding bravery and fortitude. <u>Right</u>, 20 June 1943, crowds gather for visit of King George VI.

While World War II raged on, the British government announced that Malta's "outstanding gallantry" called for "special recognition" in the grant, there and then, of £10 million for the restoration of war damage, with a further £20 million in the pipeline. The government also pledged to restore "Responsible Government" as soon as possible after the end of the conflict.

Elections in 1947 gave Malta its first Labour government under Dr (later Sir) Paul Boffa. The party proposed a referendum on whether the Maltese people, in post-war circumstances, wished to "submit Malta's case to the United States of America with a view to Malta receiving economic aid and, as a quid pro quo, the USA use of Malta as a base". It later transpired that the original draft, by Dominic (Dom) Mintoff, a former Rhodes Scholar and future premier, had left the door open for the USA or "any major power", an implicit invitation to the Soviet Union. The draft alternative was attributed to "human error" and quickly deleted.

Lost vote: Mintoff himself came to power in 1955, a quixotic politician who had once been Minister of Public Works and Reconstruction in the Boffa government and who now suggested that Malta should be "integrated" into the United Kingdom and be represented in the House of Commons. A referendum showed 67,607 out of 90,343 votes in favour of integration, but the British government, while generally sympathetic to the idea, was not confident that the result reflected the feelings of the non-voters.

The matter was still under discussion with Mintoff when it was announced in 1957 that Britain would be cutting back its defence expenditure, with unavoidable consequences for the Malta dockyard, the islands' greatest single employer – 13,000 out of a working population of 83,000. Mintoff lost his enthusiasm for integration and raised the cry for full independence. A constitutional deadlock ensued, leading to Britain taking over full responsibility for the islands' gov-

ernment. Mintoff, feeling the need for support before breaking with Britain, then resorted to one of the more bizarre political manoeuvres in Malta's history.

In 1608, Michelangelo Merisi, perhaps better known after his birthplace as Caravaggio, spent a few months in Malta in the employ of Grand Master Alof de Wignacourt. The turbulent artist soon ran into trouble, was thrown into prison, escaped and died back in Italy, but in the meantime he had painted two pictures for St John's Conven-

tual Church in Valletta, the *Beheading of St John the Baptist* and a *St Jerome*. In 1956 these pictures, which had only once before left the walls for which they were painted when they were put into protective storage during World War II, were sent to Italy in a British warship for an exhibition in Rome.

At the close of the exhibition they were returned and, to the astonishment of the Church authorities who thought they owned them, they were forcibly impounded on Mintoff's orders. Mintoff held the pictures while he prepared for a decisive break with the British government. Then, as abruptly as he had seized them, Mintoff returned the

Preceding pages: the armed forces on parade. Left, political party meeting at Marsa. Right, Caravaggio's *Beheading of St John the Baptist*.

paintings to the Church at the curious hour of one o'clock in the morning. The reason for these actions soon became clear: the paintings were held hostage to sway the Archbishop. The following day, a declaration of solidarity was issued by the Archbishop's Palace and the Prime Minister's office demanding independence from Britain.

In 1959, Malta's dockyard having outlived its usefulness (at least to Britain), the Colonial Administration published a five-year development plan in 1959 which concluded that "put briefly… Malta must get out into the world and earn its own living in other ways than it has done in the past". The means to do so clearly demanded full independ-

whether English or Italian should be the language of administration and education had long been won. The Italians were on the wrong side in the conflict and Maltese was the people's language. Only English could be the second language.

The main problems after the war concerned the economy, with worries growing that the hardships that followed World War I might be repeated. There was in addition the need for an extended settlement from Britain that would not only repair the heavy damages caused by the severe bombing but also help the construction of improved housing and infrastructure. For years Malta and Gozo had appeared poor colonial relations.

ence, and this was duly granted on 21 September 1964, albeit subject to a 10-year Mutual Defence Agreement with Britain.

The British naval base was finally closed, amid celebrations, on 31 March 1979. Independent Malta's first (and to date only) experience of a hostile foreign act came in the form of a gunboat which threatened an Italian company drilling for oil on Malta's behalf. It is not inappropriate to this history that its home port, long before Colonel Gaddafy, was on the Barbary Coast.

The European connection: Since the end of World War II, the nature of Malta's politics has changed radically. The argument over

Future employment represented a problem, too, although, for two decades, mass emigration to Australia and Canada eased the problems and softened the blow of the inevitable run-down of British service establishments which, for so many years, had been the islanders' main employer. (There are now as many Maltese and Gozitans living abroad as on the Maltese islands.)

As it transpired, by the end of March 1979 all British barracks were empty. But by that time Malta had already taken a serious step into the future by signing an Association Agreement with the European Economic Community. The first approach was made on 4 September 1967 when the Nationalist prime minister, George Borg Olivier, asked the Community for negotiations to establish "some form of relationship".

Three years afterwards an Agreement was signed. In 15 years, it was concluded, the Maltese islands would be well on the way to economic viability if they could be assured of an export market free of tariff barriers and quota restrictions, and if they were allowed to maintain for a time the protection required by their own young industries.

The objectives of the Association were clear. The government emphasised that Malta and Gozo were part of Europe geographically as well as through culture, relig-

prime minister was at pains to point out that Malta's approach to the Community was made before Britain's. The fact that Britain also planned to become a member of the European Community, he added, made it even more evident that Malta's future lay in such a relationship.

On 16 July 1990, convinced that the Association had produced economic benefits, Malta applied for full membership. Meanwhile, in the time it will take for the Commission to report on the islands' application, negotiations will take place on a transitional period of membership before Malta assumes all the obligations that Community membership implies. Already, 75 percent of all trade

ion, sentiment and way of life. Borg Olivier spoke of a growing awareness among the Maltese that they were living "in an age of economic groupings and trade areas which will make it difficult for those countries which do not join the group to achieve economic progress and this applies particularly to small countries".

Planning to forestall any future criticism from the socialist party about following in the steps of the former Mother Country, the

Left, at work in a towering crane in the islands' renowned dockyards. **Above**, ready for duty on the road, the motorbike policemen.

is with European Union countries. Malta needs to ensure that its interests in developing an export market are not subject to agreement but are accessible as of right.

Local politics are divided on how and when to achieve membership. The Labour Party believes that all conditions of membership should be stated before entry; the ruling Nationalist Party is prepared to talk once entry is achieved. However, the introduction of VAT in 1995 and various other measures have prepared the ground for Malta's eventual entry. The EU claims that Malta's neutrality remains a stumbling block.

As well as being a member of the Com-

HOW TO BECOME A RESIDENT

Islands, particularly in the Mediterranean, have an unmistakable lure. Their charm is enticing, their way of life relaxed. Inummerable travellers have landed on a brief holiday only to settle down to let the years roll by.

Malta and Gozo have their share of new arrivals and there's many a famous name here with a private corner, a villa, a converted farmhouse or a spacious apartment. The property is attractive and not expensive. There are gracious *palazzi* to choose from as well as modern apartments with views of the sea and covetous, off-the-beaten-track farmhouses that require costly rebuilding.

Government policy is to welcome foreigners as property owners as long as they adopt one of three forms of status (that is Non-resident, Temporary Resident and Permanent Resident). No employment or business activity is permitted unless officially authorised.

Laws governing residence do change periodically. The following guidelines were in force at time of going to press.

The *Non-resident* status applies to visitors whose stays never exceed three months at one time and whose property therefore comes under the category of Holiday Home. Non-residents are not subject to local tax unless they have income arising in Malta (excluding bank interest).

To safeguard the needs of housing for the local communities, the property purchased must exceed Lm15,000 in value (about £27,000 sterling).

The *Temporary Resident* status applies to visitors whose stays exceed three months and who have proof that their overseas income is sufficient for them to live comfortably in Malta. If this requirement is met and proven, a permit can be obtained from the Principal Immigration Officer. Temporary Residents are subject to local tax conditions if their stay exceeds six months in one continuous period, and they are subject to tax on any remittances of income to Maltese banks. Property purchased must exceed Lm15,000.

Permanent Residents, having been granted this

right, have the freedom to come and go as they please. But to get this status they too must first satisfy certain conditions of income. They must prove they have an annual income exceeding Lm10,000 (about £18,000 sterling) or capital of Lm150,000 (which need not be brought into Malta). The minimum income they must bring into Malta is Lm6,000 per person; the minimum tax they will pay, Lm1,000 a year.

In this category a property purchase must exceed Lm20,000 for an apartment or Lm30,000 for a house. Alternatively, property may be rented for not less than Lm1,200 a month. (Detailed current information for obtaining this status is available from the Ministry of Finance, Floriana, Malta. Permits can be obtained by applying to the Expatriates and Nationality Division, Office of the Prime Minister, Auberge de Castille, Valletta. It is advisable to make applications with the help of a local solicitor as the paperwork tends to be complicated). This status is of interest to people who want to take advantage of the special flat rate of income tax being offered them of 15 percent.

Malta has signed tax treaties with most major countries. This enables new residents to claim back tax where the income originates, or claim double taxation relief from Malta.

In a property purchase, estate agents' fees are borne by the vendor. Before purchase it is customary to sign a preliminary promise of sale agreement, a *convenju*, which is valid for three months or more. This binds the vendor and purchaser to the terms of the agreement and is subject to the searches being completed satisfactorily as well as the issue of all relative permits.

With this signing a 10 percent deposit is usually lodged with the Notary acting on the agreement. Funds to purchase must originate outside Malta and Gozo (and should the property be later resold, the full sale price and profit can be repatriated without capital gains tax being levied).

Foreigners may purchase only one property and it is permitted for use only as a home for the owner and immediate family, not as a renting investment. Although house guests are acceptable when the owner is in residence, the property may not be let or rented out. ∎

monwealth, Malta joined the United Nations in 1964 and has played its part in the Council of Europe since 1965. Malta also endorses the principles of democracy and the rule of law as embodied in the Single European Act.

Free of military alliances: Malta became neutral and non-aligned in a package deal forced on the Nationalist Party in opposition by the Labour government just before the 1987 elections. The discussions were engineered behind the scenes by Dom Mintoff, although he had already stood down as prime minister. For five years, in spite of proportional representation but with the help of cleverly drawn electoral boundaries, Labour had the majority of seats in the House of

country's protectorate were long passed.

As a result, the Nationalist Party was returned to office and immediately prime minister Eddie Fenech Adami called together all diplomats accredited to Malta to explain that Malta's neutrality was *sui generis*, a unique type. With Italy, a NATO member, undertaking to come to Malta's defence if so requested, and after consultation with NATO partners, its neutrality is indeed unique. In renegotiating the Agreement of Friendship and Co-operation with the Libyan Jamahariya, Malta dropped the clause combining the security interests of the two countries and so removed, as Italy saw it, the "odd part of the equation".

Representatives with a minority of votes.

Seeking to rectify this anomaly, it was agreed that the party polling an absolute majority of the popular vote would govern, if necessary through added seats in parliament. In exchange, it was agreed that Malta would follow the neutral path and would not participate in military alliances or permit foreign military bases on its territory, or allow foreign interference in its elections. The days when Malta and Gozo formed part of another

Left, on guard at a simple, working farmhouse. **Above**, a visiting opera production stayed at Astra Theatre, Victoria, with local chorus and orchestra.

To quote the official view: "Malta seeks to continue the development of its bilateral and multilateral relations with Europe as a full member of the European Community. Its European credentials are not in doubt; its Western democratic values have deep roots that have withstood the test of provocation; and its neutral status and unpretentious but sober efforts for peaceful dialogue are a positive contribution to a new, larger and closer, but outward-looking Europe."

Moments of misunderstanding when foreign issues were clouded in uncertainty, caused by ill-conceived statements and attitudes, seem to be over, and ambiguity has become a thing of the past. Malta has healthy relations with both Israel and Palestine and supports their rights of nationhood; it is also active in confirming the rights of all Mediterranean countries to secure their borders

Schooling remains compulsory up to the age of 16, with students prepared for both international and local school-leaving examinations. There are technical and trade schools and every town and village has a state primary school and kindergarten. Both Church-run and private schools flourish. The University of Malta is the oldest in the Commonwealth outside Britain.

More visitors: Meanwhile, lacking any resources except sea and sun, the expanding tourist industry continues to be a pillar of the economy. With more and more international visitors arriving each year, and with more money spent on improving the facilities and the infrastructure, tourism is being upgraded from its mass-market base. The modern air terminal is spacious and functional and reverse osmosis water production plants converting sea water to potable water have removed the water shortage problems that affected Malta, Gozo and Comino.

Light industry is burgeoning with considerable investment coming from European companies and, to promote overseas investment, incentives include a 10-year corporate tax holiday, soft loans, customs relief, investment and depreciation allowances, ready-made factories at subsidised rents and generous training grants. The stalwart dockyards, not to be outdone, are competitively facing today's challenges by bidding, for example, to repair and service some of the world's largest tankers and cruise liners.

To promote Malta as an international financial centre, legislation has aimed to transform the islands into an offshore centre that can compete with other offshore tax havens. And in recent years considerable attention has been given to promoting the islanders' employment potential and to attracting foreign exchange earnings by the creation of the Malta Freeport in the Marsaxlokk Bay – the spot where Presidents Bush and Gorbachev met for their memorable "seasick" summit in 1990.

Right, the islands' soft limestone quarries yield the large cream-coloured stone blocks that make the architecture so distinctive.

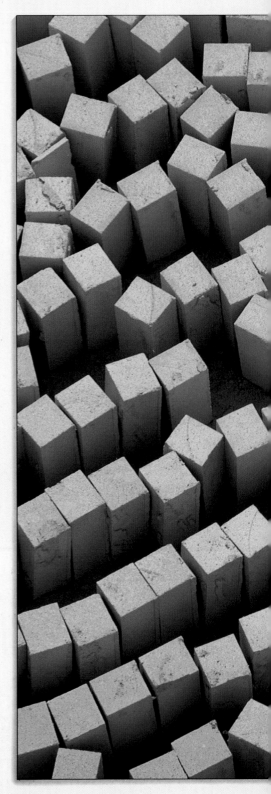

DOM MINTOFF: BOTH HERO AND OGRE

There was a time when the name Dom Mintoff was synonymous with that of Malta. Indeed, during his time as prime minister, Malta's problems were often given an airing far in excess of their worth, especially when linked to Mintoff's apparent friendship with Libya's Colonel Gaddafy. Although he stepped down in 1984, many assumed that up to 1987 his influence still held sway over political matters.

Over a period of 17 years Mintoff was prime minister four times (with Nationalist leader, George Borg-Olivier, three times). Each time he made his presence felt and his demands international news. He was inclined to come over as an ogre, both feared and disliked; but, as Britain's *Sunday Times* once recorded, had Malta been a larger country with Dom Mintoff at the helm, it would have been a country to reckon with.

Was he misunderstood? To many Maltese he is a hero, one who, were he not so patently anti-church, sometimes came close to saintliness.

The British press have always been hard on him, taking a dim view of his actions, seeing them as anti-British in spite of his English wife of patrician stock and the marriage of both his daughters to Britons. His tussles were considered racially inspired rather than what they mostly were: political. It didn't help his public relations, either, that he was apt to sue many British journalists for libel and win.

In the US, where the press was equally cool, his leftish leanings spelled Communism and although during World War II both President Roosevelt and General Eisenhower lauded the islanders' bravery Mintoff's request for Marshall Aid to help rebuild the shattered islands was turned down out of hand. It left a festering wound and barbed his tongue. Later, when he asked for US courtesy, no president would receive him.

With no foreign income to bolster the economy, Mintoff was forced to cast around. Potential friends were wary of such a volatile man. President François Mitterrand, although a socialist, took

much wooing before he issued an invitation to visit France, and the former USSR set up dialogue only through satellite states. Yet Mintoff was the first leader to be given a stupendous welcome in China, preceding all other western leaders including America's Richard Nixon.

It is said one of his dreams in those heady days was to become a world mediator, to reconcile Jew and Arab. Because of his unconcealed support for the Palestinian cause, however, his position was hardly unbiased. But his relationship with Colonel Gaddafy, although ambiguous, paid dividends. Libya provided Malta with oil at cost price as world oil prices were rocketing.

At home his supporters regarded him as being propelled by a love for the Maltese islands; his ruthless determination seen as a sign of strength as he strove to give the people a better life.

Born of humble stock in 1916 in the crowded confines of Cospicua, where the British naval dockyard was the major employer, he was very much a man of the people. The young Dominic Mintoff's dreams were formed by the poor world in which he lived, resenting the poverty and the scant regard the Maltese were given in their own country by an unthinking and insensitive regime. These were the oppressive days when Malta meant nothing but a colonial garrison. The Maltese, he determined, would prove they were as good as anyone else.

After training as an architect and civil engineer, and a spell as a Rhodes Scholar, he worked in Britain between 1941 and 1943 before returning home to help reorganise the Malta Labour Party ready for the first post-war elections. The elections took place in 1947 and Labour won.

In 1955, Mintoff, by then prime minister, suggested that, in view of the great affection he and the Maltese had for Britain, Malta should become integrated with the United Kingdom – to become, as it were, another county with representation in the House of Commons. A referendum showed that, of the 90,343 votes cast, 67,607 Maltese favoured the union. The British did not agree; the results, it said, did not indicate what the non-voters wanted. Mintoff was snubbed.

Two years later, Britain announced cutbacks in defence expenditure which would affect Malta's garrison and, in particular, the naval dockyards which employed a fifth of the islands' workforce. Most lived in parishes close to Mintoff's home ground. His enthusiasm for union evaporated. He demanded full independence from Britain. In the constitutional deadlock that followed, Britain took over the islands' government.

As was to happen in most colonies, the wheels of self-determination continued to turn. On 21 September 1964, the Nationalist Party ushered in Independence and, on 31 March 1979, the Labour Party, back in power with Mintoff as prime minister, celebrated as the last of the British forces set sail, leaving the islands to their own destiny.

In the years leading up to this long planned withdrawal, Mintoff's demands were always emphatically made, most concerning money. Malta approached other countries for aid in establishing itself in the commercial world – but only those accepting his socialist leanings would be welcomed. The result was suitors unacceptable to the West.

At home, Mintoff's actions polarised the nation. People either loved what he stood for or hated it; it was hard to be neutral. In a country where people are born to a party and never change, Mintoff could talk with charismatic oratory to the crowds of thousands, holding their attention and making promises. From the back of a workers' truck, in shirt sleeves, he would talk and inspire, harangue and re-plan. When he finished he would cry "we are strong, we shall win". Violence flared, communities divided. Maltese life became dominated by politics.

Perhaps it was simply his application, the righteous way he did things, that caused the problems. (When he stood down as prime minister, he appointed as successor Karmenu Mifsud Bonnici, who, far from being a politician, had not even stood for election.) Because of his strong personality, few would stand up to him. Cabinet ministers would feed him wrong information to make him happy.

Some say he was ahead of his time. He was, they say, educated at a time when others were not and his motives were good even if his timing was faulty. He saw the needs of his people. And, in the days when everyone was a practising Catholic, he was not. He considered the church as dangerously authoritarian and came into direct confrontation with the equally dictatorial Archbishop, Michael Gonzi, who proceeded to interdict him and so debar him from enjoying any ecclesiastical event.

The church supported the Nationalists and told parishioners to do so too. Mintoff, not one to avoid the pleasures of a clash, charged in impishly and intentionally made ambiguous statements to frighten the church. The church, he said frequently, should be seen to be poor, not rich. He attempted to confiscate their land and treasures and, in one final show-down before handing over, demanded all church schools be free. (The compromise was a form of church scholarship through State provision).

Lawyers and doctors came in for his wrath too: they exploited the workers. Not unconnected is the fact that most Nationalist MPs are doctors of law or medicine.

But he did improve the standards of living for oridinary people. Wages rose. In time all homes would have the baths, refrigerators and television sets that were only dreams before. Social services improved and government found land for newly marrieds as housing plots. Because he had seen poverty in his childhood he introduced free tertiary level education with students being sponsored so as not to be a family burden.

If he had a blind spot, it seems to have been corruption. Under Labour, no business or State transaction could be completed without a permit or an import licence. In the Latin manner, more palms needed greasing; the bigger the favour, the richer the due.

Mintoff was always a man of simple tastes. As prime minister he tried to minimise protocol, much to the distress of many visiting ambassadors and politicians. Visitors to his weekend retreat were constantly surprised by the quality of the food and the drink, though less so by the fact that he swam daily, summer and winter in the pursuit of fitness. As the years pass, so he exerts less influence on his party.

But his image remains vivid. It's an intrinsic part of Malta's public face. Mintoff took the tiny islands from being a small dependency to true independence and on the way, as the adage goes, won a few battles if not the war. ∎

George Bernard Shaw is reputed to have said: "Had priests been trees, Malta would have been a delightful place." Certainly, given the intense punctuation of the island's daily life by religious ritual and the domination of urban and rural space by the church's sacred symbols, one would not be laughed out of court for regarding Malta as the Bali of the Mediterranean.

Books on the islands by anthropologists have such titles as *Saints and Fireworks* (Jeremy Boissevain) and *Prelates and Politics* (Adrianus Koster). Popular novels with the islands as their scene of action have, typically, priests or pseudo-priests as their protagonists, ranging from the fairly ordinary parish priest of Nicholas Monsarrat's *The Kappillan of Malta*, to the brilliant scholar-forger of Leonardo Sciascia's *The Council of Egypt*, and the mystery woman disguised as a priest of Thomas Pynchon's *V.*

Big bangs: The most conspicuous feature of Maltese religion is undoubtedly the *festa*, the celebration of the feast day of the patron saints of each town and village. And the two most peculiar traits of the street-theatre which are central elements of these summer-long celebrations are band marches and firework displays; both of these were, originally, barely disguised parodies of the military force and earthly majesty put up by the British garrison from the time of its establishment here in the early 19th century.

The fireworks – called *musketterija* (musket-fire), *murtari* (mortarshots) – are fanciful variants of the saluting-battery that greeted warship arrivals and the frequent royal guests gracing the shores. Memory of those origins has become dim in the minds of most Maltese, but the passion for filling the night sky with polychrome, artificial meteors and the reverberation of big bangs shows no sign of diminution.

Festas illustrate the distinctive Maltese

conviction of the impossibility of a total separation of religion from politics. The acute and assiduous investigator of the Maltese *festa* culture, Professor Boissevain, confessed surprise when he discovered that the importance of *festas* recently seemed to be escalating, when a score of years ago all indicators would seem to have been pointing to an increased secularisation of the islands.

The British regime had, from the start, sought to maintain a collaborative relationship with the Roman Catholic bishops; the

Church network was, for all practical purposes, the sole means of communication for the colonial administration with the local people. *Festas*, organised by band clubs as a grassroot manifestation of nationalism with Roman Catholicism, had to be tolerated.

But little more than half way through the 19th century, a major social shift occurred. The change from wooden sailing ships to metal machine-driven vessels spelled the end of cotton growing (for sail-making) and for the textile activities which, for centuries, had absorbed the bulk of the landlubber workforce remaining after the thousands of others were enlisted in seafaring jobs.

The workforce shifted towards the harbour area where the naval dockyard established for the new metal ships was the great catalyst. A new technically skilled mechanic class appeared. They had political ambitions and were eventually to become the core of the Labour Party. They aspired, reasonably, to become officials of their local band clubs, the only representative roles that were available to them in recognition of leadership status apart from a few colonial government appointments.

For the most part, the lawyers, doctors and other professionals who traditionally monopolised these band club roles did not happily open their ranks to the social upstarts.

came an ever more challenging influence to the clergy, especially after he proposed integration with Britain as a preferable option to independence. Soon, his party had to build its own network of band clubs (with, often, more rudimentary and noisy youth bands) to counter those of the always *festa*-related and holy-tinctured organisations.

The Nationalist Party, in opposition, replicated this specifically political network of local bases. It therefore seemed as if the social substructure that had given extra strength to the original band clubs was being eroded. Moreover, applying some of the criteria which sociologists of religion had established as the measuring-rods for the

The result was the formation of rival band clubs in honour of the same, or other, patron saints (most often St Joseph, Skilled Worker) in the same village. Rivalry naturally led to an escalation in the demonstration of each party's respective resources. *Festas* grew and grew, not only as an expression of religious identity but also to demonstrate the relative strength of local factions.

After World War II, the path of the nearly 20-year political march to Independence was criss-crossed by the growing dramatic breach between the charismatic Dom Mintoff, Leader of the Labour Party, and the Church. Mintoff's increasing autocracy be-

secularisation of society (such as the number of priests and nuns), the process of erosion was occurring at a fast rate.

With the removal of much of the social pressure to conform, church attendance dropped, although it is still probably among the highest in Europe. Most parish priests have ceased to function as moral policemen with the ability to prescribe and enforce standards of conduct (including beachwear) within their territory. The presence of more tourists during the year than the total Maltese population has undoubtedly exercised a greater influence than most Maltese care to admit over their attitudes towards unorthodox behaviour and established authority.

There has been a marked shift from the more clerically guided, religious lay organisations to the much more individualistic, off-centre, so-called "charismatic" movements, as well as the mushrooming of hitherto un-tolerated dissident sects. These are often led by returned migrants and provide an emotive haven for souls hurt by the inconsiderate acts or dogma-mongering of the leftover relics of the old establishment. There are today self-proclaimed agnostics as well as non-practising Catholics in the Maltese parliament. Most significant are the incipient cries being voiced there for the introduction of divorce, now accepted only if obtained abroad.

But, as the sociologist who did the most extensive research on the matter, Professor Mario Vassallo, pointed out, the changes occurring have amounted to a revitalisation, rather than a weakening, of the Church.

Until a recent Vatican Council the Church authorities had undoubtedly appeared to be arch-conservatives. Nevertheless, it is remarkable that, in the 1960s, it was a Church grassroots organisation – the so-called Cana Movement, promoted by an energetic priest, Charles Vella – which campaigned with most effective public relations techniques for "responsible parenthood" as a Christian duty and set up clinics to give advice on birth control methods. Within a decade, the Maltese, who at that time had no access to contraception and who had been said by a British politician to "breed like rabbits", had achieved a stable population. The official guidelines issued by the local bishops have been recognised as among the most enlightened and pastorally practical in the world.

Another grassroots Church movement, the Young Christian Workers, which flourished with an extraordinary zest in opposition to the Integration with Britain proposals, included a former Leader of the Labour Party, Mr Mintoff's handpicked successor, Karmenu Mifsud Bonnici. He became the promoter of the idea of workers' self-management in industry and of an "economic democracy" to which both political parties have since subscribed.

Other Church-inspired initiatives in the social field included popular housing and

care of the handicapped; the provision of timely support for groups of all sorts, from the elderly to drug addicts; and the humble dedication to popular evangelism of a cohort of celibate men and women who nicknamed themselves "the Museum people" in the "fools for Christ's sake" Pauline spiritual tradition. But such initiatives did not allow the wedge driven between sections of the population and the institutional Church to result in any massive alienation from the traditional, ritual functions.

Schools paradox: Until the 1970s, state schools in Malta were generally regarded as better than the private schools which were mostly Church-run. Largely because of min-

isterial blundering in the approach to both teachers and pupils, an extraordinary exodus began from state to Church-run schools and attempts to stem the tide were equally unfortunately very heavy-handed. The result was a wholly unprecedented popular wave of support for Church schools.

To settle matters, the Labour government came to an agreement by which, through the state's financial provisions, attendance at Church schools is free and the demand more than they can cope with. Since the 1987 elections, all outstanding issues were amicably settled with the new government.

A related issue is that of Church property.

Left, nun leading exercise class at school.
Above, at prayer before morning mass.

The Labour government passed a law determined to confiscate the whole of the Church's property, ostensibly for the purpose of financing free attendance at the Church's schools; but the law was declared unconstitutional by the courts.

The subsequent Nationalist government negotiated the transfer of all Church property which was not directly used for religious purposes. It was agreed that the compensation to be paid for this move should be raised through an income based on unredeemable government bonds.

This arrangement appears to be beneficial to both parties. The Church will cease to be a major property-owner, while still receiving for their daily life and an international language, once Italian but now English, for their communication with the outside world.

The practising Maltese Catholic has a very deeply embedded consciousness of Catholicism, of belonging to a universal Church. There are almost as many Maltese priests and nuns working abroad in all corners of the world as there are in Malta. It is no accident that, soon after obtaining a place at the United Nations, Malta made its mark by proposing that ocean space be declared (in anticipation of other resources) "the common heritage of mankind".

Common good: The introduction of the principle that "common heritage" should be

adequate income to continue running its various community services. The state will be able to develop the former Church property to achieve a much higher economic yield than the income the Church was deriving from it.

Meanwhile the *festa* continues to be the symbolic enactment of the complex sacred-secular testing of truth by discussion which is so characteristic of the Maltese islands. But it perhaps represents only one side of the dual orientation which is at the base of the Maltese personality. The dualism is most clearly expressed in the bilingualism of the people – their use of a purely local language an overriding principle of international law, now generally accepted, was conceived as a practical working out of the teaching of Pope John XXIII in *Pacem in Terris*; that it was time to think, in politics, not of the "common good" of the individual state, but of the "common good" of mankind as a whole. The strong attachment of the Maltese Catholics to the See of Rome is an expression of a sense of the unity which religion fosters among the entire human race.

Above, communion during nuptial mass. **Right**, multilingual postbox with times of collection in both *Malti* and English.

GETTING TO GRIPS WITH THE LANGUAGE

Wherever they come from, visitors seem to find the national language of Malta eccentric and impossible to penetrate. Fortunately English is the second tongue and is one of the two official languages designated for use in state matters and commercial business. Also, if English is not always spoken fluently, it is at least understood.

So, too, is Italian – spurred on no doubt by the fact that Italian television appears to be more popular than the local station and the fact that it can be readily received from Italy and Sicily by satellite dishes, cable television and aerials. The influx of visitors from Europe means that German and French are frequently heard in shops and restaurants.

The first language, however, is *Malti*, Maltese. The fact that the islands still have a language all their own is in itself curious. How could such a small nation that has been subject to so many periods of domination by such a variety of invaders maintain its own ancient language? How could such a small number of people cling to a mother tongue? One answer may be self-preservation; no matter how many times the islands have been dominated, the people have remained steadfastly Maltese and having their own language was clearly an important asset to them.

ĦINIJIET TAL-ĠBIR

TIMES OF COLLECTION

7.00 a.m. – 6.30 p.m.
AS REQUIRED
G.P.O.
VALLETTA

Ittri li jkun fihom flus jew affarijiet ta valur għandhom jiġu rreġistrati f'Uffiċju tal-Posta

Letters containing coin or any article of value must be registered at a Post Office

MA JSIRX ĠBIR FIL-ĦDUD U BTAJJEL PUBBLIĊI

NO COLLECTIONS ON SUNDAYS AND PUBLIC HOLIDAYS

Malti is a living language, spoken daily in Malta and Gozo. It is a Semitic language with roots that go back to Phoenician and Carthaginian times. When the Arabs arrived later, in AD 870, they brought their own language and, because of similar Semitic roots, many of their words were taken in. Then, as the European nations began imposing their influence on Malta, so borrowed words from the Romance languages were assimilated. *Malti* expanded to become the language it is today.

In its earliest form the language was only spoken, never written. It was the language of a simple people and, possibly because of this, had a limited vocabulary. It was short of the flowery pretensions that mark the language of a sophisticated society. But as society developed, gracious words were borrowed for *Malti* and society itself began to speak the language of its protectors too. This continued even into the 20th century when, with the advent of World War II and the strengthened allegiance to Britain, Italian was superseded by English.

It is thought that the first to attempt to commit *Malti* to paper were the knights of the Order of St John after their arrival in 1530. Perhaps they are responsible for the distinctive eccentricities that make the language unique, such as dotting the *c*, *g* or *z*, or crossing the *h* as one might a *t*. Without this dot or stroke, the pronunciation is very different. In recent years a team of intellectuals has set about modifying and standardising the spelling and has successfully brought about uniformity.

There are 29 letters in the alphabet: five familiar vowels and 24 consonants. There is no *y*. The additions to the Roman alphabet are ċ (c), ġ (g), ż (z), which are dotted like an i, and gh and ħ (h). Dotting the consonant changes the way it is pronounced: dotted ċ becomes the English *ch* – as in church; dotted ġ as j in jelly; dotted ż as in zebra. (Without a dot, *z* is *ts*, as in nuts.) *Gh*, although it seems to be in every word, is not pronounced. *H* is silent unless it is crossed (ħ) like a *t*; then it is pronounced, as in hand. The vowels are pronounced long or short, depending on the position in the word.

Of course, this being a complicated language, it does not end there. *Q* is a glottal stop, faintly like a *k*, impossible to most visitors. Ask a Maltese to say *sqaq* (alley) or *tqiq* (flour). The best way to say Qawra, the name of the resort, is *ou*-(as in out)-*ra*. And *X* is pronounced *sh*. So the town of Naxxar is pronounced *nashar*. And *M* when it is at the beginning of a word is pronounced *im*. So Mdina is therefore *imdeena*. Mġarr, with both the opening *m* and the dotted-ġ, is *imJar*.

Bonġu is good morning; *bonswa* good evening. *Oqhod bil qiehda* (aw-ot bil-er-da) means sit down; saħħa (pronounce h's as in hand) is goodbye. *Int tit kellem bl'Ingliz?* (int-tit-kellem blin-gleez), do you speak English? Complicated, yes. But the Maltese enjoy explaining how it works and listening to unaccustomed tongues grappling with the phonetics. Fortunately it is not necessary to master the language; English will do. ∎

THE VILLAGE FESTA

Sometimes at weekends the sky is dotted with black puffs as petards explode with deafening reverberation above; it's as if one village has declared war on another. It's *festa* time, when villages celebrate their patron saint's feast day with bangs, bands, fireworks and processions.

The islands' public holidays list is probably the most generous one in Europe. Many, like St Paul's Shipwreck (10 February), Good Friday, the Feast of St Joseph the Worker (1 May), Saints Peter and Paul (29 June), the Assumption (15 August) and Christmas are special Catholic days. The others, like the declaration of Freedom Day, Independence Day and Republic Day, reflect party political achievements.

For the majority of the population, however, the most important date on their calendar is that of the village *festa*. Not many years ago, each one fell on the same prescribed calendar date each year between May and September when the weather was good. The date was fixed and village life planned around it. But because this mostly meant *festas* (the correct plural is *festi* but, in English, *festas* is acceptable) were on weekdays and therefore played havoc with factory workforce attendance, the government decreed that in future every *festa* would be moved to the nearest weekend, preceding or following. Little fuss was made and, as before, scant attention was paid to the church's own calendar. The result is a weekend's festivity instead of a one-day celebration.

There are some 30 different *festas*, with Lija and Victoria (Rabat, Gozo) sharing the reputation for the grandest events. Smaller village *festas* such as those held in Siggiewi in Malta or Xaghra in Gozo are usually more enjoyable and less crowded. Some, like Saints Peter and Paul on 29 June (known as Mnarija), demand a picnic in Buskett Gardens, others horse races or water sports.

But, as anyone who visits in summer will endorse, they are all noisy affairs; the noise

Preceding pages: procession of the statue of the **Blessed Virgin during** *festa* **at Zebbug, Gozo.** **Right,** band playing outside decorated parish church during the Hamrun *festa*.

starts days before they officially begin as petards herald their arrival, exploding in the early morning skies, making dogs quiver and first-time tourists expect the worst. The bangs let everyone know whose *festa* it is. These are celebratory events. Prestige hinges on their success and each villager takes great pride in their *festa* being the best.

Rural affair: The Maltese *festa* took on its present form in the 19th century. When it originated in the 16th century, it was a simple, rural affair that happened because of the munificence of local benefactors. It was often an occasion to give the poor of the parish bread or small amounts of money.

A hundred years later the celebration took

dard for celebration. Rarely participating in the village *festas*, the Order preferred to live separately. But each year it celebrated the feast day of its patron and protector, St John, and the other days that gave reason for a little outside entertainment – the election of a new Grand Master or a new Pope, for instance.

According to some historians, during Grand Master de Rohan's command, the Order's instructions were to offer such glorious spectacles as to make the islanders forget the poor social conditions in which they were living. With considerable wealth at hand, the Order invested in street decorations and more lights and in fireworks imported especially from Sicily. Parish pa-

on a more visual image as benefactors began rivalling one another in bringing fame to their villages. Bonfires were lit beside the church and extra oil lamps put out to create illumination. Competition began for brighter lights. Strolling musicians played pipes and tambourines. Soon, as a parish became wealthier through donation, so a statue of the patron saint was made so that it could be carried outside the church in procession for all to see and admire. In 1738 the first petards were fired into the sky to herald the festa of St Helena in Birkirkara.

By the 18th century the Order of St John had, wittingly or unwittingly, set a new stan-

trons, seeing these innovations, felt compelled to compete and, not to be outdone, dug deeper into their coffers.

But then, in 1800, the British arrived, bringing with them their own military pomp and ceremonial. They regarded all events as being part of the national fabric and, when villagers, enjoying the military brass bands for the first time, wanted to form their own bands, encouraged them to do so. (Today, although the ceremonial comes from the Church, the band club and its band remain the mainstay of village activities.)

Soon, seeing the poor displays arranged by the British, the Maltese started to manufacture their own fireworks. It was a skill they took to swiftly and, to this day, they produce some of Europe's finest displays.

Although there may still be some wealthy patrons, the success of a *festa* depends on the amount of money or donations collected, often door to door. There is no state participation; these are domestic affairs. The money goes towards decorating the streets with lights and bunting, towards floodlighting for the church and, of course, towards the essential fireworks. Money is also needed to pay bandsmen and, to ensure that the best possible show is put on, to hire temporary bandsmen to swell the ranks.

Of course, *festas* are not to everyone's

preceding, houses are painted outside and decorated inside. They are cleaned until sparkling, and the best pieces of crystal or silver are brought out ready to be put on show. Curtains and carpets are given new life. New clothes are bought for everyone, both parents and children, for the Saturday and Sunday evening promenades. Stocks of food and drink are readied for welcoming visitors. Everything will be at its best.

By 8am on Saturday, as petards shatter the calm air, the village streets are ready, dressed with flags, banners and strings of lights. The church around which all festivities are centred has its facade ornamented with thousands of coloured light bulbs. Whether it is

taste and, in some of the more wealthy residential areas of Sliema or the large villages of Lija, Attard and Balzan, they may even be actively disliked. At no level can a *festa* be judged sophisticated. But for anyone unused to the ways of village life they are the best way of seeing the Maltese at play, at their best and their worst. Even villages have their rowdy young.

Festas are a family affair. In the weeks

Left, during San Girgor *festa* at Marsaxlokk men gather to sing traditional *ghana*, folk songs for male voices. **Above**, musicians strolling in the band parade.

grand or humble by day, it will radiate splendour when night falls.

Inside, the church's wealth is on display. The walls and pillars are hung with red damask, chandeliers are rid of their protective plastic wrappings, the silver is polished, the altars are garlanded with flowers, and the patron saint's statue on a plinth is surrounded by bouquets presented by local dignitaries whose cards are pinned on so that the donors name might be clearly read. Later, the statue will be paraded through the streets on the shoulders of selected volunteers.

In early evening, friends and relations begin visiting, all dressed in their new clothes ready for a party. Many houses will have a long strip of bulbs and a banner hanging from a balcony and inside each one is brightly lit, with doors and windows left open so that passers-by can look in and admire the furnishings.

It is easy to be amused by these simple vanities but this is, in reality, Maltese life, warm and human. For most, unless there is a wedding or a baptism in the family, this is the only opportunity they have of greeting visitors with spirited generosity and pleasure. Prepared for their guests are the best bottles of whisky and brandy, local beers and crates of soft drinks.

The evenings are spent in constant motion.

Relatives whose houses are not on the main streets where the *festa* takes place arrive to join the more fortunate. Children run about and play with cousins visiting from other villages. Some may even have come from as far away as Melbourne or San Francisco because, even for an emigrant, the village *festa* retains its draw; if the family is going to take "the big holiday" in Malta, then they'll time their trip correctly.

A stroll to the church is optional – to see its decoration rather than attend mass. For, although this is ostensibly a religious occasion and there are masses in the saint's honour, the celebration is essentially personal. In this Catholic country, some visit their church only on this annual occasion.

As the band starts marching through the streets, so crowds follow, enjoying the music. Local bands move slowly indeed, taking time to stop, smoke and chat as well as nip in to a neighbourhood bar for a free drink. By the church, stalls set up the previous evening sell today's fast food snacks as well as traditional Maltese favourites such as *pastizzi* (cheesecakes), *mqaret* (deep-fried, date-filled pastry) and *qubbajt* (nougat that comes in different shapes, size and brittleness).

On Sunday, the statue is paraded, with confetti thrown from windows, petards loosed and young boys running around waving banners and making merry. When the procession reaches the church steps, the crescendo reaches its peak, with petards thundering, firecrackers ringing the church roof and the church bells tolling.

Each evening the signal to bring the festivities to an end is the firework display. Outside the church or in the square, tall wooden structures are covered in fireworks, ready to light up in brilliant shapes and movement. Tremendous amounts of skill, ingenuity and money have gone into preparing the spectacle. In the sky, to bring the event to a close, the brightest rockets will sweep overhead, showering explosions of colour, each display more brilliant, more exciting than the one before.

Then there is the day after: Monday. Some will go to work but many will not. Traditionally this is the day of the *xalata*, the outing.

A charabanc or two may have been hired, the rest will go by car, and they will all meet up again at a favourite beach, at Paradise Bay or Ghadira, where they can set up their umbrellas and barbecues. Here for the whole day they will sit, eat, drink and swim. The men may fish the rocks looking for *rizzi* (sea urchins) or crab, the women may find a sheltered corner to play *tombla*. Some will have *fenek*, a popular rabbit dish, for lunch.

In the evening they will leave together and drive in convoy, singing and blowing horns to let every village they pass through know they have had their *festa*. Then they have to wait for another year.

Above, fireworks bursting above illuminated parish church. **Right**, gilding and repairing the statue of a village patron saint for the *festa*.

118

A TASTE OF MALTA

Anyone who has never visited Malta may be surprised to discover that these tiny islands have a cuisine of their own. And anyone who passed this way before the 1970s may be surprised to learn that you can find it in places other than private houses.

For many years the local restaurant repertoire was limited to a kind of British style, often not particularly good. During recent years this has shifted to a proliferation of Italian, Chinese, Indian and Malaysian food outlets, besides the now de rigueur American fast food chains, McDonalds, Pizza Hut, Burger King and Kentucky Fried Chicken. However, Malta still does pretty good eggs and chips!

Cuisine is perhaps too fine a word for the cooking; its Frenchness implies sophistication and, if not just a touch of the *nouvelle* in its pretensions, at least with a wide range of chef's speciality sauces. Maltese cooking has no such artifice. Its excellence, for excellent it can be, comes from a basic, nourishing simplicity, both in its ingredients and homely treatment. It is not a dieter's food.

Given the fact that their predecessors succeeded in remaining doggedly "Maltese" over the centuries in spite of outside interference, it is little wonder that there is a local style of cooking. If the Maltese have managed to remain their own people with their own personality and impenetrable language, why not their favourite dishes, too?

Tasty mix: Geographical position has meant that the people have been subject to many culinary influences: from the north, from Sicily and Italy, and from the south, from the length of the North African coast, Tunisia to Egypt, where many Maltese communities were comfortably established until driven out by World War II.

Some of these origins show, but Maltese cooking is governed primarily by the kind of produce found on the islands – similar to that of neighbouring Sicily. So, although the likes of asparagus, brussels sprouts and the ubiquitous kiwi fruit can be readily found now, this availability is comparatively recent. Truly Maltese dishes are those produced by ingredients that are indigenous to the islands and local waters.

Walking mid-morning through the village streets, or through the residential quarters of Sliema, Valletta or the two Rabats (Victoria in Gozo is known locally as Rabat) it is not unusual to smell the most tempting aromas wafting out of the small doorways as meals are being prepared. On residential streets

such as these, it would be unusual if you did not. And often on Sundays, after the baker's bread has emerged from the ovens you catch equally delicious smells as the baker's hot oven becomes the village oven and is filled with family roasts.

This is a custom left over from the days when few houses had ovens and the oven-roast was a weekend treat. The habit continues, and on Sunday mornings baking trays covered with spotless tea cloths can be seen being carried to the village oven. Somehow the food tastes better cooked here.

Under the cloth is meat sitting on a bed of halved potatoes and onions and covered lib-

Preceding pages: early morning catch heading for the market. **Left,** *fenek* (rabbit), ready to be served. **Above,** fresh fish is a speciality at Giannini, Valletta's premier restaurant.

erally with seasoning and nobs of lard. In the bakery small metal tags are put on to each tray for identification, like cloakroom tickets, and a small charge is made. By 11am a rich aroma blankets the neighbourhood.

Ask the Maltese and Gozitans for the names of the best local dishes and you will hear the same answers wherever you are – even if some profess not to like one or two of these particular dishes themselves. Everyone knows the Maltese repertoire is made up entirely of favourite dishes, such as *timpana*, *minestra*, *kawlata*, *mqarrun fil-forn*, *bragoli* and *torta tal-lampuki*.

In praise of pasta: Two of the above, *timpana* and *mqarrun fil-forn*, are baked

dish being prepared – especially if that is squid, octopus or rabbit.

An alternative first course is soup, something like *aljotta* (a thin, clear fish broth) in summer when the fish are abundant, or *minestra* (a chunky vegetable soup) in winter. In fact, soups are staple to every Maltese family who, with much justification, have a high regard for the basic ingredients, the local vegetables.

Farms may be small but their richly worked soil produces some of the finest vegetables, salads and fruits anywhere. There is an intensity in their flavour, as if in each one it is somehow concentrated. Little is done by way of spraying to extend the life

pasta and, although a large slice of either might seem a meal in itself, here it is considered a starter. Both are made of macaroni layered with meat, eggs and cheese and, in the case of *timpana*, a casing of light flakey pastry too. They're delicious, if heavy on the carbohydrate. A variation of this recipe is *ross fil-forn*, with rice replacing the pasta. The rice is baked with minced meat, eggs and lots of saffron.

Pasta is as popular here as in Italy although it is unlikely that the average family will have it daily at home as the Italians do. It is not unusual for the spaghetti sauce to be made using the delicious juices from another

of the produce, so vegetables must be eaten within a day or two of purchase.

Because of this, housewives often shop daily and can be seen in the street markets or with the vegetable sellers with their painted trucks, selecting from the piles of seasonal produce. These include giant cauliflowers, kohl rabi, artichokes, aubergines, green peppers and *qara' bali* (a round, small marrow of the zucchini family typical to these islands and served boiled or stuffed).

Local winter favourites – meals in their own right, really – are *minestra*, *soppa tal-armla* (widow's soup) and *kawlata*. *Minestra* is Malta's answer to minestrone, although in this soup the vegetables, preferably nine or ten different ones, are cut into rough chunks; dried beans, chick peas, lentils and some small pasta shapes are then added. It is a thick, hearty and filling dish.

Soppa tal-armla consists of finely chopped white and green vegetables only. When the dish is served, a *gbejna* (a soft, round fresh goats' cheese) is placed in each bowl. And *kawlata* is a similar vegetable soup in which either a lean piece of pork or some Maltese sausages have been simmered. The meat is usually eaten separately.

Main meats: One of the pleasures of eating at home is the particular Maltese roast, beef or pork. (Lamb is mostly eaten at Easter.)

another dish worth trying, *bragoli*. This is not unlike the familiar Italian beef olive, but here the sliced topside beef is rolled, stuffed with hard boiled eggs and bacon, and simmered in red wine.

The national dish: In truth, there is no such thing – but, if there were one, it would be *fenek* (rabbit): fried, casseroled or roasted. Rabbit is everyone's favourite. As a result they are often the prizes in village raffles and there is even a special treat, an outing known as a *fenkata* when a family or group of friends get together for a picnic or in a simple village restaurant to enjoy fried rabbit with chips and lots of red wine.

It is been many centuries since rabbit ran

The meat is placed in a large greased tray, surrounded with chunkily sliced potatoes and onions, liberally sprinkled with herbs, rock salt and pepper and oil; then the tray is topped up with stock and the whole thing placed in the oven for slow roasting. As the stock evaporates, keeping the meat moist, the potatoes and onions pick up the flavours of the juices.

Unfortunately this homely skill has not spread to restaurants. But many are adept at

Left, fruit sellers at Cospicua's outdoor market. **Above**, *mqaret*, pastry with sweet date filling being deep fried to be served piping hot.

wild on the islands – though hunters, who lie in wait with their guns for the unsuspecting migratory birds who arrive seeking rest and water, say there are signs of them still on barren coastal stretches. Like the birdlife, they have been decimated by shooters. All the rabbit eaten here is specially bred for the table and is on sale, alive and fluffy, in the markets. It is not unusual for cuddly bunnies to be purchased young and taken home to be fattened up for a special occasion.

Rivaling *fenek* as the national speciality is *lampuka*, a much more refined dish. *Lampuki* (plural of *lampuka*) are *dorado*, a fish that migrates past the islands between

FRUIT OF THE VINE

Until recently, local wine was odd, and often a disappointment. It's not that it is a taste to be acquired by practice, or that it is distinctively flavoursome like Greek retsina or, indeed, headily sweet like many of the less sophisticated Mediterranean wines. It is simply that much of it had a peculiar aftertaste – sometimes described as goaty.

The old cliché that you get what you pay for seems especially apt. Although the local beers are truly excellent, commercially produced wines can be truly disappointing – especially some of the less expensive ones. As a general rule the more you pay, the better the wine.

But where once it was difficult to see how such small islands could produce sufficient quantities of grapes each summer to satisfy both the fresh fruit market and the wine producers' needs, a solution has been found. Top producers now import their grapes from France and from neighbouring Italy. Temperature controlled trucks deliver them to the wineries within 24 hours of harvesting.

Worth looking for are those wines at the top end of the ranges produced by the two major wineries, Marsovin and Emanuel Delicata. Both wineries strive to maintain consistency so that each year's wines reach the same standards. In the past many acceptable wines, like restaurants, failed to maintain their promise. Both produce Pinot Grigio, Chardonnay and Cabernet Sauvignon from imported grapes. Try also the less expensive Verdala (rosé or white wines) from Marsovin or the white wines from Delicata (their best being their Green Label).

Good wine produced privately can be fruity and delicious and largely free from the strange aftertaste or after-effects. Usually produced by the farmers themselves, the wine can be potent and, whether red or white, from Gozo or Malta, it is best served chilled. Many of the islands' better restaurants have succeeded in finding their own suppliers and now offer the local wine as house wine. It is often excellent and a safe bet.

In Maltese currency many of the wines are comparatively inexpensive, although the artificial rate of exchange in favour of Maltese Liri soon cancels out this apparent advantage. With a view to protecting local industry, imported wines are highly taxed. The result is that some of the imports appear poor value indeed. Many are already cheaper selections of wines from Italy, France, Germany and Bulgaria.

All Maltese wine is best drunk young. Prices range from 30 cents to around Lm2 a bottle. Those found in the villages made privately cost from 50 cents to Lm1 and usually come in recycled and scrubbed Johnnie Walker Red Label bottles, or take your own. Naturally prospective purchasers are expected to sample the wine before buying.

Local beer is produced by Simonds Farsons Cisk. There is a choice of lager, stout and pale ale – draught, canned and bottled – to rival any of the best beers produced in any country.

In fact, all the well-known European brands of drink are readily available in the local shops, supermarkets and bars, and many of the popular and familiar international beers and soft drink brands, such as Lowenbrau, Coca-Cola and Seven-Up, are also produced locally. The most popular soft drink, however, is Kinnie, a fizzy drink created in Malta. Made by the brewery, it is a bitter-sweet, non-alcoholic soft drink with an aromatic flavour. All locally produced drinks are sold in returnable bottles on which a small refundable deposit is paid – good news for conservationists and children wanting to make a few cents.

As for tap water, this too is safe and drinkable – for most of the time, anyway. For many years the islands suffered dramatic water shortages, with supplies being cut off for anything up to a week at a time. When the water flowed again, it was often highly salty.

The problem was overcome by the setting up of reverse osmosis plants on the coast to convert sea water into a palatable, salt-free water that is pumped into the mains system. (Until the words "reverse osmosis" entered the language, the Maltese, mishearing, charmingly referred to the new water supply as "rivers of Moses".) For purists, a variety of locally produced mineral water is sold in plastic bottles. ∎

September and November. A sleek and elegant fish, it has white flesh and a distinctive flavour of the sea.

It's a curious fact that lampuki have been caught in the same manner by Maltese fishermen since Roman times. As the season approaches, so fishermen cut and gather the large, lower fronds from the islands palm trees which they plait into flat rafts. These are taken out to sea where they are floated and the *lampuki*, finding nice patches of shade, gather beneath them. Quickly the fishermen encircle them with nets. The trick never fails.

Depending on their size, *lampuki* are grilled, fried or made into a unique, won-

pixxiplamtu, a member of the shark family; it is often passed off as swordfish. Swordfish, however, has dark shiny skin, *pixxiplambtu* does not (so it is served or sold skinned in order to disguise its species).

Fast food: Pizzas, burgers and chinese takeaways are readily available. The islanders also have their own versions It might be a slice or two of bread. Maltese bread is surely one of the world's best, good enough to be almost addictive. Made traditionally as a cottage loaf, the sour-dough is baked directly on the oven surface. It has a crisp firm crust, with a soft white centre punctured with random holes that are caused by the sourdough system used.

derful pastry-covered pie with cauliflower, spinach and olives.

Of course, these waters are abundant with other excellent fish. There are tuna and swordfish and smaller fish like sea bass, grouper, amber jack, mullet and skate. Highly favoured are saddled bream, white bream and dentex. And then there are octopus and squid, which the Maltese are adept at cooking deliciously.

The only one to be avoided is the inferior

It is full of flavour and is delicious spread with butter. But the Maltese prefer it as *hobz biz-zejt*, bread with oil, which is eaten at any time of the day as a snack. No family makes it in quite the same way; each has its own favourite extra.

To make it, first slice the bread thickly and then cut in half some ripe, tasty tomatoes. Rub them on to the bread until it turns pink. Leave the tomato on the bread and add salt, pepper and capers to taste, then generously pour some olive oil. Extras can include basil, onion, tomato purée and/or garlic.

Then there are the gloriously inexpensive *pastizzi*. Like nothing else, these are savoury

Left, local wines in labelled bottles are readily available. **Above**, crusty Maltese bread is baked and delivered fresh each day.

flaky pastry snacks that have to be eaten hot. *Pastizzi* has been translated to mean cheese-cakes because some are cheese-filled. But when they are cheese-filled, they are nothing like the sweet, American cheesecake. They are savoury. Baked on trays in special ovens, they are made of flaky pastry into which a pocket of filling is folded.

The choice is cheese (*rikotta*, seasoning and a little egg), peas (a mixture using dried peas) or, more rarely, an anchovy filling. As the *rikotta* filling is undoubtedly the best, so *pastizzi* came to be popularly translated as cheesecake. They are remarkably inexpensive and on sale most of the day from special shops or from cafés and bars. Two or three

make a favourite mid-morning snack.

Something sweet: The Maltese have a sweet tooth. Shops, cafés and stalls are laden with all manner of cakes and biscuits. Some are either garishly bright and powerfully sweet, others farmhouse-simple.

One particular inexpensive favourite is quickly recognised by a delicious aroma that wafts wherever it's on sale – for example, outside Valletta's bus terminal gate and in the evenings at *festas*. Called *mqaret*, these are small flat diamond-shaped pastry cases filled with a soft date mixture that is fla-voured with aniseed. Sold by vendors seated at small carts on which there are shallow

bubbling oil friers, *mqaret* are served deep fried, cooked to order, and eaten piping hot. It's the frying and the aniseed that give the tempting aroma.

With so much available, it's odd that menus carry few sweet dishes or desserts. In a restaurant the choice is usually limited to ice cream (mostly commercial rather than home-made) or a variety of gâteaux.

At home, although European desserts are often prepared, many families will order a *torta* from a leading confectioner when a special dessert is required: something rich and sweet and preferably with extravagant use of ground almonds. In the villages once or twice a week there are deliveries of the most delightful, simple biscuits, made by local bakeries. Like the crops many of the most popular Maltese sweets are seasonal.

For the Carnival weekend that heralds Lent, for example, there is *prinjolata* (a kind of gâteau made with pine nuts). During Lent there is *kwarezimal*, a sweet almond biscuit covered with honey and pistachio that origi-nally answered the prescribed Lenten rules because it contains no eggs or shortening. And, in the winter months, there is *qaghaq tal-ghasel*, a ring of sweet pastry filled with a mixture of dark treacle, semolina and can-died peel. In fact, these are so popular that they can often be found year round.

The best, however, are *figolli*, an Easter treat. These are biscuity cakes shaped into figures, decorated with bright coloured ic-ing, a small chocolate Easter egg and, the most important part, old-fashioned oleo-graph faces to give them character. In the biscuit there is a layer of sweet almond paste. On the whole, the more expensive it is, the thicker and better its almond centre.

As final proof of the passion for sweets, there is *qubbajt*, the local nougat sold at every *festa* from decorated stalls set up along the roads, each with a large pair of chrome scales as centrepiece. The choice is hard or soft – that is, dark brittle-sweetness or pale almond-chewiness. To entice the buyer, tiny samples are offered to passers-by. Like so many of the islands' favourites, *qubbajt* is particular, and delightful too.

Above, ready for the oven, *qassatat*, rikotta pies, larger versions of savoury cheesecakes. **Right**, in Gozo small terraced fields are still worked with simple methods.

VENERABLE VEHICLES

There are about 150,000 cars on the two tiny islands with a total population of 350,000: that is more than one car to every two adults. Almost every family runs one. And if there are adult offspring, they will usually have one each. New cars are not cheap – not even relatively. The most basic models free of any luxury can cost more than the average worker will earn in two years. Yet cars proliferate. Few are scrapped and such is the reverence attached to owning one that many achieve heirloom status.

At least 20 per cent of the islands' cars are more than 20 years old and look it. These are loved but they are not seen as the kind of cars that are accorded classic status in Europe and polished until they shine. Cars like those in 1950s British movies are commonplace; they never attract so much as a passing glance. A significant proportion of the remaining 80 per cent are between 10 and 20 years old too. The Maltese do not change their cars regularly; that sort of north European custom is not the national habit. This is not because of parsimonious conservation. When a Maltese does buy a newer model it is because he or she wants a bigger, more expensive car to emphasise upwardly mobile status, not because the older one is fit only for the scrapyard.

But this habit may be slowly changing. Younger people are becoming aware of the trade-in syndrome and there is an upsurge of interest every time a major European or Japanese car manufacturer launches a new model with customary hyperbole.

What happens to the older cars they replace? Nothing much. They get handed on or are sold for not much less than when they were first bought, which creates a buoyant, pricey secondhand market.

Because of the importance accorded to cars, old vehicles are not sold at bargain rates, they are sold for good hard cash. The used car market is ever thriving. The introduction of cheaper marks like Skoda, Lada

Preceding pages: the islands' old buses lavished with exterior ornaments and detailing are a reminder of the past. **Right**, one of many figureheads gracing buses and trucks.

and Dacia from the Eastern bloc countries has affected it to some extent but not so effectively as to force the old rusting models to be scrapped. There will always be those who would rather spend a sum on a car of doubtful condition from a prestige manufacturer's range rather than spend the same amount on a car with doubtful origins. Fords are the most popular – if not a Capri or Escort, then at least an Anglia or Prefect.

With no regulations or tests to ensure roadworthiness, except for commercial vehicles, Malta and Gozo's old and dilapidated cars are allowed to run on and on belching noxious fumes and diesel clouds. Silencers seem unimportant too. However, MOT-

style tests are in the offing and for which EU-type legislation is being drawn-up. In the meantime a start has been initiated on public transport. Front seat belts are now statutory.

Most drivers of the old-timers also insist that the cost of spare parts and regular trips to the mechanic/electrican/insurance man are less expensive than the amount it would take to buy something flashier. And the islands' mechanics appear to have a near magical way of whizzing up spare parts no matter how old the vehicle. Could this be because similar cars are constantly being stolen for spare parts? There is a high rate – and low recovery rate – of stolen cars on the islands.

Mechanics have a way of multiplying like hamsters too, operating from private garages in quiet neighbourhoods and driving residents to distraction. So do their colleagues the panel beaters. Car repair could be considered a steady job.

Many of the cars carry stickers on their rear windows. Some of these make commercial points – like Cloud 9 (a discotheque), Libyan Airways and Evermond (cosmetics) – or speak religious texts – like Jesus Loves Me and Think God.

On the buses this religious mode continues. There is often a neon sign behind the heads of the drivers reading Ave Maria. Others have a small plastic statue of the Virgin surrounded by an arrangement of dried flowers in a glass vitrine like a treasured Victorian piece. The more enlightened, or so it might appear, hang pictures of musical superstars such as Michael Jackson, Prince and that other Madonna. However, the days of this quaint habit are numbered because all displays – whether religious or otherwise – are prohibited by the public transport authority.

Buses can seem older than the oldest cars. Passengers often hold their breath when one of the great originals strains up a hill then plummets down the other side. They are unbearably hot in summer because most were originally driven on English roads where heating was important, not air-conditioning. But they are a cheap means of transport and the introduction of new buses is very imminent.

Trucks and vans are sometimes museum pieces too. At one time every truck seemed to be painted red and green but now there are all colours, including some remarkable builders' trucks dressed up in glorious pink. Bakers' vans are cream with a red stripe on the back door; butchers have a blue stripe.

Almost all have a name painted on the sides of their bonnet. Names like Tarzan, Rio Rita, Fat Boy and Red Devil as well as the more inspirational names of today. Yes, Sue Ellen and Dallas. There is even a giant, 30 year old mobile crane called Lambada Dance and a bus called Paul's Toy. Paul's Toy? Well, why not? This is Malta.

Above, souped-up Ford Prefect complete with message from the driver. Right, trucks and buses are given names, from Elvis to Madonna.

MALTESE ARCHITECTURE

Considering the abundance of historical architectural splendour that covers the islands – the two cities, the fortifications, the grand buildings and the churches – it is somewhat surprising to discover that there were periods in Malta's history when, architecturally, the islands were dormant.

The first time they reached a peak of achievement was around 3000 BC. The archaeologist Professor Colin Renfrew describes the Maltese Neolithic temples of that time as "the earliest free-standing monuments in stone in the world" and the "memorably imposing" facade of Gozo's Ggantija temples as "perhaps the earliest architecturally conceived exterior in the world".

Later, during days of antiquity, the excellence of Maltese houses that were "very beautiful and ambitiously adorned with cornices and stucco works" caught the attention of the Sicilian-Greek historian Diodorus Sicullus (80–20 BC). At that time Malta was ruled by Romans and, as elsewhere, they built temples, town houses, baths and villas. There was an active harbour in the Marsa basin end of the Grand Harbour with quays built with massive masonry blocks that were perfectly cut and jointed. The capital Melita (where Mdina and Rabat stand) was a sprawling city with well-built houses. Only the merest traces now remain.

The Dark Ages came over Malta as they did the rest of Europe; but, while the latter emerged triumphantly out of the torpor to beget the great monuments of the Romanesque and Gothic period, the Maltese islands slumbered on. All through the Middle Ages the islands remained desolate, sparsely inhabited and isolated. At that time Mediterranean shipping tended to hug the continental coastline, shying away to avoid shipwreck and the pirates that might be lurking in Malta's coves and bays. Outside influences passed them by.

Indigenous Maltese architecture of the medieval period is almost non-existent and such buildings as there are, were strongly influenced by Arab tradition. The islands were subjected to Arab domination from AD 870 to AD 1090 which was ended only when Christianity returned with the conquest of Malta by Roger II of Sicily.

There were a number of troglodytic churches decorated with Byzantinesque figures, while the few free-standing churches consisted of small, flat-roofed, cubical structures. Internally many were ornamented

with brightly coloured wall paintings; externally they were plain, the only ornamental features consisting of a deep hood-mould over the slightly pointed doorway with, sometimes, a small circular window above.

Raising the roof: In Mdina, Birgu (Vittoriosa) and in Gozo's Citadel there are some late medieval houses still, with windows on the first floor of a characteristically Catalan inspiration – with round-headed double lights separated by an excessively slim colonette. There was a cathedral, too, in Mdina that dated from the 13th century but this was enlarged a few centuries later by the addition of transepts and a choir, while the

Preceding pages: the stones of Vittoriosa turn golden in the setting sun. **Left,** the imposing portals of Auberge de Castille, the prime minister's offices. **Right,** wooden balconies give domestic architecture character.

roof was raised by the adding of a clerestory.

It was in 1530, at the height of the Renaissance, that Charles V handed over the islands to the Order of St John. It was a momentous event, ushering in a long period of building activity that would produce the finest architectural monuments.

With the arrival of the Order, Malta was linked once more to international currents and with owners who represented a concentration of wealth combined with an incredible reserve of human resources. The rich aristocratic knights, particularly the Grand Masters, would shower their riches on their new headquarters and endow the islands with fine buildings and works of art. Eminent artists, military and civil engineers, architects and artisans would be "lured" to Malta; the Order was good paymaster. Painters such as Mattia Preti and Antoine de Favray, and engineers and architects such as Francesco Buonamici, Mederico Blondel and Charles François de Mondion, called in at Malta for a few days but stayed on to benefit the whole island.

The knights chose Birgu as their base because its position, straddling a promontory in the Grand Harbour, had deep creeks on either side to provide shelter for their fleet. As they had never ceased in their campaign against the Turkish infidel, they were fully aware that their immediate task was security; the new Malta headquarters would be regarded as a centre for Christian piracy that offended the mighty Ottoman.

In true terms of defence their position was at first untenable; but with the help of some of the foremost military engineers of the day provided by Christian states, walls were built that rendered it sufficiently strong to withstand a great Turkish force sent by Suleiman the Magnificent.

After the Great Siege in 1565, the Order decided to build a new fortified town on the higher promontory (Mount Scebberas) that dominates Malta's two main harbours, the Grand Harbour and Marsamxett. Pope Pius

IV sent Francesco Laparelli da Cortona, one of his best engineers and an assistant to Michelangelo at St Peter's, to advise and supervise the project.

The first stone was laid on 28 March 1566 and the city was named Valletta after the heroic Grand Master who won the Siege. The massive fortifications that encircle the town were completed in less than five years with a local labour force being augmented by foreign labour from Italy.

When Laparelli left the island, in late 1569 or early 1570, the task of completion was put into the hands of his able assistant, a Maltese architect, Gerolamo Cassar (*circa* 1520–

92). It was he who subsequently designed the new city's principal buildings: the Grand Masters' Palace, the Conventual Church of St John, the seven auberges of the knights, the Hospital of the Order, the slaves' prison, the Ferreria (arsenal), and several churches and monastic buildings. Many survive.

Before embarking on his task Cassar was sent on a short tour of the foremost cities of Italy, and the buildings designed by him rose in a rigid variant of Italian Mannerism (although it was Laparelli who designed the rigid grid plan of the city streets).

Gerolamo Cassar's buildings, as it transpired, perpetuated many features that appear on early buildings in Mdina and Birgu,

nating, the whole tied in with "rusticated" corners – that is, with sunk joints and roughened surfaces. These corners became his hallmark and, as he progressed, so the rusticated quoins (cornerstones) became wider and more deeply cut and powerful than any he might have seen abroad. The conventual church (Co-cathedral) of St John is his masterpiece and here, in its monumentality, simplicity and deep solemnity, one can truly appreciate the talent of the architect.

The church was once as severe internally as it is externally, a severity that was intended to express the character of the Order whose church it was, as well as reflect the surrounding fortifications of Valletta. Cas-

but they set the character of all the buildings in Valletta and, to a great measure, influenced all subsequent building in following centuries. Cassar's facades were all astylar (that is, without pilasters or columns) and when storeyed, with an exceedingly tall first, upper, floor. Straight-headed windows were widely spaced in long uniform rows.

The emphasis was strongly horizontal, with huge masses of plain masonry predomi-

Left, Valletta, housing above the bastion walls facing into the Grand Harbour. **Above**, Richard England, Maltese architect with an international reputation.

sar believed all his buildings should echo the fact that they were built in a fortified city and have, therefore, a military cast. The interior was subsequently transformed, mostly by the Calabrese painter Mattia Preti, into the magnificent baroque interior we see today.

During the first part of the 17th century a number of parish churches were built in a style strongly reminiscent of the Italian Quattrocento with the addition of the occasional element recalling the late medieval Maltese church. Unfortunately, as parish wealth increased, many were later enlarged and, in the process, ineradicably changed.

One, however, the parish church of Attard,

DOMINATED BY CHURCHES

It is generally believed the islanders between 3000 BC and 2000 BC avoided warring and tribal hostility by channelling their energies into non-destructive competition: each chiefdom apparently trying to outshine its neighbour by building a bigger and finer temple. This kind of parish rivalry has continued ever since and, as a result, is responsible for the cathedral-sized churches to be found in many villages and for the stunning magnificence of their interiors.

True, many were made an excuse for cheap ostentation and, in some, there is the occasional disappointing sameness. But ignore the indifferent and commonplace and you are still left with a wealth of outstandingly beautiful buildings.

In the Middle Ages, the islands were backward and poor; the free-standing churches consisted only of small, cube-like structures – externally severe, sturdy and squat.

The system used for constructing these first churches was conditioned by the fact that the only building material available was the soft, fine-grained limestone from the local quarries. Stonemasons learned to make everything from the stone – not only the walls but also the roofs – but, they quickly discovered, 6 ft (2 metres) is the maximum length a narrow slab of limestone can span, so arches became an integral support feature.

Because of this limitation, the interiors were divided into a series of bays created by the arches. The walls were plastered and painted with murals that were predominantly in red, yellow ochre, verdigris and a dark blue-grey.

Only a few of these late medieval churches survive – the Annunciation at Hal Millieri, Santa Marija at Birmiftuh, old St Gregory at Zejtun – the best descendants of this indigenous type.

Similar to these small vernacular churches are slightly larger, domed, versions with foreign inspiration. Embedded into the urban core, they are found everywhere, from the Marina outside Valletta to countryside isolation. Perhaps the most memorable are the church of Sarria at Floriana,

and Ta' Liesse on the Grand Harbour's waterside road into Valletta. In the fields near Siggiewi is the church of Tal-Providenza.

During the first half of the 17th century parish churches had the same fundamental, rectangular form but, with the addition of transepts and a choir, their plan became cruciform. The crossing was roofed with a low dome and the nave divided into three bays for side altars. They were quite moderate in size and remarkable for their pleasing proportions, the result, no doubt, of the good schooling of their architects in Renaissance theory. The best surviving example is the church of Santa Marija, the parish church of Attard. The old, partly collapsed parish church in Birkirkara was similar, but more richly decorated. Its remaining facade has two very fine Corinthian capitals.

A contemporary of these is the church of St George in Qormi (1584–1684). With a basilican plan similar to Brunelleschi's Florentine churches of Santo Spirito and San Lorenzo, this was the first of Malta's big parish churches and has a two-towered facade that is both graceful and stately.

From the late 17th century, the move was to build baroque churches – generally on a large scale with florid western towers. The vaults were invariably painted and the altars had big altarpieces and big sculptured retables.

The parish churches of Zebbug and Siggiewi are outstanding examples of the Maltese baroque with their paintings, rich carving and liberal application of gilt and multi-coloured marbling.

Quite a number are masterpieces of architecture. The most striking of all ware the cathedral in Mdina, St Catherine at Zejtun; St Helen at Birkirkara; St Paul, Rabat; St Lawrence, Vittoriosa; St Saviour, Lija; St Nicholas, Siggiewi; Our Lady of Graces, Zabbar and Santa Marija at Gudja. On the island of Gozo there is the Matrice and parish church of Gharb.

Also in Gozo is the simple, classical 18th-century cathedral within Victoria's Citadel walls with its *trompe l'oeil* painting to give worshippers the feeling that there is a dome above (it was never completed). Perpetuating the tradition of fine church building today is Xewkija's new basilica dedicated to St John. It dominates Gozo and rivals the giant Mosta dome in Malta. ∎

was almost untouched and is the best example of this period on Malta. Another, Santa Marija, in Birkirkara, was saved by the accidental collapse of its vault preventing further alteration. It is remarkable for the richness and crispness of its carving.

It was Francesco Buonamici, an architect from Lucca, who designed the first important baroque buildings in Valletta. He was the Order's resident engineer between 1634 and 1659 and was primarily responsible for overseeing the extensions to the Order's fortifications (notably those protecting Floriana) as well as the maintenance of all other fortifications. His designs, in the then current baroque style, include the church of Vittoriosa. In the first two facades Buonamici shows how it was possible to articulate a long facade by means of panelling while at the same time retaining the columnless treatment of Valletta's earlier palaces.

By the mid-17th century Mederico Blondel from France had succeeded Buonamici as resident engineer. He is on record as having designed the splendid facade of Valletta's church of St Mary of Jesus (1689), but it is quite likely that he was also responsible for St Rocco and St Francis (both 1681) and, in Mdina, the Carmelite church (1650–72). This centralised church, with its oval plan similar to that of Vignola's Santa Anna dei Palafrenieri, was built by Fran-

St Nicolas in Valletta, the plan of the church of St Paul at Rabat with the adjoining church of St Publius, part of the facade of the church of St Philip in Zebbug and several altar retables (the frames enclosing decorated panels behind the altars).

His civil buildings include the Jesuit College and Hostel de Verdelin in Valletta, Wignacourt's College at Rabat and, possibly, the facade of the Inquisitor's Palace,

Left, Zabbar's baroque splendour, the parish church of Our Lady of Grace. **Above**, the fortifications of Valletta towering above the Grand Harbour.

cesco Sammut and Lorenzo Gafa'.

Gafa' is Malta's greatest baroque architect. After beginning life as a sculptor, he turned successfully to architecture and is responsible for some of the finest churches to be seen in Malta or Gozo. His is the work that seems to symbolise the Maltese islands, the Maltese image. The churches include St Nicholas (1676–93), Siggiewi; St Lawrence (1681–97), Vittoriosa; Santa Maria (1685–1712), Qrendi; St Catherine (1691–1778), Zejtun; the Matrice (1697), Gharb; and the cathedral (1696–1702), Mdina. This latter masterpiece, set in its dramatic position on the ramparts of the old city, is a wonderful sight. The encircling walls of the city look like parts of the church building itself and the whole is surmounted by a dome such as only a baroque sculptor could have fashioned.

During the 18th century a number of florid baroque buildings rose in Valletta and Mdina. They were designed by Romano Carapecchia who worked in Malta for 30 years from 1706, and a Frenchman, Charles François de Mondion, resident engineer from 1715 to 1733. Their buildings are on a par with those erected on the mainland.

The major building that dominates Valletta, however, is the Auberge de Castille designed by Gerolamo Cassar but remodelled by Andrea Belli in 1741. A Maltese architect who had studied in Italy and travelled through Austria and Germany, Belli designed several other outstanding buildings that give Maltese architecture its authority. His are the Bishop's Seminary (1733) in Mdina (now the Cathedral Museum), the Augustinian Priory in Rabat (1740), the Archbishops Curia (1743) in Floriana and in Valletta's South Street, the building that houses the Museum of Fine Arts (1761).

Another architect of note during this period was the Sicilian, Stefano Ittar. He was responsible for the neoclassical Biblioteca, the National Library (1786–96), and the Customs House on the quay below the city walls in the Grand Harbour.

The 19th century saw a number of important new buildings swelling the ranks of architectural treasure. In 1833 the Mosta Dome, the church of Santa Marija known as the Rotunda, was designed by Grognet de Vasse. In 1841 St Paul's Anglican cathedral, designed by William Scamp, replaced the Order's Auberge d'Allemagne. Then, in 1860, the Royal Opera House was designed by Edward Middleton Barry, the architect of the Royal Opera House in London's Covent Garden. Sadly, this was destroyed, with so much more of interest, in World War II.

Since then, Maltese architects have made their mark – some good, some indifferent, some excellent. But the talent is here and so, fortunately, is the soft limestone that gives the islands their architectural quality.

Right, like many others, this patrician building in Valletta has been converted for use as shops, offices and apartments.

It does not take long to discover that the Maltese islands wear a very modest décolletage, so to speak, and the rest is camouflaged, but tempting none the less.

Take, for example, the Palazzo Ferreria in Valletta's Republic Street, whose Francia family died out only in recent years. In the 1920s and 1930s, audiences at the Royal Opera House across the road would twist and crane their necks to get a glimpse of the huge Francia diamonds worn on gala occasions. The secret of the whereabouts of these great gems, purchased from Russian refugees at the time of the Revolution, was lost with the demise of the family.

Great residences in Valletta are few, but once, before they were adapted to offices or divided into flats and shops, they were abundant. The Maltese Barons Azzopardi, in their palace cornering South Street, kept liveried flunkeys well into this century; their carnival parties were legendary and their life-style was well-suited to the belle époque. Their Château Bertrand, a shooting box at Wardija, still stands as a small but rare and charming example of Ludwigian architecture in Malta stone.

Treasures dispersed: Still in Valletta, stretching out along Christopher Street, between Republic and Frederick Streets, the great house of the admiral of the Order, the Palazzo Rocca Grande, stood as one huge facade. Until recent years the Maltese Count Sant lived in one half and the Sicilian Conte Messina in the other. The great collection of the Messinas was dispersed only in the second quarter of this century, and one still hears comments such as, "those flower pictures belonged to the Conti Messina".

All the great collections are dispersed, but they have not gone far. The great treasures of the knights that were not removed by conquerors have made their way up to the great rooms of the smaller palazzi spread through the length of Malta. A great candelabrum may be gathering dust on the *piano nobile* as it awaits its day of glory. Immured collections of silver are stored away safely. An age-old trick as protection against thievery was to cut a narrow slit into the top of an internal door, which then became the resting place of many hundreds of gold coins: one still hears stories.

Private collections kept in secrecy still surpass the stock held in the national collections. In spite of legislation enabling a beneficiary of a will to opt for his or her chattels to be legally declared as only five percent of an inheritance, there is doubt about how the tax authorities would interpret the law. If the testator had an "accumulation", all would be well; if it is deemed to be a "collection", then it would have to be declared and paid for.

Until this uncertainty is resolved, private houses may never be open to the public and the great private collections never be seen.

Mdina on its own would, in any list of historic houses, offer a Magnificent Seven. Here, within the city walls, lie treasures of untold importance to the history of Malta. Porcelain, pottery (including those wonderful pharmacy jars of the Order), silver that even in Rome and Venice would look elegant and never provincial. There are paintings by Mattia Preti, portraits and rare landscapes by Antoine de Favray, rumours of a Caravaggio or two, landscapes from the 17th and 18th centuries, pictures by unknown artists of suffering martyrs, triumphant saints, shipwrecked St Pauls, Virgin Marys, and perhaps most important of all, acres of naive ancestors painted locally.

In such portraits, the lucky woman who bore a son was traditionally depicted with a flower in the right hand. Wimples were worn by the ladies, prelates wore gold and sometimes jewelled pectoral crosses, priests and monsignori were always in their finery and usually abundant in lace. Children wore coral jewellery to drive away the Evil Eye

when presented for admiration. They are the embodiment of a culture, a unique record.

The oldest Maltese pedigree seems to belong to the Inguanez family, descendants of that splendid character Cikku Gatto. He was ennobled in 1350 and made Governor of Malta. His will is a delightful document in which he remembers and mentions his "natural" as well as his legitimate heirs. It is likely that perhaps half of the residents of

Mdina are able to trace their ancestry back to him. His tombstone has survived in the gardens of the Palazzo d'Aurel in Gudja.

Like many country houses, Palazzo d'Aurel is situated in a village. In its heyday, it was the residence of Marchesa Bettina Dorrell, lady-in-waiting in Naples to Maria Carolina, Queen of the Two Sicilies, sister of Marie Antoinette. The gardens were laid out in their present form under her direction and the outlook is magnificent. There are belvederes, follies, temples and even a watchtower which commands a coastal view of 180 degrees. The main house is architecturally of a higher standard than usually achieved by the nobility, and it stands today, well-preserved with its *trompe l'oeil* frescoes, one of the most important examples of grandeur unrelated to the knights.

Casual visitors to Malta and Gozo do not really get the opportunity to view the grand houses, but they do exist and they are more beautiful and plentiful than even the average Maltese resident imagines. An exception, however, one that gives an idea of Maltese wealth, is the building that is now the Casino. This was the 19th-century Italianate summer residence of the Marquis Scicluna.

Huge diamond: The Villa Bologna in Attard, named after Pietro Bologna, in recent history became the residence of Gerald Strickland Bologna, Count della Catena, who inherited it through his mother. He was part-English and became a member of the British Parliament as well as Prime Minister of Malta. When he married a Hulton Press heiress, Villa Bologna and the gardens achieved a great infusion of new splendour. The Countess accompanied her husband to London for the coronation of George VI, buying for the occasion a diamond for her tiara just slightly larger than one old penny.

A list of the great houses in Mdina would include Casa Inguanez in Villegaignon Street which, remarkably, is still occupied by the descendants of a 14th-century ancestor, plus the palazzi Bonici, Mangione and Sant Manduca. Then there are Villa Preziozi (renamed Francia), Villa Parisio, il Palazz L'Ahmar and Casa Barbaro. Who knows what riches they once held?

Superstition and traditional wariness are important facets of the national character. Most of it is secular but some is religious. Everyone has something that is lucky or unlucky, that he will or will not do, particularly when away from sophisticated town society. But even in town there is many a mother who will not tempt fate by wearing green the day her child is to sit an exam.

The Catholic ethic of behaviour is learned at an early age and many soon find a favourite saint to pray to for the rest of their lives for protection and intercession. Where most university students make their promises to St Jude the patron saint of students (and have printed a few lines of thanks in the local *Times*) others invoke the likes of St Rita, St Anthony and the Virgin Mary.

In churches like the Ta' Pinu shrine in Gozo there are naive votive paintings donated to the church after a miraculous rescue had been effected after invoking the name of the patron saint in prayer. In Ta' Pinu's side corridor are paintings of shipwrecked sailors being saved by the Virgin Mary as well as macabre rememberances of miracle cures – like gall-stones in jam jars, discarded crutches and trusses.

There are holy images everywhere, in banks, shops and even buses. By the driver, most buses have little shrines lit by a small bulb and before the bus starts older passengers cross themselves and will do so again if the bus passes a shrine beside the road.

Time for the devil: To confuse the devil who roams, churches have two clocks in their towers, one real, the other *trompe l'oeil*. Tradition has it that the devil is confused by these, cannot tell the time, and so cannot come to collect departing souls – though cynics point out few churches could have afforded two real clocks when their towers were built. Warding off evil in the pagan manner, many houses in rural communities have bulls' horns tied, pointing outwards, on the highest corner of a roof or perhaps above

the front door. Mixing the religious with the pagan, most will also have a saint on another corner or in a niche cut into a wall. It's the best of both protections.

In the 18th century young girls in society were given simple coral necklaces to ward off evil and, until recently, men sometimes wore tiny horn-shaped amulets made of ivory or coral on a chain around the neck. In the old peasant Latin tradition many men still stick out the fore and little fingers of the hand in the form of horns when they think some-

one has the evil eye or is wishing them ill. Children can often be seen surreptitiously making this sign when playing games in order to bring bad luck to their opponents.

As bad luck is not confined to humans, to ward off evil, horses pulling carts or *carrozin* often have red tassels or feathers attached to their harnesses or bridles.

And the *luzzu* and *dghajsa*, the beautiful brightly coloured, traditional boats of these waters that have been used by Maltese sailors since Phoenician times, have their pagan protection too. Each craft may be named after a Catholic saint but each also has on either side of its prow a wide-open, ever

Preceding pages: wall shrine alongside bar, Marsaxlokk. **Left,** holy reliquary at St Paul Shipwrecked Church, Valletta. **Above,** white bow tied to door knob to signal wedding day.

alert, painted eye ready to ward off the worst.

Many old beliefs have faded away. There were old wives' tales with old wives to help keep them alive, especially where fertility and birth were concerned. For example, it was deemed that the best months for marriage were January, April and August when bodies are at their most fertile; that women should not work in fields or at pickling vegetables during menstruation for the produce will be ruined; that black underwear ensures pregnancy, white the opposite; and, if a pregnant woman craves special food and does not eat it, her child will have a birth mark in that shape.

Young mothers are especially wary of the

evil eye. It may be possessed by someone, invariably female, who does not know that she has it. It works this way: she says to the mother "what a beautiful baby you have" and the next day something awful happens to the baby. The child "has been given the eye". The child will develop spots, a cold, a squint. A mother seeing a neighbour with the evil eye approaching will cross the road with her child to make sure the women does not look at the child and compliment it. (The effects of the evil eye always come after a compliment.) She's not regarded as a witch. Like poisonous snakes, Malta doesn't have those.

(Tradition has it that St Paul was responsi-

ble for removing the poison from the snakes of Malta having been bitten by one soon after his shipwreck. Cynical tradition continues by saying that after removing the venom from the tongues of vipers he put it into the tongues of the Maltese, many of whom enjoy malicious gossip.)

A more enjoyable custom with babies, but dying out, is the *quccija*. On a child's first birthday the family gets together for a small party. There they assemble a tray of small items, the objects varying slightly for a boy or girl. Among the objects might be a thimble, pen, rosary, an egg, some money. The tray is put in front of the child for it to make a choice. The object chosen foretells the child's future – tailor, clerk, priest, farmer, banker, or whatever.

There is a ritual at home that mimics the pagan one of harvest rebirth, one that has become incorporated into Catholic ritual too. About two weeks before the Christmas crib is assembled near the Christmas tree, the child is given saucers or shallow bowls on which to sow seeds of wheat, *qamh*, or canary seed, *skalora*. They are then kept in the dark and watered every two days. As soon as long pale shoots begin to sprout, the bowls are brought out by the child and put near the Baby Jesus, as the child Jesus is called here.

Food, too, comes into consideration. Boiled grasses can provide both a laxative and a slimming regimen; boiled lettuce a liquid that induces sleep even to an insomniac. An onion sliced in half and rubbed on a balding head will, like the licks of a cow, encourage regrowth.

As for catching a cold, the easiest way to do so, it is said, is to go out of a warm house into the cold winter streets without first lowering the body temperature. Many therefore will stand for a few minutes just inside the front door with their wrists pressed against the cold stone wall. This, they say, reduces the temperature of the blood.

Should a member of the family die in the house, a glass of water or a saucer of salt is often placed near the front door. The spirit must never leave the house thirsty or without salt to flavour its food.

Above, in Zabbar church museum, votive paintings and models illustrate miracles received. **Right**, most boats have watchful eyes on the prow to ward off evil.

Fifty-eight miles (93 km) due south of Sicily, in the middle of a remarkably clear and unpolluted expanse of blue Mediterranean, the Maltese archipelago consists of three inhabited islands, Malta, Gozo and Comino, and two minuscule uninhabited rocks. The total area adds up to only 122 sq. miles (316 sq. km) and the population to just 350,000. As the islands are low lying and relatively flat, they are not easy to identify from a distance. Malta is the shape of a wedge which slopes from the southwest to the east. Most of the resort development is to the east, along a coast indented with harbours and bays, with rock beaches and sheltered coves. Most of the western side is sheer cliff.

Valletta, the capital, is the seat of government as well as the centre of commerce. Its resident population is about 10,000 but numbers are dwindling as younger people move out to more modern surroundings. After 7pm the city closes its doors; nightlife is elsewhere. Architecturally superb, Valletta was built by the Order of St John who laid its foundations in 1565 after the Great Siege of Malta when the Order and the Maltese defeated the invading Ottoman Turks. Now being restored to its former glory after years of neglect, Valletta has a wealth of historical splendour.

On a plateau in the centre of the island, Mdina, the old capital, is one of the world's finest examples of an enclosed medieval walled city still inhabited. Known as the Silent City – because that is what it is – its houses are patrician, its cathedral superb. The silhouette of Mdina seen as one approaches is unique.

Sliema, the main residential town, has rapidly developed with its satellites, St Julians and Paceville, into the most important resort area too. This is where the middle class once chose to live, a comparatively sophisticated place. Leading hotels, the casino, beach establishments and the best of the island's restaurants are here too. Further north are the newer resorts of Bugibba, Qawra, St Paul's Bay and Mellieha, all constantly expanding as visitors flock in. And, although it may seem as if Malta is over-built, true countryside does exist. A car will help you explore and get off the beaten track.

If some place names prove unpronounceable, the Maltese, a friendly people anyway, are always delighted to provide a phonetic equivalent. *Malti*, the Maltese language, can seem impenetrable to any non-native. But most Maltese speak English too and many have a smattering of Italian, French or German. It might be nice to say *kif int?* (how are you?), *x'hin hu?* (what time is it?), *kemm?* (how much?), or even *grazzi* (thank you). But English will do.

Preceding pages: Dwejra as the sun sets; tiny wayside chapel surrounded by fields; Gozo's harbour of Mgarr. Left, Marsaxlokk glows beneath an evening sun in summer.

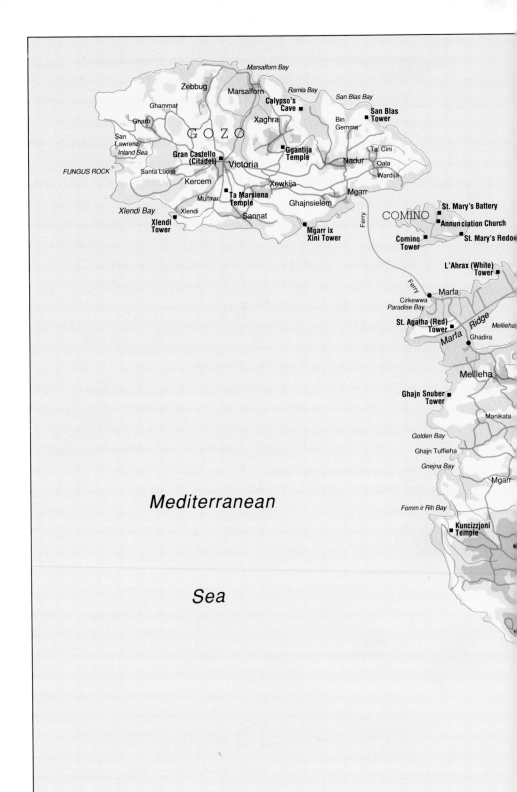

Marsalforn Bay

Zebbug

Marsalforn

Ramla Bay

Calypso's Cave ■

San Blas Bay

San Blas Tower ■

Ghammar

Xaghra

Bin Gemma

Gharb

G O Z O

San Lawrenz

Inland Sea

Ta' Cini

Gran Castello (Citadel) ■

■ Ggantija Temple

Nadur

Qala

FUNGUS ROCK

Victoria

Wardija

Santa Lucija

Kercem

Xewkija

Munxar

■ Ta Marsiena Temple

Ghajnsielem

Mgarr

Xlendi Bay

Xlendi

Sannat

COMINO

St. Mary's Battery ■

Annunciation Church ■

Xlendi Tower

■ Mgarr ix Xini Tower

Ferry

Comino Tower ■

St. Mary's Redoubt ■

L'Ahrax (White) Tower ■

Ferry

Marfa

Cirkewwa
Paradise Bay

St. Agatha (Red) Tower ■

Marfa Ridge

Mellieha

Ghadira

Mellieha

Ghajn Snuber Tower ■

Manikata

Golden Bay

Ghajn Tuffieha

Mediterranean

Gnejna Bay

Mgarr

Fomm ir Rih Bay

■ Kuncizzjoni Temple

Sea

adid

ST. PAUL'S ISLAND

Qawra Tower

ul's   Bugibba   **Ghallis Tower**

Quawra   Salina Bay

St. Mark's Tower

Bur Marrad

San Pawl Tat-Targa

Mosta Fort   Gharghur

St. Julians   St. Julian's Bay

Sliema Point Tower

San Gwann

Naxxar   **Sliema**

Mosta   Gzira

Msida   Marsamxett Harbour

Cumbo Tower   Balzan   Birkirkara   **Valletta**   Grand Harbour   **Fort St. Rocco**

Ta' Qali   **San Anton Palace**   Kalkara   **Inquisitors Palace**

Attard   Pieta Floriana   **Fort St. Angelo**

a   Hamrun   Senglea   Vittoriosa

Mdina   **Roman Villa Museum**   **Cospicua**

M A L T A   Kordin   **Kordin Temples**

Rabat   Hal Muxi   Qormi   Marsa

Zebbug   Hal Mula   Ghammieri   **Paola**   Fgura   **Zabbar**

Hypogeum   **Tarxien Temples**   Marsaskala

Luqa   Santa Lucia   Zejtun

Verdala Palace   Siggiewi   St. Thomas Bay

Luqa Airport

Mqabba   Ghaxaq

Inquisitor's Palace   Kirkop   Gudja

Qrendi   Safi   **Ghar Dalam Cave**   **Fort St. Lucian**

Zurrieq   Marsaxlokk

Birzebbuga   *Marsaxlokk Bay*   **Fort Delimara**

Hagar Qim and Mnajdra Temples   Bubagra

Nigred

Wardija Tower   Kalafrana

Dolmen   **Fort Benghisa**

Ghar Hasan Cave

VALLETTA

"Our fair capital with its cosmopolitan connections may not inappropriately be considered to be an apt seat for a Council of European States." When Prime Minister George Borg Olivier wrote these words in March 1966, he could scarcely have imagined that, 23 years later, the leaders of the two most powerful nations on earth would find Malta an appropriate location to hold a superpower summit. (In fact, the Bush-Gorbachev summit did not actually take place in Valletta, but Valletta is where it would have taken place had not massive security considerations deemed it necessary to float the momentous 1989 meeting aboard a warship in Marsaxlokk Bay.)

Certainly, Valletta, with its deep historical roots, seems well suited to this role. After successfully withstanding the prolonged siege of 1565 and emerging the battered victors and defenders of Christianity, the inhabitants realised that, in order to be ready for a second Islamic invasion that must surely come, it was tactically essential to build a new and better fortified city in Malta. The Turk, they believed, always returned and the island represented a Christian outpost, a stepping stone to the Christian mainland on the shores of the Mediterranean. The forces of Islam would not fail to strike again and try to conquer in the name of their faith.

The ground around Birgu that the knights and the Maltese had so bravely defended was reduced to rubble and no amount of repair or rebuilding could render it strategically safe. The situation appeared so dire that many of the knights favoured abandoning the islands altogether and returning to the safety of Europe's mainland. If the Order were to remain on Malta, it would better serve Christianity if a new and impregnable city were to be built.

The site chosen was virgin territory across the great harbour (now the **Grand Harbour**). It was a high, barren, uninhabited rocky peninsula known as Mount Sceberras that, with the tiny fort of St Elmo at its tip, both commanded the entrances to the harbours and dominated the lands on either side of it. It was from this unguarded superior position that the Turks had managed to rain down their fire with such devastation. The knights would not make the mistake again of leaving such a strategic position available to the enemy.

The land belonged to the Inguanez family, whose descendants still live in Mdina. Their rent was agreed as an ear of wheat and a glass of water, to be proffered annually by the Grand Master himself. (The water was drawn from a well-head which can be found behind a grill in the grand Corridor of the Palace of the Grand Masters).

After much political argument and discussion, plans that had been drawn up by the Vatican architect, Francesco Laparelli, were accepted. One of the most important planned towns of the Renaissance would now be built. Laparelli's Valletta would be a city laid out in rigid grid plan – that is, with all

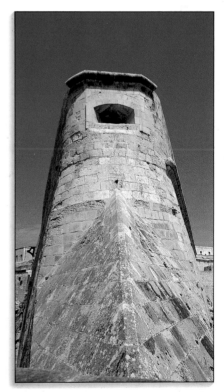

roads running straight and crossing each other at right angles. There would be main squares and secondary squares.

To make the city beautiful there would be uniformity of house design. Noxious trades would be zoned together to protect the residential quarters. Laparelli planned an imposing space for a Grand Masters' palace to be built "as large as Palazzo Farnese in Rome", and there would be excellent sites for the conventual church and hospital as well as for eight auberges for the different langues that formed the Order. As the promontory was so hilly and much had yet to be levelled it was impossible to estimate the number of houses that could be built.

On the morning of 28 March 1566, with great pomp, the foundation stone was laid. There, where the the chapel of Our Lady of Victory would be built, a richly decorated altar was set up and High Mass celebrated in honour of Santo Spirito. The air filled with sacred music. The new city that would rise was christened Valletta after Grand Master Jean Parisot de la Valette, who had led the Order to victory.

In spite of the enthusiasm and urgency, work was slow and laboured. Hard rock had to be turned into a plateau before building could begin. After a few years Laparelli returned to Rome and the work came into the hands of a Maltese architect, Gerolamo Cassar.

New glory: Cassar, then in his late forties, had worked with Laparelli and during the siege, while only a boy, had helped repair fortifications and invent war weapons. He had studied in Rome at the expense of the Order. Slowly the city took shape. Today, although masked by a plethora of modern shopfronts and advertising hoardings, the city remains a delight, combining as it does Laparelli's original designs and Cassar's magnificent architecture. Some is restoration (necessitated by the bombing campaigns of World War II) but the restoration is excellent. And, even now, the restoration of Valletta to its true glory continues with governmental aid and with the help of Malta's

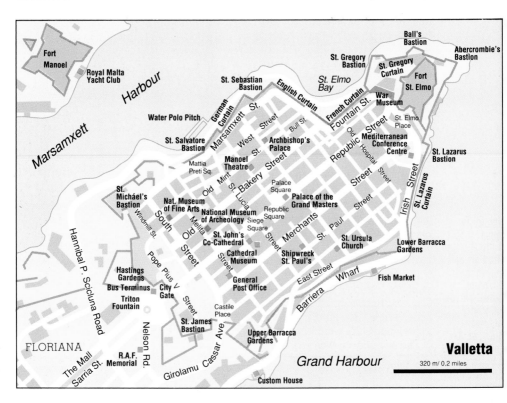

leading architects committed to the capital's rebirth.

In fact, the dramatic outline of the city, with its superb bastion walls wrapped protectively around it and its skyline of rectangular masses varied only by a cupola or church spire, remains an impressive sight, whether viewed from the Sliema side of Marsamxett Harbour or from the other side, across the Grand Harbour. And by night, floodlit to perfection, it is a moving sight.

A walk through Valletta refreshes the spirit. It is a city of palaces, churches, art galleries and museums, unlike any other. Enter on foot from **Republic Gate**, from the busy confusion of Malta's central bus terminus, or by car from the grand sweep that leads to the Auberge de Castile, the Office of the Prime Minister.

Manoel Theatre, with composer Charles Camilleri.

Although it is not open to the public, start at the **Auberge de Castile**. A wonderful example of baroque, it was redesigned under the instructions of Grand Master Pinto in 1741 by Andrea Belli a Maltese architect from Zejtun. The high doorway, flanked by a pair of cannons, is approached by an elegant flight of steps. The exterior is magnificently decorated with carved stone and inside there is a particularly fine staircase and an attractive paved courtyard.

Abutting Castile in **Merchants' Street**, around the corner, is **Palazzo Parisio**, another government office, this one the Ministry of Foreign Affairs. When Napoleon Bonaparte took Malta on his way to the Egyptian campaigns bringing to an end the Order of St John's reign, it was the Palazzo Parisio he used as his quarters, and the office currently used by Foreign Ministers contains an alcove which the Emperor used as his bed chamber.

Cut into **Republic Street**. This is the city's main artery, leading from the Republic Gate entrance to Fort St Elmo at the tip of Valletta's promontory. It is the main shopping street, with popular boutiques, shopping malls and cafés. What appears to be a bomb site near the gate is just that. This was where, until

World War II, the grand and gracious Royal Opera House stood.

On the corner of Republic Street and narrow **Melita Street** is the imposing **Archaeological Museum**, a large edifice with small shops tucked into its hem. This was one of the original auberges, the Auberge de Provence. It suffered some war damage but has been restored and, as a museum, contains collections of prehistoric pottery, sculpture and personal ornaments recovered from the megalithic temples that dot the island. There are also some typical examples of tomb furniture of the Punic and Roman periods. Special exhibitions are mounted here, usually of photographs or paintings.

To the right, continuing along Republic Street, is **St John's Square**, with **St John's Co-cathederal**, one of the most important and remarkable monuments on the islands. Although its frontage, designed by Cassar, is somewhat plain, the interior is awe-inspiring in its wealth and detail. Almost all the facings of the walls are carved with high relief and painted in rich Renaissance colours and gilded. The novelist Sir Walter Scott said it was the most striking interior he had ever seen.

All the design directs the eye to the high altar. The floor is paved with marble slabs, each the tomb of a knight and bearing his arms in intricate marble inlay. The frescoed vault is painted in oils by Mattia Preti and in the oratory hang two of Caravaggio's great paintings, *The Beheading of St John the Baptist* and *St Jerome*.

Further along the main street, to the left, are the **Law Courts**, a modern, post-war building complete with massive pillars. Beyond are the two grand squares that give the city its centre.

The first is **Republic Square** (until recently Queen's Square), with the statue of Queen Victoria, a permanent resting-place for pigeons, surrounded by open air cafés. To the left is the flank of the Palace, but lending its imposing presence as a backdrop is the **Biblioteca**, the National Library.

Under the arches is the entrance, with

Seated in front of the Great Siege monument, carved by Antonio Scibberas (1879–1947).

tall doors and an imposing staircase that leads to the vast room above. Designed by Stefano Ittar, a Sicilian, in 1786, it was the last building of importance erected in Valletta by the Order of St John. There are said to be more that 300,000 books and documents in the building including, in the archives, more than 10,000 priceless manuscripts dating from the 12th to the 19th century. Among the letters is the signed bull and accompanying letter in which Henry VIII proclaimed himself the head of the Church of England. When Napoleon Bonaparte conquered Malta, he ordered all the records of the Order of St John to be destroyed; fortunately his orders were never carried out.

Then there is **Palace Square**, regrettably serving as a car park, with the **Palace of the Grand Masters** on one side and, facing it, the **Main Guard** and, an elegant building, currently the **Italian Cultural Centre**. The Main Guard once housed a ceremonial guard, but originally it was the Chancellery of the knights. Above its Doric portico is a royal coat of arms, erected by the British, carved in limestone with an inscription dated 1814 recording in Latin the compact between Malta and Britain. Under the plans for the rehabilitation of the city, this spread of buildings may become government offices.

A large room in the Palace, the President's official office, serves as the **House of Representatives**, Malta's Parliament. There are plans to rehouse this in a building backing on to the Office of the Prime Minister at the Auberge de Castile and return this room, once the Armoury, to its former glory.

Within the Palace, whose grand rooms are used for state occasions, is a wealth of splendour. Guides are available from **Neptune Courtyard**, one of the two square courtyards around which the Palace is built. On the grand floor above visitors see the **Corridor**, **Throne Room**, **Hall of St Michael and St George**, the **Red Room** and the ornate **Council Chamber** which is hung with superb Gobelin tapestries.

A short distance from the Palace, in

Relaxing at the open-air cafés in Republic Square with the Biblioteca in the foreground.

Old Theatre Street, is the **Manoel Theatre**, a gem of an 18th-century theatre with gilded boxes rising in tiers to the ornate ceiling. It is reputed to be the second oldest theatre still in use in Europe. Built in 1731 by Grand Master Manoel de Vilhena as a theatre for the people, mostly with money from his own pocket, it was, he declared, "for the honest recreation of the people". It opened on 9 January 1732 with a presentation of *Merope*, a grand tragedy in the classical manner by Scipione. The knights were the actors.

Its success continued. There were many grand evenings and, on 4 December 1838, three decades after the islands had come into British hands, Queen Adelaide, widow of King William IV, accompanied by cheers, anthems and guards of honour, attended a performance of Donizetti's *Lucia di Lammermoor*. But, with the opening of the Royal Opera House designed by E.M. Barry (who had also designed the Royal Opera House in London's Covent Garden) able to welcome far larger audiences, the Manoel fell into disrepair. In time, as its fortunes changed, it became a dosshouse for beggars, a dance hall and, more recently, a cinema.

In response to public appeal, the theatre is now owned by the nation and, after delicate restoration, has been officially declared Malta's National Theatre. There are plays in Maltese and English, some of them by touring British companies, and concerts with such artists as Yehudi Menuhin, Rostropovitch, Vladimir Ashkenazy, Kiri te Kanawa, and Louis Kentner.

Devastating losses: Back on Republic Street, the slope leads down to the tip of Valletta, to the Fort St Elmo and the National War Museum. At No. 74 is **Casa Rocca Piccola**, the only patrician house in Malta open to the public. Not a museum, the house is still lived in.

Established in 1488, **Fort St Elmo** played a pivotal role in the defence of the islands during the Great Siege. Unfortunately, because of the high ground which overlooked it, the Turks were able to breach its defences and the knights suffered devastating losses. Except for a handful of Maltese who were able to swim to safety across the harbour, all the brave defenders were slaughtered.

With the creation of Valletta, the land bordering St Elmo was levelled; the fort was repaired and enlarged to form a classical star-shaped fort as part of the defensive bastion walls that encircle the city. During World War II its bastions were manned by the coastal and anti-aircraft batteries of the Royal Malta Artillery. As well as containing the **National War Museum**, it is part of the Armed Forces of Malta establishment.

Just a few minutes' walk away is the **Mediterranean Conference Centre**, an uninspired title for a fascinating place. For more than two centuries this landmark was the Sacra Infermeria (the Holy Infirmary) of the Order of the Knights of St John of Jerusalem. Work on the foundation began in 1574 and extensions were added over the next century. Not only was the nursing of the highest standard, it also came to have the world's longest hospital ward

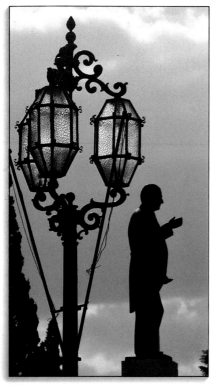

Memorial statue of former Prime Minister Borg Olivier.

which, in 1666, was described as one of the "grandest interiors in the world".

By 1787 the hospital had a complement of 563 beds which could be increased to 914 in time of emergency. The infirmary received male patients of every class, foreigners as well as Maltese. Patients were fed from silver plates. Non-catholics, however, could not remain in the great ward for more than three days if they declined to accept religious instruction from the chaplains. There are no records of conversion, however. The School of Anatomy and Surgery that would become the Medical School of the University of Malta was established at the Infirmeria in 1676 by Grand Master Cottoner.

After the departure of the Order, the French declared the hospital for the exclusive use of their troops, and so it became a military hospital – a role it would also play for the British Military Forces from 1800 to 1920.

During World War II four direct hits from bombs reduced sections of the vast building to rubble, but what remained of the long hall soon became known as Command Hall as it changed its colours to become an entertainments hall for allied troops, There were visiting concert parties, dances and film shows.

It was not until late 1978 that energetic steps were taken by the government to reclaim the devastated and derelict building and, while returning some of its former architectural glory, to turn its impressive space into an excellent fully equipped Congress Centre. In February 1979 the revived building was inaugurated and its superb restoration won the Europa Nostra Award.

In fact, as everyone who has attended an event in the building will confirm, the restoration is spectacular. The Long Ward is now the **Dar-il-Wiri**, ideal for large shows or exhibitions, and the five additional converted halls are fully equipped conference halls capable of accommodating 70 to 1,000 delegates. There is also a large restaurant and, in another hall, a multi-screen show, *The Malta Experience*, which dramatises the islands' history using the latest pro-

The stepped street of St John.

jection techniques. The commentary is in four languages.

Of the eight auberges designed by Gerolamo Cassar for the various langues of the knights, only five stand. The most imposing is the **Auberge de Castile** (the Office of the Prime Minister). The others are the **Auberge d'Aragon** (a government ministry) in Pjazza Independenza, the **Auberge d'Italie** (the Post Office) in Merchants' Street the **Auberge de Provence** (the Archaeological Museum) and the **Auberge d'Angleterre et Baviere**, known as the Baviera used as government offices but awaiting new designation, on the English Curtain section of the bastion road near Fort St Elmo.

Three have disappeared. The first was **d'Allemagne** which was demolished in 1838 in order to make way for **St Paul's Anglican Cathedral**, designed by William Scamp. Queen Adelaide laid the foundation stone during a visit in 1842. Two were ruined in World War II. The **d'Auvergne** (in Republic Street), has been replaced by the Law Courts, and **de France**, on the corner of South Street and Old Bakery Street, is now the austere, faceless headquarters of the General Workers Union (GWU).

Also in South Street is the **Museum of Fine Arts**, an elegant palazzo that long ago was built as a private palace but was taken over in British times to become Admiralty House. Lord Louis Mountbatten, as Admiral of the Fleet, had his headquarters there. In the museum are fine foreign and Maltese paintings. Exhibitions are held throughout the year.

Valletta is a city that repays exploration. There are remarkable churches to happen upon, for example. Wander in and there, for everyone to see and admire, is a wealth of baroque detailing and paintings of quality. Especially notable are **St Nicholas**, **St Mary of Jesus**, **St Rocco**, **St Francis** and **St Paul Shipwreck**. Near Castile are **Our Lady of Victories**, desperate for loving repair but the first church built in Valletta, and, facing across the narrow road, the almost matching church of **St Catherine**

Left, in Argotti Gardens with the dog. **Right**, selling videos in the market.

which adjoined the original Auberge d'Italie and, also ripe for restoration, even now has mass in Italian and an Italian congregation. (In Republic Street, mass in English and German is celebrated at **Santa Barbara**.) Rebuilt since the war is the tiny Greek church of **Our Lady of Damascus**, in Archbishops' Street to the side of the Palace, in which hangs an icon dedicated to Our Lady, brought to Malta by the knights in 1530, plus 36 icons by the Russian painter, Gregriur Malzeff.

Then there are things particular to Valletta. Like the streets of steps – **St John**, **St Lucia** and **Scots** are just three of them – where the steps were designed just high enough for men in heavy armour to climb without too much effort. (They swung their legs at the hips, raising their feet a matter of inches as they pivotted to meet the new step.)

Then there's the magnificent view of the **Grand Harbour**. The days when the harbour was busy with liners, warships and toiling tugs are long passed. No more the busy activity between ships or the countless numbers of *dghajsa* ferrying people aboard or ashore. (Rarely seen now, the *dghajsa* is the colourful water taxi, the Maltese equivalent of a gondola. It was propelled by the oarsman standing – as they still do in annual races. Today, working *dghajsas* are more likely to have outboard engines.) The Grand Harbour today is tranquil, its traffic the occasional container ship and the daily visit of some of the Med's finest cruise ships.

But it was not long ago, in some people's memories, that this was the target of enemy war planes, when the Grand Harbour was the home of the Mediterranean Fleet and haven to the convoys of merchantmen determined to keep Malta alive and steer victory the way of the Allies. The best vantage point is from the **Upper Barrakka** public gardens near Castile. This is the highest point on the 16th-century bastion walls that the knights of the Order of St John built to protect and encircle their city of Valletta.

The panorama here is incomparable.

From left to right, there is the breakwater entrance to the harbour with, across the water facing Valletta, **Fort Ricasoli, Bighi** (well known once as a naval hospital but now state housing), the **Fort St Angelo** standing majestically perfect, the witness of so much history, and directly ahead, the town of **Senglea**, dwarfed suddenly by the size of today's giant tankers that have come in for servicing at the famous dockyard. To the right are more dockyard workings and a towering grain silo. Below this vantage point are the **War Rooms** (open to visitors) where Malta's defensive strategy was plotted.

View from the sea: Another good way to see the Grand Harbour is by harbour cruise. Launches with well-informed guides leave Sliema's Strand daily and, after a tour of **Marsamxett Harbour**, head out to sea, then skirt Fort St Elmo before turning back into the spacious waters of the Grand Harbour. This is the way to see the fortifications as seamen have for many centuries.

Of course, as the capital of the Maltese islands, Valletta is also the commercial and business centre. There are shops and boutiques and pharmacies with trained chemists dispensing all kinds of international medicines.

In **St Lucia Street** are a dozen tiny jewellers' shops selling gold and silver, most of it made locally with faultless workmanship. In **Merchants' Street**, a street market has bargains in casual clothes such as T-shirts, jeans and sweaters, and an indoor market has a variety of tiny shops selling excellent fish, meat, fruit and vegetables. There are innumerable places to buy souvenirs of doubtful taste.

Of doubtful taste, too, is **Strait Street**. But it's a landmark and must conjure up memories for anyone who served in Malta during World War II. Known then as "The Gut", this narrow long street once consisted of nothing but ever-open bars and dance halls with ever-available hostesses. It has seen better days and better income and most larger establishments have been replaced by offices. The survivors at the far end, where surroundings are seedy, serve egg and chips all day.

And there's a wide selection of cafés, some outdoors like those in **Republic Square** alongside the Palace, others air-conditioned and indoors. Each has its patrons who would go nowhere else. **Caffe Cordina** facing on to Republic Square has a fine reputation and is the meeting place of businessmen and lawyers who collect there in the late morning beneath the painted ceilings, standing around the bar. Cordina is known for its confectionery, the gâteaux and seasonal specialities, which make delightful presents. The Maltese have a great weakness for anything sweet.

In the city, too, are a number of small **Lotto offices** with their small boards of five numbers hanging outside. It is here that tickets for the islands' National Lottery, with its generous prizes, can be purchased, as well as tickets for the two popular weekly tombola lotteries. A stake on three numbers in the Saturday draw can cost as little as 20 cents. Luck plays an important part in Maltese life. It always has, and history proves it.

Left, the *carrozin*, horse-drawn sightseeing. **Right**, small bars offer cooling refreshment.

The Palace of the Grand Masters

In every stone and every picture of this stupendous Palace one can read the long and varied history of the Order of St John, of British colonial rule and the establishment of the newly born Republic of Malta. It is one of the islands' great historical legacies.

It was 1571, when Valletta's fortifications were considered safe enough to resist a fresh enemy attack, that the Order of St John transferred its seat from Fort St Angelo and the Borgo, (Vittoriosa) to the new city. La Valette's successor, Pietro del Monte (1568–72), in an effort to persuade the knights to leave their residences in Vittoriosa for the yet uncertain comforts of Valletta, purchased a newly constructed small house belonging to his nephew, intending to convert it into a much larger building which was to become the Magisterial Palace.

Work was started in earnest the following year under the next Grand Master, La Cassiere (1572–81), with Gerolamo Cassar (1520–92) entrusted with its design and construction. From the time it was completed a few years later until the end of the Order's stay in Malta in 1798, the Palace was used by all successive Grand Masters, and then, until 1964, by the British governors. Since 1976 it has housed the offices of the President of the Republic.

By profession Cassar was a military architect and became proficient in civil architecture relatively late in life, mostly as a result of his visit to Rome and other Italian cities in 1569. Even so, his style remained, to a considerable extent, severe, no doubt further inspired by the military character of the Order hardened by the steel and fire of battle.

The main facade of the Palace which opens on to Republic Street is plain and generally disappointing, and was even more so before the addition of its only decorative elements, the two Doric gateways and the long wooden balconies that were constructed during the time of Grand Master Emanuel Pinto de Fonseca (1741–73). The excessive length of the facade and the irregular arrangement of the rooms on both floors made it difficult for Cassar and the other architects who followed to retain coherence in the rhythm of the windows and the walled spaces between.

Corner pilasters with ponderous rustications, so characteristic of 16th and 17th-century Valletta, rise the height of the building, giving it a visual impression of strength. At the same time they confer a note of finality on a building which, because of a complete absence of articulation, would otherwise have been difficult to define. A bold projecting cornice runs along the whole building, topped by a high balustrade.

Upstairs, downstairs: The sumptuous interior of the Palace more than makes up for the austere aspect of the facade. All state rooms, as was usual in important buildings of the period, are on the first floor, while the ground floor was reserved for stables, coach-houses, kitchens, servants' quarters and stores.

Some fine masonry work in local

limestone, the groined cross-vaults, saucer-domes and plain vaulting supported on massive walls, can be seen in most of the ground-floor rooms and corridors, especially in the older sections of the building. An open corridor runs round the main courtyard. Its balustraded arcading, sub-tropical trees, small flower-garden with the bronze statue of **Neptune** and the sculptured marble and stone fountain bearing the coat-of-arms of the Aragonese Grand Master Ramon Perellos (1697–1720), make it one of the finest of its kind in Malta. It is here, in **Neptune Courtyard**, that visitors can find the official guides for a tour.

Two large vaults at the rear of the Palace contain **The Armoury**, which has one of the most important collections of arms and armour in the world.

The Armoury was, since the time of Grand Master Pinto, originally housed in a long hall in the upper floor of the Palace but was transferred to its present location in 1976 when the hall was converted into the Chamber of Parliament.

On permanent exhibition are splendid suits of armour, some of them sumptuously engraved, rapiers, swords, daggers, halberds, pikes and lances, and flintlocks, arquebuses, pistols, mortars and small ordnance. A limited number of Turkish arms and trophies completes the collection.

At the back of another courtyard, named after Prince Alfred to commemorate the first visit to Malta by the second son of Queen Victoria in 1858, stands a high bell-tower with an interesting clock which has been chiming the hours since 1745. Four bronze figures, representing Moorish slaves, strike three gongs with a hammer every quarter of an hour. Its four dials show the hour and minutes, the phases of the moon, the month, and the day.

The first floor is reached by a marble winding staircase with unusually shallow steps, said to have been purposely constructed for the benefit of old and gout-ridden knights and Grand Masters. The newel (the staircase's centre pillar) is a hollow masonry cylinder

The Tapestry Room.

with balustraded openings, while a handrail is carved into the wall. The barrel-vaulted ceiling, which follows both curvature and slope of the stairs, is a rare masterpiece in masonry work and a tribute to Malta's ancient craft of stoneworking.

At the foot of the stairs, a marble slab fixed to the lobby wall gives the names of the Grand Masters of the Order of St John who ruled over Malta between 1530 and 1798; another marble inscription at the top of the staircase lists the British civil commissioners and governors who represented the British Crown when Malta was a British dependency between 1800 and 1964. The two inscriptions provide an admirable exercise in historical continuity.

The first floor, or *piano nobile*, contains the main apartments built round wide corridors overlooking Neptune Courtyard. Of special mention is the Council Chamber, also known as the **Tapestry Room**, and the Supreme Council Hall (also called, until a few years ago, the **Hall of St Michael and St George**). Both halls have timber ceilings, with decorated wooden beams of red Sicilian chestnut resting at their ends on carved supporting brackets designed to reduce the span. Cross-beams richly painted and gilded, placed at frequent intervals, provide an elaborate coffered effect.

In the Council Chamber, the senior members of the Order met regularly to discuss day-to-day matters pertaining to the administration of the island. The tradition was continued by the Maltese Parliament which held its sittings here between 1921, when self-government was granted, until 1976, when Parliament moved to the former Armoury.

A set of **Gobelin tapestries**, donated to the Order by Grand Master Ramon Perellos in 1710, embellish the Council Hall. Known as *Les Tentures des Indes*, they depict in vivid yet subdued colours jungle scenes recalling the hunting expeditions of a German prince in Brazil, the Caribbean Islands, India and tropical Africa undertaken between 1636 and 1644. Wild animals, a striped horse,

Recent floor mosaic.

elephants, forest bulls and ostriches vie for prominence against a background provided by luscious and exotic flora with a wealth of detail culled from the illustrations of a botanical handbook.

Above the hangings around the four walls of the Chamber is a frieze made of rectangular panels showing galleys of the Order in action against Turkish vessels. The frieze incorporates allegorical figures representing Faith, Charity, Fortification, Virtue, Manhood, Vocation, Providence, Munificence, Victory, Hope and Justice. At one end is a large painted crucifix on which Grand Masters and members of the Council took solemn oaths during their deliberations by extending their hand towards it.

Superb painting: The Grand Master summoned his Supreme Council, consisting of the 16 most senior members of the Order, whenever important decisions on domestic affairs or on foreign relations had to be taken. Gianbattista Tiepolo (1693–1770) immortalised one of the sessions of the Grand Council held in the Supreme Council Chamber

with a superb painting which hangs in the Museo Civico in Udine, Italy.

The frieze, by Matteo Perez d'Aleccio (1547–1628), painter, engraver and probably a pupil of Michelangelo, is a reliable pictorial depiction of the Great Siege of 1565, painted between 1576 and 1581; the event was described to him by eye-witnesses. One can follow the dramatic episodes of the arrival of the Turkish armada in May, the landing of the Turkish troops in Marsaxlokk Bay, the epic month-long siege of Fort St Elmo and its fall on the eve of St John's Day. The assault on Fort St Michael and the Posts of Castile and Allemagne at the Borgo, with Grand Master La Valette wounded at the head of his troops, is graphically illustrated with evident feeling. Perez d'Aleccio completes the pictorial history of one of the major events of Malta's history with a vivid panorama of "the entire war", the arrival of the Little Relief and later of the Great Relief, sent by Garcia de Toledo, Viceroy of Sicily, and the final withdrawal of the Turkish army on 7 September.

The Siege panels are separated by allegorical female figures representing Justice, Happiness, Prudence, Fortitude, Temperance and the three theological virtues of Faith, Hope and Charity. At one end of the hall is a modified version of the original throne used by the Grand Masters and later, during the colonial period, by Governors representing the British monarchs. At the opposite end is a singers' gallery, previously in the private chapel of the Grand Master, decorated with scenes from Genesis, said to have been brought by the Order on their flight from Rhodes.

The Supreme Council Chamber is also known as the Hall of St Michael and St George, a name derived from the fact that since 1818, when the chivalrous order was instituted by King George IV, originally for citizens from Malta and the Ionian Islands, the first and many subsequent investitures were held in here.

Adjacent to the Supreme Council Chamber is the **State Dining Hall**, a room of beautiful proportions, in which

Detail from Gobelin tapestries, known as *Les Tentures des Indes*.

the Grand Masters and British governors gave sumptuous dinners in honour of important visitors and local dignitaries. The hall originally had a timber ceiling like all the state rooms of the Palace, but this was unfortunately destroyed by aerial bombardment during World War II and replaced by a concrete roof painted with a copy of the original design. Paintings of British royalty adorn the walls: King George III, during whose reign Malta became a part of the British Empire, George IV, Victoria, Edward VII, Alexandra, George VI and Elizabeth II.

On the other side of the Supreme Council Chamber is the **State Room** or **Ambassadors' Room**, where Grand Masters received the credentials of envoys to Malta, a practice retained to this day by the President of the Republic when accepting the credentials of new ambassadors accredited to the islands. The Ambassadors' Room is decorated with a high frieze of paintings depicting episodes from the Order's earlier history during its sojourn in Acre, Cyprus, Rhodes and Viterbo, and a splendid series of personages from the Old Testament. Impressive paintings of European monarchs, Louis XIV, Catherine II of Russia, Louis XV and Louis XVI, in heavy gilt frames, decorate the walls.

Next to the Ambassadors' Room is the **Pages' Waiting Room**, or **Yellow Room** (so called because of its gold damask hangings). The painted frieze, also by Perez d'Aleccio, depicts incidents from the beginnings of the Order's history in Jerusalem, and a set of 10 fine allegorical figures.

The wide **corridors**, all in marble paving, which provide an independent entrance to all the state rooms, have a decorated ceiling of canvases painted in 1724 by Nicolo Nasoni (1664–1730) and a vast array of lunettes recalling naval engagements between vessels of the Order and Turkish galleys. The Palace corridors are also veritable picture galleries, with portraits of Grand Masters, European royalty, Spanish Infantas, princes and dukes. History can be read in every stone and picture.

Also in the Tapestry Room: wild animals in a botanical landscape.

ST JOHN'S CO-CATHEDRAL

When the knights of the Order of St John took formal possession of the Maltese islands in October 1530, the Grand Master and his entourage set up headquarters in Fort St Angelo, close to the entrance of the Grand Harbour. The knights themselves settled in the Borgo, a small township to the east of the fort. The Order had already been in existence by then for more than four centuries, and, among the small dwellings of their new territory, they put their auberges, the treasury, armoury, hospital and other institutions required for the smooth running of government.

But they were, above all, an essentially religious brotherhood, and the Conventual Church was therefore their most important building. In the Borgo they found one of the oldest churches of the island, second only in importance to the cathedral at Mdina. Known at the time as St Lawrence by the Sea, it was built as a small chapel in 1090 and was enlarged in 1508. In November 1530 it was declared as the principal church of the Order and remained so until the knights transferred their seat of government to the new city of Valletta in March 1571.

By this time the fortifications of Valletta had been completed and the knights put their resources and efforts into the construction of the main buildings of the city, houses, palaces, churches and auberges. In November 1573 work was begun on the Conventual Church dedicated to St John the Baptist, the patron saint of the Order. Its design and construction were entrusted to the Order's chief architect, Gerolamo Cassar. Originally it was planned for lower Valletta close to the Holy Infirmary; but, realising that the ringing of the bells would disturb the sick, the Grand Master changed the site to its present position at the heart of the city.

Cassar's basic training was in military architecture. This explains the austere lines of the facade, which has been described accurately as that of a fortress-church and a continuation, in conception, of Valletta's fortified lines.

Despite its severity, the composition is restful and the proportions of its several articulations are in perfect harmony with the facade as a whole. Cassar constructed a screen facade of two storeys, wide enough to hide the heavy stone buttresses at the sides. Above are three-storeyed towers, topped by octagonal spires, at the flanks. The two western towers, quite rare in Renaissance and baroque Rome, set the pattern for future Maltese church architecture and there is hardly a church on the island without the characteristic twin bell-towers on its front.

Bronze bust: The great mass of plain walling is relieved by the central portal which is flanked by two Tuscan columns and two tall round-headed niches. On the upper level there is a ceremonial loggia and an open, balustraded balcony. A high-relief figure of Christ in bronze, attributed to the Bolognese sculptor Allessandro Algardi (1598-1654), fills the tympanum. The bust

Preceding pages: St John's Co-cathedral, high altar; the frescoed ceiling by Mattia Preti. Left, during high mass. Right, side corridor linking the chapels.

does not belong to the original church design, but was put there in 1853 after being removed from the Church of The Saviour on the Valletta Marina which was being demolished.

But if the facade of St John's is bleak, the interior is an unqualified triumph. Art critic Nikolaus Pevsner described it as the first complete example of high baroque anywhere.

As one leaves the sun-lit square and walks through the main portal into the semi-darkness of the cathedral, one is overwhelmed by an almost incredible sense of contrast. The rigid plain lines of the exterior change, as if by a magic wand, into a dazzling blaze of colour and marvel of decoration which made Sir Walter Scott exclaim with delight in 1831: "This is the most magnificent place I saw in my life."

For a few moments the eye moves gradually along the richly painted vault, down the arabesque carvings which cover every inch of the walls, and past the multi-coloured marble slabs which cover the floor from end to end. Slowly but surely, a sense of harmony takes over as the pattern of the orderliness emerges from the effect of the impact caused by initial surprise.

The building was completed in 1577 at the expense of Grand Master La Cassiere (1572–81), and blessed by Monsignor de Torres, Archbishop of Monreale, Sicily. Important additions, however, were made well into the 18th century. The Oratory of the Decollation was constructed in 1603, and the sacristies the following year. The two plain buildings on either side, the residences of the Grand Prior and the Vice-Prior, followed in 1667, and the long galleries parallel to the nave in 1736.

The plan of the church is simple: a vast rectangular chamber with an **apse** at its eastern end, a slightly-pointed barrel **vault**, originally coffered, and **chapels** at the sides behind high arches. Cassar, obviously uncertain of the structural and static possibilities of the local limestone, used extra thick walls between the side chapels as supports for the heavy buttresses above, so count-

Corridor and ornamented side chapel.

eracting the enormous lateral thrust of the huge vault.

Very narrow doors (opened years after the church was completed) lead from one chapel to the other, small enough so as to interfere as little as possible with the stability of the supporting walls. The vault is divided into six bays by wide ribs, each resting on the pilasters between the arches of the side chapels. In each bay, an oval window gives light to the ceiling and the church itself, although the light is somewhat restricted due to the presence of the buttresses outside.

Just before the painting of the vault in 1661, a suggestion was made to the Grand Council for the widening of the windows; but this was turned down as it was feared that the operation might weaken the structure. Only the window of the facade, originally in the shape of a *croce guelfa*, was altered to its present form and size. In the absence of a regular cornice in the nave, the vault springs directly from a shallow architrave with a small projection, creating an impression of much greater width and height.

For more than 70 years after its completion, St John's remained a vast cavernous stone structure barren of all decoration. Then, in 1661, Grand Master Rafael Cotoner (1660–63) commissioned Mattia Preti to decorate the ceiling. Known as *Il Cavalier Calabrese*, Preti was one of the most outstanding artists of the Italian Seicento. Born in Taverna, Calabria, in 1613, he studied in Rome and Naples, where he came under the influence of the art of Caravaggio and the Venetian Masters of the 16th century whose two main traits characterise all his artistic works.

Preti used oils on stone on which there was a sort of light priming, a technique which has created problems over the years because of the porous nature of the soft limestone and its easy absorption of moisture. During the 19th century, when mould had been affecting the paintings for some time, attempts were made at restoration with disastrous results and it was only through the expert intervention in 1962

Pavement floor made up of marble memorial tombstones.

of Rome's Istituto Centrale del Restauro that Preti's original work was again revealed in all its glory.

Preti divided each of the six bays of the vault into three sections by means of painted architectural devices such as balustraded balconies, cornices and elaborately decorated archways, thus creating 18 spaces in which he depicted episodes from the life of John the Baptist. Using surprisingly skilful illusionistic effects, dexterity in the use and combination of colours and, above all, perfect draughtsmanship, he succeeded in turning the glory of St John's into his own artistic triumph.

The two Cotoner brothers, Grand Masters Rafael (1660-63) and Nicolas (1663–80), under whose rule the decoration was brought to fruition, are given a place of honour in the large lunette over the main door. They are represented against scenes depicting the dual characteristics of the knights as hospitallers and defenders of the Faith.

In the vivid colours of the vault, one can read the entire biblical narrative of the life of the Baptist, from Zachary in the Temple to John's Birth, his Encounter with Christ in the Desert, Christ's Baptism, John's Preachings in the Wilderness, the Reproval of Herod, the Dance of Salome and the final episode of the Beheading. Figures of Saints and Heroes of the Order, dramatically illuminated on each side of the oval windows, are considered among the best in Preti's baroque decorative art.

Preti completed his masterpiece in less than five years, while working concurrently on the preparation of drawings for the elaborate full-relief sculptures of the nave and aisles. The plain stone surface of the pilasters, arches, walls and ceilings of the chapels, perfect material for the carvers' chisel, was transformed into a riot of gilded flowers, scrolls, shells, winged angels and escutcheons – all the design motifs that are characteristic of baroque ornamentation.

Each of the eight langues, or national sections of the Order, had its own chapel where the knights prayed and heard **Detail from marble memorial.**

mass. The chapel nearest the entrance on the right, is that of Castile, Léon and Portugal, dedicated to **St James**. The altarpiece and the lateral lunettes, representing episodes from the saint's life, belong to the first phase of Preti's work. The Portuguese Grand Masters Antonio Manoel de Vilhena (1722–36) and Manuel Pinto de Fonseca (1741–73) are commemorated in two splendid monuments of marble and bronze.

The next chapel, dedicated to **St George**, is that of the Langue of Aragon, Catalunya and Navarre, whose altarpiece and all other paintings are by Preti too. The chapel contains two of the most beautiful Grand Masters' mausoleums in St John's, both exquisite examples of Italian baroque sculpture, that of Nicolas Cotoner (1663–80) and of Ramon Perellos (1697–1720). Here, as in the other chapels, are works of art in their own right, in marble and bronze: panoplies, armour, banners and cannon; effigies proudly crowned; coats-of-arms held up by cherubs or supported on the aching backs of slaves in chains.

Part of the sumptuously decorated walls.

The **chapel of Auvergne**, with an altarpiece and other paintings depicting scenes from the life of St Sebastian, comes next. It has, along with the chapel of Italy, the oldest surviving altar-front in St John's, with two fluted and twisted columns so typical of Roman baroque. The monument commemorates Grand Master de Chattes Gessan (1660) who died only four months after his election.

At the end of the right aisle, enclosed by a silver gate, is the **chapel of the Blessed Sacrament**, formerly known as the chapel of Our Lady of Philermos, so called after a Byzantine icon brought by the Order from Rhodes that was placed there. The painting was taken by the knights when they left Malta in 1798 and was eventually presented to Paul I of Russia when he became Grand Master of the Order. It was replaced in 1954 by an effigy known as Our Lady of Carafa, removed from the chapel of the Italian Langue.

The chancel and choir, and indeed the whole of St John's, is dominated by a magnificent marble group representing

the *Baptism of Christ* by Giuseppe Mazzuoli (1644–1725), with a gilt bronze *gloria* as background, the work of Giovanni Giardini (1646–1721), an Italian sculptor and silversmith. The **high altar**, certainly the richest in Malta, is made of lapis lazuli and other precious marbles, and enriched by a relief of the *Last Supper*, also in gilt bronze, in its centre.

At the end of the left aisle is the **Chapel of the Holy Relics** with an altarpiece of *St Charles Borromeo*, and renamed the chapel of the Anglo-Bavarian Langue in 1794. Next to it is the **chapel of Provence** with a contemporary copy of Guido Reni's *St Michael*, and the mausoleums of the two Provençal Grand Masters, Antoine de Paule (1623–36) and Jean Lascaris Castellar (1636–57).

Next is the **chapel of France**, dedicated to St Paul. This chapel was shorn of its original Preti-designed sculptural decoration in the 1840s, when a short-lived iconoclastic movement appeared in Malta, and was replaced by motifs representing the British royal crown, the fleur-de-lys and the eight-pointed cross. The mausoleum of Grand Master de Rohan (1775–97), which was also adversely tampered with, and that of Adrien de Wignacourt (1690–97), adorn this chapel. Another fine monument commemorates the Vicomte de Beaujolais, who died in Malta in 1808; it was erected by his brother, King Louis-Philippe of France, in 1843.

Adjoining the chapel of France is that of the **Langue of Italy**, with an altarpiece of the *Mystic Marriage of St Catherine*, one of Preti's finest works in Malta. The chapel contains the monument of Grand Master Carafa (1680–90), with a fascinating marble relief of the Battle of the Dardanelles fought in 1656 by the galleys of the Order St John with Carafa as the Captain-General of the fleet.

The last chapel is the **Three Kings of the Langue of Germany**, with the monument of Grand Master Zondadari (1720–22), a splendid mausoleum in bronze and black marble.

Walls are carved and gilded.

On certain days of the liturgical calendar, a magnificent set of 14 **tapestries** is hung in the nave of the church. Donated by Grand Master Perellos, they were executed by the famous Flemish *tapissier*, de Vos, after cartoons by Rubens and Poussin, and portray scenes from the Life of Christ and religious allegories.

The Beheading of St John by Michelangelo Merisi da Caravaggio (1573–1610) in the church oratory is undoubtedly the most famous painting in St John's – and, indeed, the Maltese islands. A crucial landmark in the history of European art, it was one of Caravaggio's last works, and certainly considered one of his best. In 1957, the large canvas was taken to Rome and masterfully restored by the Istituto Centrale del Restauro.

In the oratory, Caravaggio's *Beheading of St John*. The history of the Order, of its knights and admirals, its warriors and heroes, of their deeds and achievements across three centuries, is emblazoned on **marble tombstones** which cover the floor of the nave, aisles and oratory.

Latin inscriptions set into the marble under heraldic coats-of-arms with many quarterings, scrolls and patronymics, resound with brave deeds on the field of battle or at sea and record names of the most of the aristocratic European families of the time.

Other servants of the Order, perhaps with less spectacular achievements but no less famous in their time, have their remains interred close to their other brothers in religion. The floor of St John's is a history in marble of one of the most famous chivalric Orders.

William Makepeace Thackeray wrote of St John's in 1846: "The Church of Saint John, not a handsome structure without, is magnificent within: a noble hall covered with a rich embroidery of gilded carving... the main structure, of which the whole is simple, and the details only splendid: it seemed to me a fitting place for this wealthy body of aristocratic soldiers, who made their devotions as it were on parade, and though on their knees, never forgot their epaulets on their quarters of nobility."

MDINA

The Romans called their town *Melita*, the Arabs *Medina*, and in the early days of the knights it was known as *Citta Notabile*. When the knights completed the building of the new city of Valletta, the old capital was rechristened *Citta Vecchia* (Old City) to distinguish it from the new. The Maltese, however, corrupting the Arabic, preferred **Mdina** and that's the name that stuck. It is also one of the world's finest examples of a still-inhabited medieval walled city.

Because of its commanding position on a high ridge that runs on the southwest of the island, there have been settlements here since the Bronze Age. At 500 ft (150 metres), it is simple to defend; below, it is surrounded by fertile fields able to produce abundant vegetables and fruit to satisfy a growing population. In AD 60 this was where Publius welcomed St Paul after his shipwreck on the way to Rome and was

Preceding pages: picking oranges at Buskett; Mdina skyline at sunset; triumphal Main Gate into the old capital. Left, the walled city of Mdina.

himself converted. In AD 870, after the Aghlobite Arabs had invaded and taken Malta, the Arabs began to extend its perimeter walls along the plateau ridge to encompass a suburb of dwellings they would call Rabat.

It was after 1090, when Roger the Norman, Count of Sicily, conquered the islands in the name of Christianity, that he decreed a cathedral would be built within the walls to make the city fit for Christians. Soon a Romanesque cathedral rose on the ruins of a small sanctuary built where Publius' house had once stood, a site sacred to the memory of the first Bishop of Malta.

As the years passed and Malta fell into different hands, so the city flourished. Beautiful palaces gave the city a remarkable, patrician air. In 1429, when the Saracens attempted to conquer Malta, Mdina stood firm because, as legend has it, St Paul appeared riding a white charger and brandishing a flaming sword to exhort the Maltese defenders. Fired with bravery by their faith, the city did not fall. In recognition of ceaseless bravery, Alfonso V of Aragon, into whose hands the islands had now passed, demanded the city be rechristened. The new name, he signified, would be one of honour: Citta Notabile.

Then, during the Great Siege, the city acquitted itself further and changed the fate of the Order of St John. Its brave cavalry attacked the Turkish base camp just when victory was within enemy grasp. The skirmish forced the Turks to pull back; the tide of war was turned.

Silent City: As the capital, it was the seat of power of the ecclesiastical, military and civil authorities. It was – and still is – the home of the oldest Maltese families. Within its boundaries are grand palazzi, monasteries, churches, cathedral and museum. For many years it was known as the Silent City because its narrow streets were unsuitable for much traffic and its use was purely residential. Now, although only residents with permits may drive in with cars, restaurants, bars and cafés can be opened in the historic buildings.

The streets were built deliberately narrow and angled so that the limited

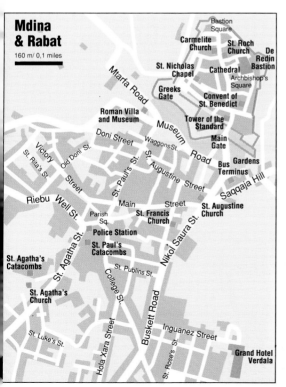

Mdina & Rabat
160 m / 0,1 miles

Bastion Square
Carmelite Church
St. Roch Church
De Redin Bastion
St. Nicholas Chapel
Cathedral
Archbishop's Square
Greeks Gate
Convent of St. Benedict
Marfa Road
Roman Villa and Museum
Museum
Tower of the Standard
Doni Street
Waggons St.
Main Gate
Main Road
Bus Terminus
Gardens
Old Doni St.
Victory Street
St. Rita's St.
St. Paul's St.
St. Augustine Street
Saqqaja Hill
Riebu
Well St.
Main Street
St. Francis Church
St. Augustine Church
Parish Sq.
Police Station
St. Agatha's St.
Nikol Saura St.
St. Agatha's Catacombs
St. Paul's Catacombs
St. Publins St.
College St.
Buskett Road
St. Agatha's Church
Hola Xara Street
Inguanez Street
St. Luke's St.
St. Rose's St.
Grand Hotel Verdala

space would be used to best advantage and cooling draughts of air would be circulated. The tall buildings themselves would be able to cast shadows on each other and so keep them cooler still in the hot summer.

The city's fortifications were completed after the Great Siege. As the Order built Valletta, so they repaired Mdina and gave it the bastion walls that ring it today. There are three entrances, the **Main Gate**, the **Greek Gate** and the **"Hole in the Wall"**. The Main Gate leads from the gardens of Rabat outside the walls. The Greek Gate opens below into the moat's wide ditch and takes its name from the colony that lived in that area. The "Hole in the Wall" is exactly that; it was cut into Mdina's walls when Malta's steam railway was in operation and the citizens demanded easier access to the station below on the road leading to Mtarfa.

The Main Gate was constructed in 1724 on the instructions of Grand Master de Vilhena. A baroque triumphal archway with imposing pillars, rich carving and an ornate superstructure, it was reached by drawbridge across a dry moat. This gate replaced an earlier, simple gate still visible in the outside walls to the right. On the inside are the arms of Antonio de Inguanez which were removed during the short occupation by French forces in 1798 and replaced by a statue of Liberty. The present arms were placed there in 1886 by order of the British governor, Sir Lintorn Simmons.

Inside, to the left, is the **Tower of the Old Standard**, currently the police station but dating back to the 16th century. It was on the top of this tower that bonfires were lit to warn the population that Corsairs had landed or that the island had been invaded.

Facing the tower is the Magisterial Palace, the **Palazzo Vilhena**, designed by Maltese architect Giovanni Barbara in 1733, the year he died. Now the **Natural History Museum**. Malta's original governing body, the Universita, had its offices here until they were devastated in an earthquake in 1693. When he opened the new gate into the

Carrozin for hire outside the cathedral.

city 40 years later, Grand Master de Vilhena took the opportunity to replace them with his own new palazzo.

Opposite the gate, the fourth side of this small square dedicated to St Publius is the forbidding **nunnery of St Benedict**, founded in 1418 but substantially rebuilt in 1625. The sisters are an austere order with strict rules of seclusion that, until recently, decreed that, even after death, a nun could never leave the nunnery but must be buried within its walls. No man is permitted to enter unless he is a doctor and even then only with the permission of the bishop.

To the left is Mdina's principal thoroughfare, **Villegaignon Street**. It leads to **Bastion Square** with its elevated platform that offers the most spectacular views across the countryside, sweeping from Mtarfa to the left to Valletta on the right. In the middle distance is the church known as Mosta Dome, with what is reputed to be the fourth largest unsupported dome in the world. By night the view turns to a sparkling carpet as, below, the lights of Malta flicker in the ink-blue darkness.

Adjoining the convent walls are the **chapels of St Peter and St Agatha**. In St Peter's the altarpiece is by Mattia Preti, who has ornamented so much in Malta. It shows the Madonna with Saints Peter, Benedict and Scholastica. The original church of St Agatha was built in 1417 but remodelled in 1694 by Lorenzo Gafa'. Its altarpiece of Santa Agatha is by Giuseppe d'Arena.

Along the length of the street are Malta's finest houses, preserved by the island's ancient families. Many have private art treasures that would be warmly welcomed by museums in any country. At No. 6, Casa Inguanez dates back to 1350 and has been in the family's hands since then. It is the oldest of the Mdina families; the Governorship of Malta was held by a Baron Inguanez until supplanted by the Order of St John upon their arrival in 1530.

On the corner of Casa Inguanez is Mesquita Street, leading to Gatto Murina Street with the **Palazzo Gatto-Murina**. The building has grace and

style and is a fine example of 14th-century workmanship.

It was from a window at No. 11, the **house of Notary Bezzina**, that Captain Masson, the Commander of the French garrison in Mdina, was hurled in 1798 by an infuriated mob in a rage that sparked off the Maltese revolt. Under Napoleon, the French had taken Malta from the Order of St John and banished the knights, but within weeks had become so unpopular that insurrection seemed inevitable.

This "defenestration" came about when the people, enraged that the French were auctioning tapestries taken from the nearby Carmelite church, rose in fury. It signalled the final assault to the Maltese outside the city and the French garrison was practically annihilated. It was the prelude to the invitation extended to Britain to take the islands under its protection.

On the corner of **St Paul's Square**, the spacious forecourt to the superb cathedral, is the **Banca Giuratale**, built by Grand Master de Vilhena to house the Universita when he took over their dilapidated palazzo inside the Main Gate for his Palazzo Vilhena. Further along is **Palazzo Santa Sofia**, on the corner of Holy Cross Street, reputed to be the oldest house in Mdina. Its ground floor is 13th century (the first floor dates from 1938). A few yards further along is **Palazzo Falzon**; originally this was also single-storeyed, built in the 14th century, but its additions are 15th-century. Known as the **Norman House**, it is, unlike other private houses here, open to visitors.

God among Mammon: Between the grand houses are the religious. There is a little **chapel** dedicated to **St Roque**, rebuilt in 1728. Until that time, St Roque formed a part of the Chapel of Santa Maria della Porta at the gate to the city. When Grand Master de Vilhena carried out his rebuilding plans and the old gate was replaced, the chapel was moved. Known locally as *Madonna tad-Dawl* (that is, the Madonna of the Light), the chapel altarpiece is a painting by the Portuguese Emanuel Pereira.

The Catacombs of St Paul's, Rabat.

On a much larger scale is the **Carmelite Church** with its priory. A mendicant order, the Carmelites arrived in 1370 from Sicily and took up residence in Rabat. In 1659 they moved into Mdina and in 1680 their present building was completed. The church contains four side chapels and seven altars with, as the main altarpiece, an 18th-century painting of the Annunciation by Stefano Erardi. The 19th-century paintings of St Simon and St Elijah are by the Maltese artist Michele Bellanti.

The cathedral itself is dedicated to St Paul and, according to tradition, stands on the site of the house that belonged to Publius, Malta's first Christian convert and Malta's first bishop. The present building was erected between 1697 and 1702 after an earthquake in 1693 demolished the original.

Many of the treasures not pillaged by the French during their short occupation are on exhibition in the **Cathedral Museum**. One special curiosity is a painting of the Madonna and Child, said to be the work of St Luke who came to Malta

in AD 60. This building, erected in 1733, was once Mdina's seminary.

In Inguanez Street where it meets St Paul's is the **Herald's Lodge**, where heralds would read proclamations made by the city's council, and the **Corte Capitanale** (now a part of the Palazzo Vilhena but once the Courts of Justice). Beneath the latter are dungeons and cells. Tradition says a tunnel connects this to the Archbishop's Palace alongside the cathedral. The ancient building alongside, a grand family home and later an eccentric hotel called Xara Palace, awaits new designation.

Commercial centre: Outside Mdina's fortified walls is the suburb of **Rabat**, a sprawling town isolated from the city to which it was attached in Roman times. First to create its artificial separation were the Arabs, who wanted to give their city more strategic protection; this is where the island's wealth was manifest. They cut a ditch into the plateau to isolate the city and shaped its outer perimeter to make scaling its walls a hazardous venture. Centuries later, the

Mosaic floor, Roman Museum, Rabat.

knights built the dry moat and the steep impregnable bastion walls that ring the city today. To ensure impregnability, the knights provided only two gates to give access to Mdina.

Rabat is the commercial centre of this rural part of the island with banks, offices, souvenir shops, a vegetable market and inexpensive restaurants.

A number of religious orders have settled into the imposing buildings that serve as large monasteries, priories and nunneries. They are probably here because there was not enough space for them to be accommodated in either of the cities of Valletta or Mdina and the cool seclusion of Rabat was more conducive to meditation. The most interesting is the priory of **St Dominic** in St Dominic Square, a fine 16th-century baroque church with monastic cloisters.

During the French occupation, Napoleon declared that religious orders would in future be permitted to own only one religious house each, so during the French occupation the monastery became, temporarily, a hospital. Only the church is open to visitors. In Nicolo Saura Street is the **Santo Spirito Hospital**, the first hospital ever built in Malta. Records show it was functioning in 1370. It closed its doors in 1968.

The charming church of **St Agatha** is dedicated to the young woman who fled Sicily in AD 249 to take refuge in Malta rather than marry Quintanus, the Governor of Catania. She hid in Rabat's catacombs but later returned home to be tortured and die a martyr to Christ rather than submit to marriage. Beneath the church are the catacombs in which she hid, decorated with many frescoes, including one dating from AD 395–870 the islands' Byzantine period.

In Roman times it was customary for the bodies of the dead to be cremated and burial on open ground was not permitted. But Palestinian Jews who did not believe in cremation adapted to the laws and introduced burial in subterranean vaults, and it was an idea quickly accepted by Christians. Soon these catacombs would also serve as refuges in times of persecution, places where

Verdala Palace from Buskett Gardens.

Christians could hold their religious services in comparative safety.

It is believed that underground churches and catacombs abound in Malta, some known but buried under later buildings and others, so it is said, currently in use, with tiled floors and whitewashed walls, as household cellars. In Rabat two separate catacombs open to visitors are in St Agatha Street: the **Catacombs of St Paul** and of **St Agatha**. Both are eerie, vaulted tunnels with stone-cut tombs, niches and canopies and the *agape* table on which food was prepared by Christians celebrating the Last Supper.

The church of **St Paul** is reputed to be the first recognised parish church on the Maltese islands. Below it is the **Grotto** where the saint is believed to have spent much time after his shipwreck. Legend has it that its walls are miraculous and that scrapings from it will cure the sick if kept by their beds. For centuries visiting pilgrims have scraped pieces off the walls and yet (miraculously?) the grotto has stayed the very same size.

The church itself was built at the expense of a noble woman, Cosmana Navarra, and above its high altar is a painting of St Paul's shipwreck by Stefano Erardi. The adjoining church of **St Publius** was built as an act of piety by Giovanni Beneguas, a Spanish nobleman who lived for some time as a hermit in the Grotto. The crypt contains a marble statue of St Paul and traces of frescoes. In the inner room are a marble statue given by Grand Master Pinto, lamps donated by Pope Paul VI and a Christian temple with an *agape* table.

On the perimeter road that separates Rabat from Mdina is the most important of the Roman remains found in this area, the **Roman Villa**, clearly the house of a merchant of some standing. Its foundations were discovered only in 1881 and over its mosaic flooring has been built a small museum of Roman antiquities, with a collection of the relics and statuary found nearby. On the country road outside Mgarr leading to Ghajn Tuffieha are the traces of **Roman Baths**.

On the outskirts of Rabat leading to-

Terraced fields along Dingli Cliffs.

wards **Dingli Cliffs** is **Verdala Palace**, a silent, romantic castle surrounded by olive and fir trees, set above the green orchards of **Buskett Gardens**. A delightful spot, cool in summer, ripe with oranges in winter, this is Malta's largest wooded area.

Designed by Gerolamo Cassar in 1586 for Grand Master Fra Huges de Verdale, Verdala looks a traditional medieval castle as it stands on elevated ground surrounded by woodland. But, half villa and half fort, it was not designed to withstand serious assault, although its four corner towers are positioned to afford excellent musket fire should it be required. It has been enlarged and embellished over the centuries – with the British in their later years installing plumbing and sanitation as they converted it into the Governor's family's summer residence.

It has a quiet grandeur, with frescoes in the main room depicting highlights from the life of Grand Master Verdale. There is a fine staircase to one side leading to the roof from which there is a superb view of the countryside. Within its stone walls is a concealed chamber with rings in the floor and wall where prisoners were chained and tortured.

In the grounds is the Chapel of St Anthony the Abbot, built in the 16th century and, seen from Buskett below, it is possible to see the *trompe l'oeil* windows painted to create the impression of symmetry.

Buskett is popular with picnickers and for more than 300 years, on 29 June, one of the most popular *festas* has been celebrated here, **Mnarja**, the feast day of Saints Peter and Paul. Its name comes from the Latin *illuminaria*, used originally by the clergy to describe the lighting up of the churches of Mdina and Rabat in honour of the two saints.

The day traditionally starts with horse and donkey races on a road that leads up to the Saqqija hill entrance into Rabat; here there is a stone balcony on which successive Grand Masters and governors sat to watch the races, and later present banners to the winners. These, in days passed, were taken back to the villages to be used as altar cloths. During the day, crowds gather in Buskett to cook rabbit, drink wine, play *tombla* and sing into the night. Not far away is **Dingli**, a small village near Malta's highest spot, Dingli Cliffs, with its enigmatic cart tracks at "Clapham Junction" and cliff-top road leading to the **Hagar Qim** and **Mnajdra** temples.

Following the country road away from Buskett, down the lush valley to Siggiewi, you reach the **Inquisitor's Summer Palace**. A remarkable and beautiful house concealed on the side of the hill, it was built in 1625 by the Inquisitor, Horatus Visconti, as his summer residence. The elegant building is only one room deep, with all rooms interconnecting. There is a small chapel at one end and beneath its terrace apron are deep caves where the Inquisitor's staff are said to have lived.

For years the palace lay abandoned and prey to vandals. It has been renovated and is used by the Prime Minister as his summer residence and so is not open to visitors. Pot-holers can explore the caves.

Left, the Oval Staircase, Verdala Palace. **Right**, decorated ceiling, Carmelite Church, Mdina.

MDINA CATHEDRAL

The closing years of the 17th century heralded a new and exciting architectural period. It was a time when an all-important local idiom began to assert itself. Self-assured and vital, it was a baroque evolution, Italian and Sicilian in origin, but with a character distinctly its own. Mdina's cathedral is probably the finest example of this development in the Maltese Islands.

The site on which the cathedral, and the others that preceded it, were built, is, according to hallowed tradition, the site of the house of the father of Publius, the chief man of the island, who, as related in Acts: XXVIII, lay sick with fever and was healed by St Paul in AD 60. He later became first Bishop of Malta. (In the side chapel dedicated to the Blessed Sacrament is an icon of the Virgin said to have been painted by St Luke.)

Although it is known that there were other churches before it, the first documented cathedral dates back to the late 12th or probably the early 13th century. It is depicted in two frescoes painted by Matteo Perez d'Aleccio in the Palace of the Grand Masters in Valletta and appears to have been built in the South Italian Romanesque style, with a single nave, a high-pitched timber roof and a squat belltower to one side.

In January 1693 the old cathedral was destroyed by a great earthquake which shook the whole of the Central Mediterranean region and badly hit many towns and villages in Sicily and the Maltese Islands. Only the apse at the back of the cathedral survived, a credit to the renowned Maltese architect Lorenzo Gafa' (1639–1702) who, while rebuilding it a few years earlier in 1681, decided to strengthen its structure.

Gafa' was again commissioned to design and supervise the new building which he commenced in 1697. He was then 58 and, having benefited from the work of other Maltese pioneers and

Left, facade of Lorenzo Gafa's cathedral, the islands' finest domed church.

with a wealth of experience in church-building behind him, he had reached full architectural maturity. He struck a perfect balance between the light-heartedness of some of his earlier churches and the ponderous.

The monumental facade, with its interplay of balanced vertical and horizontal lines in the true spirit of the Roman baroque, is constructed with two superimposed orders, the Corinthian in the lower level and the Composite above. Both extend the width of the facade. The central feature projects a little forward of the side wings and carries a fine square-headed portal with full mouldings. This is surmounted by a broken pediment containing the crest of the head of the diocese then in office and the Maltese national emblem in heraldic symbols of red and white. It is flanked by the coats of arms of Grand Master Ramon Perellos (1697–1720) and of Bishop Cocco Palmieri (1684–1713).

The two side doors have surrounds of unornamented mouldings and a segmental pediment which help to fill the blank expanse of walling on each side of the centrepiece. A central window, redolent of the circular and oval eyes of earlier church architecture but now a fully fledged opening, provides an effective visual link between the main door and the crowning pediment.

The slightly recessed side bays carry two towers with richly ornamented spires containing six bells, the oldest of which was cast in Venice in 1370. Curious is the position of the two clock dials which break the entablature and actually touch the cornice. This seems a deliberate device by Gafa' to give height to the squat bell-towers.

The plan of the cathedral is in the form of a Latin cross, with a central vaulted nave and two aisles with small side chapels. The transepts, chancel and choir are of generous proportions, while the two small chapels on each side of the chancel are small gems of architecture.

The floor is a superb patchwork of inlaid multicoloured marble slabs, some macabre, some gaudy. They commemorate leading Maltese ecclesias-

A richly ornamented side chapel.

tics, bishops, prelates, monsignors and canons, as well as prominent laymen, most of whom belonged to the Maltese nobility and aristocratic families.

For decoration, the cathedral has a nave ceiling painted in fresco in 1794 with scenes from the life of St Paul, to whom the cathedral is dedicated, executed by the two Sicilian brothers, Antonio and Vincenzo Manno. The interior of the dome was painted by Mario Caffaro Rore in 1955.

Mattia Preti (1613–99), who is responsible for much of Malta's glory, is the author of the altar-piece of the choir, the apse above and the two lateral panels, all depicting various episodes in the life of Malta's patron, Saint Paul. The Royal Arms of Spain take pride of place in the centre of the arch surrounding the apse and recall the munificence of Emperor Charles V who donated the islands to the Order of St John in 1530 after their seven years of homelessness since abandoning Rhodes.

Two interesting relics which survived the earthquake that demolished

the earlier cathedral are the marble baptismal font (1495), and the Irish oak sacristy door which is a marvel of carving in wood (1520). Both bear the national emblem, a shield divided vertically in the traditional red and white Maltese colours, and are witness to the antiquity of the islands' emblem.

Gafa's architectural masterpiece, however, and the culmination of all his artistic work is undoubtedly the cathedral's magnificent baroque dome. Bold and dynamic, more sculptural than architectural, seen from a distance, it rises high above the hill of Mdina and dominates the surrounding countryside for miles, around a miracle in stone. The superb, unique profile of the Old City's skyline is, rightly, one of the island's most famous silhouettes.

The two cannons outside the cathedral date from the early 17th century and were once taken to London for display at the Artillery Museum in Woolwich. In 1888 they were returned with many others on the instructions of Malta's governor.

Mdina Cathedral is dedicated to St Peter and St Paul.

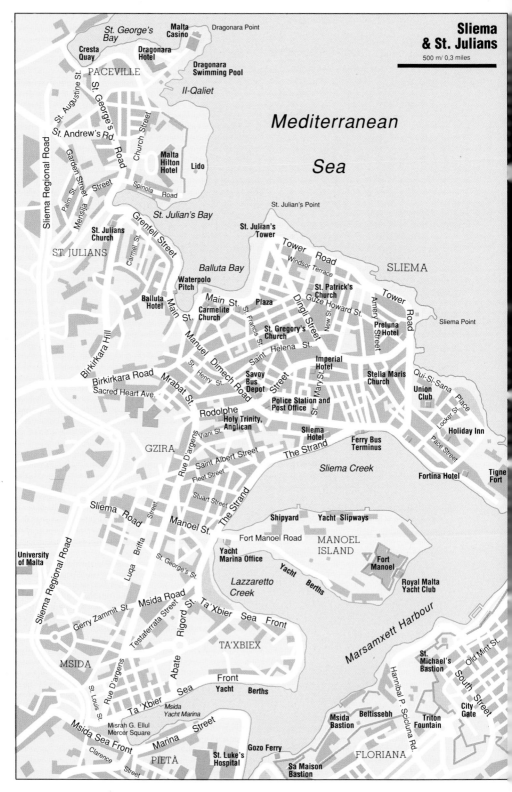

Sliema
& St. Julians
500 m/ 0,3 miles

St. George's Bay
Malta Casino
Dragonara Point
Cresta Quay
Dragonara Hotel
PACEVILLE
Dragonara Swimming Pool
St. Augustine St.
St. George's Road
Church Street
Il-Qaliet
St. Andrew's Rd.
Garden Street
Palm Street
Mensija Street
Malta Hilton Hotel
Lido
Spinola Road

Mediterranean

Sea

St. Julian's Bay
St. Julian's Point
St. Julians Church
St. Julian's Tower
ST. JULIANS
Grentell Street
Carmel St.
Tower Road
Windsor Terrace
SLIEMA
Balluta Bay
Waterpolo Pitch
St. Patrick's Church
Tower Road
Balluta Hotel
Main St.
Plaza
Guze Howard St.
Amery Street
Sliema Point
Carmelite Church
St. Francis St.
St. Gregory's Church
Preluna Hotel
Main St.
Manuel Dimech Road
Saint Helena St.
Dingli Street
Birkirkara Hill
St. Henry St.
Imperial Hotel
St. Mary St.
Stella Maris Church
Qui-Si-Sana Place
Union Club
Birkirkara Road
Mrabat St.
Savoy Bus Depot
Street
Locker St.
Sacred Heart Ave.
Rodolphe
Police Station and Post Office
Holiday Inn
Holy Trinity, Anglican
Pace Street
GZIRA
Rue D'argens
Viani St.
Saint Albert Street
Sliema Hotel
The Strand
Ferry Bus Terminus
Fortina Hotel
Tigne Fort
Fleet Street
Sliema Creek
University of Malta
Sliema Regional Road
Sliema Road
Briffa Street
Stuart Street
The Strand
Shipyard
Yacht Slipways
Manoel St.
Fort Manoel Road
MANOEL ISLAND
Luqa
St. George's St.
Yacht Marina Office
Yacht Berths
Fort Manoel
Royal Malta Yacht Club
Lazzaretto Creek
Msida Road
Ta'Xbier Sea Front
Gerry Zammit St.
Testaferrata Street
Rigord St.
TA'XBIEX
MSIDA
Abate
Rue D'argens
Sea Front
Yacht Berths
Marsamxett Harbour
St. Michael's Bastion
Old Mint St.
Ta'Xbier
Msida Yacht Marina
St. Louis St.
Hannibal P. Scicluna Rd.
South Street
Msida Sea Front
Misrah G. Ellul Mercer Square
Marina Street
City Gate
Clarence Street
PIETÀ
St. Luke's Hospital
Gozo Ferry
Msida Bastion
Beltissebh
Triton Fountain
FLORIANA
Sa Maison Bastion

SLIEMA AND ITS SATELLITES

The main resort areas of Malta are found around Sliema, Bugibba and, in a much smaller way, Mellieha. Development has crept along the eastern coastline which, on this side of the island, shelves gently into the water and has a number of safe bays and coves for swimming.

Sliema, however, is not only the major holiday area, it is also the main residential area. This is where prestigious apartments sell to the newly upwardly mobile at what are, locally, exorbitant rates. It is also where Malta's wealthy middle class live, where children can walk safely to and from friends' houses in the evenings and where Standa, Stefanel, Body Shop and St Michael cater to residents rather than to holidaymakers visiting the islands on a two-week break. There are some excellent hotels and restaurants here, but the core remains residential.

The town started to take shape as a small resort for the residents of Valletta. With its pleasant coastline indented with small coves and its smooth white rock beaches facing the clear blue sea, Sliema was where they would come in summer to swim and take the fresher air. There was a small fishing community, some smallholdings and a military presence in Fort Tigne which was built in 1761 by Grand Master Pinto and, with Fort St Elmo across the water, guarded the entrance to Marsamxett Harbour.

Gradually, as the wealth and size of the population within the city of Valletta increased, so Sliema began to take shape. Families moved out of the city. Villas and elegant houses were built, land was developed, shopkeepers set up business and it became an elegant place to live.

By the turn of the century fine domestic architecture in cream limestone gave Sliema an enviable, subtle grace and elegance of its own. So much so that, while Valletta remained the capital and centre of business, those whose families had not already gone to the Three Villages of Lija, Attard and Balzan where the families with longer established roots had moved (opting for rural space close to San Anton Palace rather than the salt winds off the sea) now moved to Sliema. Saying one lived in Sliema implied a certain status.

With land at a premium, the Sliema boundaries came to include Balluta and St Julians. Later they encompassed Spinola and St Andrews, where the British established a large barracks.

Much remains the same as it was, but there are changes. Most are designed to accommodate the new wealthy Maltese, as well as the tourist. Today, as many of the children of old families marry and look for homes, the new generations have begun to settle in the villages a short drive from the Sliema satellites – in **Naxxar** or **Gharghur**, for example. There they have more privacy, more space and, in the current vogue, go about being Green.

Also, as property prices in Sliema are the highest on the islands, they get more for their money elsewhere. The young

cannot yet afford the high prices of the new apartments that dominate Tower Road, the main coast road of Sliema that looks out over the rock beaches, or the villas on High Ridge and Madliena, two prestige patches just beyond St Andrews. Nor would they want to live within the latters' crowded confines.

But, for every one ready to move out, there are two or more ready to move in, people for whom the status of being able to say they live in Sliema counts. Sliema has cachet. It is not without reason that the people on the south of the islands refer to Sliema people as *tal pepe*, meaning snobs.

However, the price of this progress is being paid for by the loss of aesthetic pleasure. As developers woo the original residents of the fine houses with inducements that include money and a new highly functional modern apartment or two in exchange for the old family house, persuasion is hard to resist. (Parents can have one apartment, children the other, and neither will have the perennial problems that living in old limestone houses brings: rising damp and rusting pipes.)

Change for the worse: Sliema is, as everyone will confirm, not the place that it once was. In a matter of a few recent years the wonderful seafront houses that created an elegant vista and made the promenade what it was have gone. In the creation of such an idealised vista, the land on which they stood became increasingly valuable and coveted. In their place are towering faceless blocks of flats and large hotels. Even the quiet backstreets are not safe; apartment blocks, hotels and restaurants are moving in here too.

Of course, none of this shows to first-time visitors. At the **Strand**, for example, where the boat cruises set off around the harbours or to Comino and Gozo, life bustles. This is where Sliema begins. On the water there are motor launches and holiday craft; with Valletta as their backdrop, yachts sail past as they head for the nearby marinas of **Msida** and **Ta' Xbiex**.

There are cafés for snacks like *pas-*

St Julians Bay.

tizzi or *timpana*, creamy cakes, ice cream, cold drinks and cappuccino. There are local boutiques with names like Square Deal for inexpensive fun fashion and Marks and Spencer for British imports. By the car park and gardens are bus stops for services to Valletta or, in the other direction, to St Julians and Paceville. It was here in the good old days that steam ferries had their jetties and carried passengers to Valletta and back for a few pennies.

At the top of the hill, **Tower Road** and **Bisazza Street** meet. These are the two major shopping streets with butchers, banks, chemists, money exchange offices, a supermarket, jewellers and even newsagents where, by 6pm, British and Italian daily newspapers are on sale. This is where residential Sliema does its serious shopping.

To the right is **Tigne**, a quiet quarter with the hotels Holiday Inn, Fortina, Tigne Court and Plevna. Along its **Quisi-Sana** waterfront (its name means "here one gets healthy") there are beach concessions with pools, bars and chang-

ing facilities. Many better quality self-catering apartments are here; so, too, is the reverse osmosis plant that converts sea water to drinking water. Most of **Fort Tigne** has long been government housing, but it is soon to be converted into an upmarket holiday complex.

Then, along **The Front** – as locals refer to this stretch of Tower Road – there are more hotels, restaurants and the free (public) rock beaches where Sliema folk and a few tourists swim. (Locals are inclined to prefer rock beaches – not that there are many sandy ones.) In the cool of the evening this becomes a busy promenade. Generations of Maltese have enjoyed this *passegiata*, walking, talking and socialising. This is where boy meets girl. There are ice-cream sellers, soft-drinks kiosks and men with baskets of roast almonds, hazlenuts and peanuts.

The road passes through tiny **Balluta Bay** where one of the island's best waterpolo teams, Neptunes, has its club and poolside lido with a casual summer restaurant. Games are played on Satur-

White rock beaches line Sliema coastline.

day evenings. Here the road reaches its busiest junction, **St Julian's** (signposts sometimes read **San Giljan**, the Maltese spelling).

This is not a place to come shopping. Once a simple, peaceful but picturesque residential corner where fishermen would land their catches in the evening – and some still do – it has now developed into a busy corner with a waterside walkway, a splendid collection of restaurants and constant traffic congestion. San Giuliano and Dolce Vita, two of the island's most popular restaurants, are here, along with popular bars, specialist restaurants and pizza parlours. Evenings begin here.

Within walking distance at the top of the hill is **Paceville**, a little tawdry but with less expensive eating houses, bars, clubs and discos and a smart cinema complex. At night in summer the streets are crowded with a cosmopolitan mix. Sometimes, late at night, it can be a little rough and not to everyone's taste.

In quiet corners, however, are the grand hotels like the Malta Hilton,

which was enlarged and rebuilt. And jutting out to sea on a promontory with a beach club and scuba-diving school is the **Casino**. A converted summer house that once belonged to a wealthy Maltese family, it has been transformed into the islands' only gambling casino with tables for roulette, blackjack and baccarat. It is run on highly professional lines with skilled croupiers; there is a small entrance fee and a dress code which bars informal dress such as jeans.

Minutes away are the discos, Euphoria and Axis. These are perfect examples of how discos should be. Close by, at St George's Bay, is a popular lido and another scuba-diving school and the five-star hotel Corinthian San Gorg.

It was further along this coast road, at St Andrew's and St George's, that the British garrison was stationed in barracks built stylishly in the local limestone. Story has it that the original plans were destined for India but, owing to clerical error, found their way to Malta. Now with the military presence long gone, by apparently random conver-

The Malta Casino, Dragonara.

sion, the buildings have become a mixture of commercial enterprise and government housing.

This road, sweeping along the beautiful coastline, passing the white rocks and fun park at **Bahar-ic-Caghaq**, reaches **Salina Bay** with its hotel and salt pans. To the right across the bay is **Qawra** with its impressive Suncrest Hotel and the road leading to the fastest developing resort area, **Bugibba**. Further on is **St Paul's Bay** with, on the far side of the bay, the small rock, St Paul's Island, where tradition has it that St Paul was shipwrecked.

It is this coast road, from Sliema to Qawra, that the Maltese find particularly appealing; at weekends they will drive from miles away to park their cars in one long ribbon from end to end. They will stay until late at night, picnicking. On Saturday and Sunday nights, expect slow-crawling traffic.

As the Sliema district is primarily a residential area that has welcomed tourism, it naturally carries on with daily family life. And its religion. There are a considerable number of parishes, their church domes breaking the skyline or peeking out between the tall buildings, their bells tolling during the day.

This means that in the summer there is a *festa* on most weekends, with a number of streets decorated and with bands and the patron saint's statue paraded through the streets. Crowds gather to walk, talk and enjoy the fireworks displays. Although not the largest parish, the St Julians *festa* in late August has become very popular and restaurants with tables overlooking the bay, where diners can enjoy the fireworks spectacle, are booked early.

Swimming, too, is excellent along the coastal road of Sliema, from the far end of the Strand alongside the Fortina hotel with its waterside pool as far as Bahar-ic-Caghaq (which may be pronounced, by foreigners, *bahhar-i-tchark*). It is worth exploring to find a quiet spot – but no topless bathing here, the beaches can be seen from the road.

Of course, along this stretch swimming is from rock, but much of it is

St Julians' restaurants open late.

white and smooth. If it is not, avoid it, for it will be sharp. Watch where the Maltese swim; they know the best spots and where it is easy to get in and, more important, where it is easy to clamber out again. Anyone who cares to dive will find that the experience approaches paradise: the water is so clear you can see the bottom and only the deepest diver, or the myopic, risks hitting the bottom. Beginners with flippers and a mask can have hours of pleasure skimming along the edge.

Disco dancing: Disco life on Malta has a subtle divide. It is probably the Great Social Divide – although, to be less undemocratic, it might perhaps be better termed the Great Territorial Divide, for that it is too. The more cosmopolitan youth of Sliema and the neighbouring areas of equal social pretension differ hugely from the young people in outlying towns and villages.

Most discos open at 6pm on Saturdays and Sundays and during the week too in summer months. Early, yes – but for a very good reason. First on to the floors are teenagers from the islands' remoter villages who flood in early and leave by 10pm. They have to if they want to get home by public transport before parental curfew and before the last bus services at 10pm.

Often the management of Sliema's two most popular venues organise minibus shuttle services from central pickup points to their disco and then back to each person's doorstep. The 14-year-old crowd don't drive. With the vast amounts of money spent on doing up the discos, this is one way to fill up a place at an otherwise empty time.

The cosmopolitan crowd, however, from Sliema and environs, the local fashionable crowd, rarely arrive much before midnight. With this trendsetting group, disco is an addiction and they go home only when they are ready. Thanks to their spending power, the big discos like Axis and Euphoria have had huge sums of money lavished on them – sums even some London clubs might envy.

<u>Right</u>, summer and winter, the Paceville discos draw a cosmopolitan crowd.

THE THREE CITIES

When Charles V of Spain gave Malta to the homeless Order of St John they settled in an area known as Il Borgo. Malta was not their first choice for a new home but it was preferable to Tripoli, their only other option. The Maltese nobility in the city of Mdina was far from welcoming so the knights made their home in Il Borgo. At least its creeks would shelter their galleys. Il Borgo was the home of a small but flourishing community and set deep in the safe reaches of the harbour opposite which, after repelling the Turkish invasion, they would come to build Valletta.

This spread of land consisted of two promontories with flat ground between; Birgu (now **Vittoriosa**) and Isola (now **Senglea**) with Bormla (**Cospicua**) between. Jutting out from Vittoriosa was **Fort St Angelo**, the only means of defence. Curiously, to this day, the Maltese living in this area cling to old names handed down from the days of the knights and call the Three Cities, respectively, **Birgu**, **l'Isla** and **Bormla**. Today's road signs, as if designed to confuse rather than aid, use either.

During the knights' long tenure, considerable sums of money were spent creating the kind of buildings the Order required and the whole was wrapped in defensive bastion walls similar to those that protected Valletta. Later the British garrison brought its additions.

But little remains. This is the location of Malta's famous dockyards, the target of most of the bombing in World War II as the Axis partners tried to flatten the dockyard and the ships undergoing essential repair. Cospicua and Senglea suffered considerable damage. Houses and streets were reduced to rubble, families were evacuated. Since then, of course, the whole district has been totally rebuilt, but much of it hastily. The small amount of historical or architectural interest that remained after the conflict is masked by post-war building and development. It is much neglected and in need of the restoration and reha-

bilitation being lavished on Valletta.

Cospicua took the brunt of the bombardment and, having done so, has become in its re-establishment a commercial centre around the dockyard gates. Its **Church of the Immaculate Conception**, built in 1637, narrowly escaped total destruction.

Senglea, named after Grand Master de la Sengle who fortified the promontory and founded the community in 1554 by distributing free building plots, has, despite the destruction that rendered it uninhabitable, regained a picturesque charm. Once, during Malta's boom period of the 1970s, it had all the makings of becoming an artists' colony when foreign painters, writers and sculptors moved in to the houses and apartments overlooking the harbour. Now, with just a sprinkling of emigrés, it has returned to familiar local life.

Senglea's appeal stems from its excellent view over the Grand Harbour. The harbour may not be as busy as once it was, but from the gardens with their Vedette sentry post at the tip of its

promontory both Valletta and the fort of St Angelo look superb. Valletta is particularly fine floodlit by night and it's little wonder Senglea is the proposed seat of a *son et lumière* show.

Below, ringing Senglea at the water's edge, is a pleasant walkway that heads towards Cospicua. In the cool of the evening, the still waters in the creek take on the appearance of a tranquil lagoon. The parish church, **Our Lady of Victory**, was built after the war. Inside are two statues, the Redeemer, which is highly venerated, and Our Lady of Victory, which is paraded on Senglea's big day, 8 September, which is also a national holiday, Victory Day.

Then there is Vittoriosa. The least damaged of the three, it is not yet a place for lengthy visits as there are no cafés, no restaurants and only the tiny local shops to serve the neighbourhood. But there is the Inquisitor's Palace (now used as a folklore museum), the majestic Church of St Lawrence (San Lawrenz) and the most perfect example of a walled fortress, Fort St Angelo.

The **Inquisitor's Palace** is a 16th-century palazzo that once housed the court, residence and prison of the Office of the Inquisition. As the Pope's delegate, the Inquisitor was accommodated in style. Though its role was to combat heresy and protect the Catholic faith, this Office was not quite as dogmatic when it was first established as the infamous Spanish Inquisition. It was only as the Inquisitor's power base grew stronger that it took on a more ruthless rule. Two Inquisitors went on to Rome to become Pope. Alexander VII (1655–67) and Innocent XII (1676–89). The Office also provided 25 cardinals.

Restoration of the interior is now complete and the exterior seems unprepossessing, but inside there is an interesting grandeur. The Inquisitors were men of standing and the building reflects this. There are some fine murals and the ceiling of the main hall has coats of arms of the 62 Inquisitors carved in wood.

There is also a prisoners' cell that leads directly into the Judgement

The walls of Senglea seen across the creek from Cospicua.

Room. Its door was deliberately low so that each prisoner was forced to bow to the presiding Inquisitor on entering.

The **Church of St Lawrence** (San Lawrenz) on the waterfront facing Senglea was originally the conventual church of the Order of St John and contains many relics of the knights. Built in 1723 to replace a smaller church erected by Count Roger the Norman, it is a magnificent church in a picturesque corner. In front of it stands a small memorial erected in 1979 to commemorate the withdrawal of the British forces.

At present **Fort St Angelo** is officially closed to visitors but it is hoped this will soon change as it is one of Malta's most interesting sites, both historically and architecturally. Under British rule it was a naval headquarters and maintained in excellent condition. Since then it has been neglected, awaiting its next designation.

According to the records, the fortress was originally established in AD 828 by the Arabs when they took Malta. Before that a Phoenician temple stood here until it was replaced by the Romans, who built a new temple to the goddess Juno. In 1090, however, when Roger the Norman, Count of Sicily, defeated the Arabs in the name of Christianity, a small chapel dedicated to the Blessed Virgin was erected on the spot instead.

By 1430 the plateau had developed to such an extent that there was a thriving community and a rich family called De Nava had built themselves a grand house and a small chapel dedicated to St Anne. Both still exist.

It was in 1530, when the Order arrived, that Grand Master de l'Isle Adam took over the De Nava house and set about converting this high ground into a fortress. During the Great Siege, St Angelo was the pivot around which the battles were fought.

In 1912 the fortress became HMS St Angelo, headquarters of the British navy. The Commodore occupied the original De Nava palace. Further buildings were erected to house the extensive naval station and submarine base. The history of Fort St Angelo is as old and as

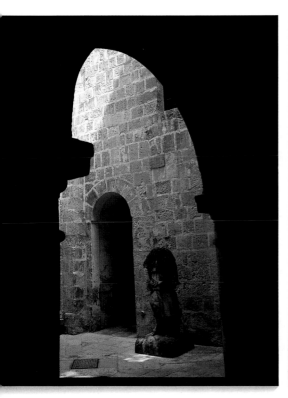

glorious as that of Malta and Gozo.

Nearby is **Kalkara**, a small pretty harbour with all the potential for making an excellent yacht marina. At present it is a quiet creek; many of Malta's traditional boats are repaired here or wintered alongside the few craftsmen who still build the *dghajsa*.

On the far side of Kalkara's creek is **Bighi**, once a large patrician villa but converted by Britain in the 19th century to make an impressive hospital. It closed with the departure of British forces in Malta and since then has been carved by roads and converted into a trades school and government housing.

Beyond, with its breakwater thrusting towards Valletta, is **Fort Ricasoli**, built in 1670 facing the sea and guarding the entrance to the Grand Harbour. In the days of the Order it had a complement of 2,000 soldiers. In World War II it received some damage and since the departure of the British navy has lain idle except for a small civil unit set up to clean the holds of tankers.

Also facing the sea a short distance away is **Fort St Rocco**, one of the many small forts created by the knights as part of Malta's coastal defence. These were an addition to the 13 isolated watch-towers already ringing the island. Within sight of one on either side, their look-outs could relay signals back to central garrison.

Beside the ancient fort a modern enterprise flourishes. These are the unique **Mediterranean Film Studios**, where many a sea or water-action scene for major international movies is shot. In the height of summer it is not unusual to see tall icebergs or pirate galleons floating ready for action.

The studios offer two superb water tanks overlooking the sea, both positioned in such a way as to give the cameras natural sky as their backdrop. One tank is a specially designed deep-water photography tank where scenes can be shot under water in controlled conditions. Both film and television companies use the facilities. Amid all the history for which Malta is famous, here is 20th-century expertise.

Below, serving some of the world's largest cruise ships and tankers. Right, business from a barrow.

STREET MARKETS

I n Latin countries, street markets are a way of life. To the casual visitor they may simply appear colourful places to pick up a bargain or fruit for a picnic, but to the local residents they are an essential part of the fabric of everyday living. In Malta and Gozo, this is especially true. Here, like the islands themselves, the fruit and vegetable markets are tiny but they are the hub of a community where gossip and news can be exchanged at the same time as shopping for the daily needs.

There is a market in almost every village or small town, although it may well be hidden away in a quiet square or on a side street. Also, it will probably have vanished by 11am – the best produce is sold early, usually after morning mass. Nor will it be there every day.

Take a Monday, for instance. Because few farmers work on Sundays, very little produce reaches wholesalers and there is nothing to buy. And on Saturdays, if a stallkeeper does open, he will rarely have anything but second-grade goods because his best will have gone on Friday, the traditional day for stocking up for the weekend. Few market traders have cold-rooms for storage and, as local produce is grown with the minimum of crop spraying and preservatives, its shelf-life is limited – perhaps to a day or two. Unsold items would therefore rot, unprofitably. (Shops, however, are different. Most have full cold-room facilities.) The best market days are Tuesdays and Fridays.

In certain districts a large street market appears one day a week when a road is blocked off – in Cospicua and Marsa, for example. Alternatively, as in Pawla (Paola), there is a market on a square which functions Tuesday to Saturday. Trestle tables are lined side by side, in rows. At one end there is seasonal produce like giant cauliflowers, carrots, cabbages and oranges in winter; tomatoes, green peppers, aubergines and figs in summer. Often there is fresh fish. At the other end are carpets, bolts of fabric and expanses of clothes. Between are groceries, potted plants and household items, from ovenware to whimsical china figurines. The clothes are similar to the T-shirts, jeans and sweaters that cover the stalls on Merchants' Street alongside St John's Cathedral in Valletta or hang outside the waterfront boutiques in the resort areas. Most are made for export in local factories.

Wherever they are and whatever they sell, the markets are crowded. They are great meeting places. There are bargains to be had.

Many neighbourhoods also have sellers who travel from door to door, pushing a converted pram laden with fresh produce from their own fields. Or a decorated truck, its bonnet emblazoned with the name of a hero like Elvis Presley or Mad Max, may take up a regular position three or four times a week on a street corner. In the cool of summer evenings these are the trucks that service the coastal towns from Sliema to Mellieha.

Shoppers don't stand in line at either truck or stall. They lean to catch the eye of the salesman and call out their orders. It is customary to ask for a bag and help yourself, passing back each bag for weighing. The only time self-selection is discouraged by stallholders is when soft fruits like peaches or apricots are in season: these bruise if handled too much.

The law dictates that all prices must be marked, though sometimes they are not. Some sellers hike the price by a few cents for tourists.

Until the introduction of the metric system all weights were either Maltese, based on a *ratal* (28 oz/790 grams) or Imperial. But the Maltese were quick to accept metrication and decimalisation, and kilos and divisions of a kilo are now the norm. (So is Celsius; mention temperatures in Fahrenheit and everyone is confused.)

Valletta has an excellent indoor market in Merchants' Street, behind the Palace of the Grand Masters, selling food. An old building that has recently been restored, it now offers some of the best value available. One floor is devoted to fresh fish, meat, poultry and delicatessen goods, another to fruit and vegetables.

In Gozo, the centre is the picturesque market square of It-Tokk below the Citadel in Victoria, now under threat of being converted to a permanent car park. Meanwhile its stalls sell clothes and household items while the narrow lanes edging it sell local produce and fresh fish. ∎

THE VILLAGE CHURCHES

Dominating Malta's countryside are tall limestone churches, their generous round domes painted ruby red or silver, their pairs of pointed belfry towers standing sentinel. No two are identical. They are what make the landscape so special, each one a unique architectural signpost, parish church and focal point for village life. All merit a brief visit.

To a less noticeable extent, churches dominate Valletta and Sliema, too – although, in Sliema, the uncontrolled building of tall apartments and hotels has begun to change the skyline and screen them from view. Mdina, however, remains superb. The cathedral, with its stone dome so much a part of the city's battlement walls, creates a unique and moving silhouette.

Unique charm: Although Valletta's churches, like Mdina's cathedral, contain artistic treasures no village can match, most have, nonetheless, a church of majestic splendour and, as anyone exploring the island by car will testify, each one contains a considerable amount of grandeur and charm all its own. Most are excellent examples of the baroque. They are a matter of great pride for the villagers, whether they are churchgoers or not.

It's worth noting that in Malta there are two cities – that is, Valletta and Mdina – and the "Three Cities" of Vittoriosa, Cospicua and Senglea. The only designated towns are Sliema and Rabat. The rest, even though many certainly are town-size, are called villages. This is a custom dating back to times when they were villages and has nothing to do with accuracy or the size of the population.

The most distinctive church is at the crossroads in the centre of **Mosta**. Dedicated to St Mary, its **Mosta Dome** can be seen from almost any vantage point in Malta. Villagers here take great pride

Preceding pages: the superb Mosta Dome dominates the community. **Left,** parish church and village square, Gharb.

in its impressive scale and the fact that its dome is reputed to be the fourth largest unsupported dome in the world, surpassed only by St Peter's in Rome, St Sophia in Constantinople and (though they are not much amused by this recent addition), the new church dedicated to St John built at Xewkija in Gozo.

Whether it truly is fourth largest or not does not matter. It is a remarkable church with an elegant interior and was built to the design of Giorgio Grognet de Vasse with almost total voluntary labour drawn from the parish. The first stone was laid in 1833 and 27 years later the main structure was completed. Its generous size came about because it was erected around a church already on the spot. The original one had become too small for the growing parish but could not be demolished until an alternative was available.

During World War II a bomb pierced the dome and landed unexploded on the church floor. Defused, it is now on display in the church.

Lija, **Attard** and **Balzan**, are often referred to as the "Three Villages", villages where property prices remain constantly high and where there are some superb patrician houses that date back to the 17th century. This is where many wealthy families came to live as peace returned to the islands during the reign of the Order of St John and as Valletta became overcrowded.

The three have grown into one mass with their boundary lines known only to the residents. The President's official residence is in Attard, the **San Anton Palace**, an elegant and stately palace. It is not open to visitors but its gardens are.

The Lija *festa*, around 8 August, takes place in front of **St Saviour** designed by Giovanni Barbara in 1694. This popular *festa* is renowned for superb fireworks.

The first of the big parish churches, built to accommodate expanding parish boundaries with their fast growing populations, were **St George** at **Qormi** and **St Philip, Zebbug**. They were erected to show village wealth as much as the visible face of the church. But it is **Attard**'s parish church dedicated, like

Young parishioners being baptised at Mosta.

246

so many others, to **Santa Marija** that heralds the splendours to come.

It was designed by Tommaso Dingli in 1613. A prolific architect, he designed the parish church of **Santa Marija** in Birkirkara, a triumph of indigenous design and sculpture, a fine example of a Maltese Renaissance church. Later he went on to Naxxar, Gharghur, Gudja and Zabbar. Not that they all remain, like Attard, as he envisaged them. As the parishes grew, alterations were made; many were proving too small for their growing congregations.

In fact, Dingli's Birkirkara church was never completed because even then they knew it would be too small. And Our Lady of Graces in Zabbar was not only expanded but much later given a new dome as the original one was damaged by cannon fire from the French lines in Cottonera in 1800 after the Maltese had risen against the occupation of their islands. It was this skirmish that was part of the prelude to the arrival of the British that year.

Dingli's Gharghur church, **St Bartholomew**, contains a statue made of plaster and real bones – like so many on the islands. His church in Gudja is not far from the delightful chapel of **Birmiftuh** which was built in 1436. Also dedicated to St Mary, this was one of the first parish churches on the island and served the neighbouring hamlets until they grew large enough to become parishes themselves. Its original parapet was consecrated and considered sanctuary. The right of churches to offer sanctuary was ended during the rule of the knights. The bell tower is a "new" addition, having being added in 1578.

The cathedrals of Mdina and Victoria (that is, Rabat, Gozo) were designed by Lorenzo Gafa' who was also responsible for three of the most distinctive large-scale baroque parish churches: **St Nicholas** at **Siggiewi**, **St Lawrence (San Lawrenz)** at **Vittoriosa** and **St Catherine, Zejtun**. Of course, these three have had their alterations too but they still show the skill of this master architect. A short distance from St Catherine in Zejtun is the charming but sim-

ple church of **St Gregory**, one of the oldest on the islands, built in 1436.

The most spectacular example of local church building is deep in the unremarkable streets of **Birkirkara** at the centre of the island. Dedicated to St Helena, it is considered the climax of local baroque. This is the church that replaced Tommaso Dingli's design. Conceived by 27-year-old Domenico Cachia – who later designed the superb Auberge de Castille in Valletta – it is powerfully proportioned with a rich interior of frescoes, painting and carving.

Plain and simple: The Maltese are emotionally attached to the vast number of attractive small churches and chapels that seem to be sited only in picturesque, sheltered corners of narrow streets or outside a village in the countryside where cars pass by at speed. Once these tiny edifices, Wayside Chapels, served the country faithful who came from isolated farming communities that were gathered together as if in hamlets, their parish priest travelling to be with them. All are architecturally delightful and usually simple, small, plain box-like buildings consisting of one square room with, perhaps, some external buttressing and a bell tower over the plain front door. Few open their doors to visitors or worshippers on a regular basis.

The first came into being around 1436 when the Bishop of Malta created 10 new parishes outside the main conurbations of Valletta, Mdina and Il Borgo (where the Three Cities would be established). Until then, as the population of the islands was sparse, churches in the open countryside were mostly troglodytic and cut into the rock or caves where they were safe and less likely to be seen by the Corsairs who constantly raided the islands stealing what they could and taking the peasants as slaves to sell in the markets of North Africa.

After the knights came in 1530, the clerical (and secular) architectural face of Malta changed. Malta would assume its distinctive appearance, and church buildings would become an art form.

Left, the richly decorated interior of the parish church of the village of Nadur.

TEMPLES

Although the islands are known for their long association with the knights of the Order of St John and, in more recent times, for the incalculable bravery of the people during World War II, they are also renowned for their prehistory, with remains dating back more than 6,000 years. Here, in unknown times, men built. With simple tools they scooped out the ground or piled high large masses of heavy stone. Had their work been carried out today, it would still be impressive.

Who these people were is a mystery. There is nothing to explain where they came from, nor what happened to them. At times the population may have been quite large – how else could they have erected such impressive monuments? At other times the islands seem to have been abandoned. Whoever they were, from Stone Age to Bronze Age, they left behind them for future generations a considerable amount of building and cause for endless conjecture.

Prehistoric chronology is still a matter of debate; experts using carbon dating argue that many prehistoric cultures in Malta are even older than is currently recognised. Some dates and sites, however, are commonly accepted. From the Stone Age, there is Ghar Dalam (5000 BC), Birzebbuga (pre-3600 BC) and Skorba, Zebbieh (3600 BC).

From the Temple Period, there is Xemxija Tombs, St Paul's Bay (3600 BC); Mgarr Temples; Kordin, Marsa; Mnajdra and Hagar Qim, Qrendi; and Ggantija, Xaghra, Gozo (all 3600–3000 BC), and the Hypogeum, Paola (2400 BC). From the Bronze Age, there is Tarxien cemetery and Borg-in-Nadur, Birzebugga (1500 BC), and cart tracks from the Bronze Age.

Ghar Dalam, the Cave of Darkness, is on the main road to Birzebbuga. It is a natural cave where, in addition to traces of Stone Age man, the bones of prehistoric animal life have also been found. These, mostly from dwarf elephants and hippopotami, have fuelled

the speculation that the islands once formed part of a land bridge between the African and European continents, between Sicily and Libya or Tunisia. Theory has it that a major earthquake broke up the land and caused severe flooding. This created the Maltese archipelago and separated the two continents, north and south.

Traces of human life indicate that Ghar Dalam was used again during the Bronze Age and by the constantly moving traders, the Phoenicians, when they arrived around 800 BC.

The **Skorba** site is on the main country road to Ghajn Tuffieha at Zebbieh, not far from the small village of Mgarr, the site of the earliest known settlement in Malta. There are signs of two temples and a number of houses, indicating that a flourishing farming and fishing settlement must have been here.

Two kinds of pottery have been found here, grey and red; by dating these it would seem that Skorba was a flourishing place for more than 1,000 years, even into the Bronze Age. A number of

specialist papers have been written about the Skorba people, offering conflicting theories. Some date the settlement to pre-3800 BC.

The **Xemxija** tombs are on the hill above St Paul's Bay leading to Mellieha. Not a major site, they are interesting because here the dead were buried in womb-like tombs cut into the rock. This suggests a return to the womb of Mother Earth. The **Mgarr temples**, although historically significant, have little to offer the non-expert, although their monumental frontage pre-dates those of the islands' most spectacular Neolithic temples, Ggantija in Gozo and Hagar Qim and Mnajdra in Malta.

New research proves Ggantija was the first to be built. To add to the temples' appeal, carbon-dating technology suggests that they are the oldest freestanding monuments in the world, perhaps even older than the first pyramid in Egypt. The shapes of the temples and the positions of altars and smaller chambers make their use easy to understand, guides are on hand to add colour and can make a visit more interesting.

Often considered the most impressive, **Ggantija**, on the outskirts of the village of Xaghra, sits on a sheltered slope facing inland. Many of the huge slabs of limestone that form its monumental walls are 20 ft (6 metres) high and weigh several tons. How these early people were able to move these – or the similar stones at Hagar Qim and Mnajdra – and then to stand them upright too is yet another matter for conjecture. A favoured theory is that they were transported on stone balls, but how they were hoisted up into position has still to be explained.

Ggantija is really two temples with a common forecourt. One consists of five rooms; the smaller one, only three. There are chambers, altars and niches, all of which were used in the ceremonies of ritual worship. Fragments of plaster and red pigment found here indicate that the temples were originally plastered and painted.

In Malta, the **Hagar Qim** and **Mnajdra** temples outside Qrendi are on

Hagar Qim's complex chambers.

the land slope facing the tiny rock island of **Filfla**, which more recently was used for target practice by British warships. Two-tailed lizards are reputed to live here among the unexploded shells. Filfla has been declared a nature reserve but law-breakers, instead of landing, now pass by on boats to shoot the resting migratory birds. Because of the mysterious way the rock stands out in the water and the way the midsummer setting sun catches it, the island may have been an integral part of temple ritual and may have been the reason why the temples were built in this exposed position.

Hagar Qim is at the top of the hill, with Mnajdra (closed for restoration) tucked somewhat more magically into the dip below. Like Ggantija on Gozo, the temples were used for sacrifices with libations of milk and blood presented at the altars. The temples were shrines to Mother Earth and it is thought that the dead returned to her womb only if sacrifices were offered. In the chambers there are decorated stones, libation altars and tie holes where curtains were hung in order to conceal the priestesses.

Hagar Qim and Mnajdra are a distance from public transport and, unless you are travelling as part of a group, they are accessible only by car, especially in the heat of summer. The advantage of a car is that you can also reach, close by, the tiny picturesque rocky inlet of **Wied-iz-Zurrieq**. There, the traditional Maltese fishing boats (the *luzzu*) are moored in the water in great numbers or hauled ashore to be repainted in fine colours.

It is a spectacular drive into Wied-iz-Zurrieq along the cliffs. From its jetty beneath the simple cafés and souvenir shops, small boats ferry visitors to the **Blue Grotto**. The best time to go is in the early morning when the light reflected through the caves brings out the colour. It is wise to negotiate the price of the boat trip before setting out.

To the other side of the temples, towards Dingli and Buskett Gardens, the road passes another popular spot, **Ghar Lapsi**. Little happens here, but it is a favourite place to come for walks in

Ggantija outside village of Xaghra.

winter and spring. In summer swimming is passable rather than good – except for scuba divers, who find the underwater world worthwhile. There is a small casual restaurant of the egg-and-chips variety offering spaghetti, fresh fish and *fenek*, Malta's favourite rabbit dish. To one side of the valley, below a stone quarry, is one of the island's many reverse osmosis water plants, which convert sea water to drinking water.

Probably the most fascinating temple, however, is the **Hal Saflieni Hypogeum** at **Paola**. Unlike the others, the Hypogeum is underground, carved deep into the soft limestone. It was discovered accidentally by builders in 1902 when they were preparing the foundations of a house. It is closed for major restructural works.

The Hypogeum was dug out of the rock around 3000 BC by people using flints and hard rocks. They created a network of corridors and deep chambers on three levels. At the deepest level there appears to be a secret granary which is reached by seven uneven angled steps that turn sharply to the right and have a sheer drop into a narrow chamber on their left. This deliberate drop is said to be a device to trap would-be thieves as they approached in the enveloping darkness.

The Hypogeum was a place for both ritual and burial. When discovered, it was full of fragments of bone and pottery, of which only a little has been kept. An estimated 7,000 bodies were interred here. The chambers are well finished on a well-proportioned scale. The most impressive, commonly referred to as the "Holy of Holies", has pillars and lintels that are architecturally remarkable. The room was probably used for the sacrifice of animals.

There are patterns and symbols on the walls and there is an oracle chamber where a square niche was cut into a wall to serve to echo the priest's voice around the temple. When a man speaks into the niche, the sound reverberates around the chamber; when a woman speaks into it, nothing happens. Two "Sleeping Lady" figurines were found

Prehistoric cart tracks near Dingli.

256

in the middle chambers but, like the other artefacts from the Hypogeum, these have since been moved to the Museum of Archaeology, Valletta.

A short distance away are the temples of **Tarxien**, discovered in 1914 and excavated with great care. A group of four temples, these at Tarxien are remarkable for the quality of their carvings which not only include subtle decorative spirals but also friezes of farm animals, among them a bull and a suckling sow. The bull represents virility, the sow fertility.

Of considerable historical importance was the discovery here of the large base of a monumental statue to Mother Earth. It indicates that these early peoples had created the first known free-standing statue of a deity. Had it survived, it would have been at least 8 ft (2.4 metres) high.

Certain walls and floors are discoloured with a curious dark patina and experts believe this was caused in the later Bronze Age by the funeral pyres of a new people arriving at the temples.

These were people who cremated their dead. The original dwellers did not.

On both Malta and Gozo there are strange Bronze Age cart tracks, deep ruts along which sledge-like carts were dragged. Always on the high ground, they were carved by hand into the hard, uneven rocky surface of the barren countryside to ease the movement of the carts as they were pulled along with their shaft ends resting on the stone. Unsignposted, in Malta they can be found at **Mtarfa**, **San Pawl-tat-Targa** and **Bingemma** and near **Dingli**, where so many cross each other that the group has become known as Clapham Junction after the London railway junction. In Gozo the most evident are on the cliffs by Ta'Cenc Hotel at **Sannat**.

The deep cart tracks were undoubtedly part of a regular system of transport but it is not clear where they went to, or why. They are cambered on corners. Some lead straight off the cliff edges and add graphic evidence to the theory that Malta and Gozo were once joined to mainland Europe.

Sophisticated workmanship in stone at Tarxien temples.

THE BEACHES

The coastlines of the islands are indented with harbours, bays and creeks. And the surrounding sea is the clearest, cleanest and bluest in the Mediterranean, free of the kind of pollution that affects the coasts of Italy or the south of France. In summer it is remarkably refreshing and inviting; in August it can even appear to be warm. It is one of the islands' incomparable assets.

There are no real tides, no treacherous currents and no known dangerous fish. The wide variety of fish that do swim in these waters, big and small, are delight to both fishermen and cooks.

As for the islands' beaches, there are not many if, by definition, "beach" would imply sand. Of these, there are only 11 on Malta, two on Gozo and two on the tiny island of Comino, not all of them large or good.

But the islands more than make up for this apparent shortage of sand with a vast number of excellent rock beaches where children can swim and play with equal safety. The Maltese themselves generally prefer swimming from the smooth rocks anyway. From these you can dive in where the waters are deep or walk in easily where the waters are shallow. And for anyone keen on scuba-diving or simply starting out to enjoy the pleasures of underwater discovery with mask and flippers they are a joy.

Taking to the air: There are also beach establishments and lidos with cafés, beds and umbrellas, showers and the opportunity to water-ski, windsurf, jet-ski and sail. The less energetic can rent a pedalo or canoe. In places like **Mellieha Bay** it is also possible to parascend from the water's edge harnessed into a multi-coloured parachute and be towed by speedboat out to sea to view the coast like a gull. Only surfboarding is impossible – these islands never have waves big enough.

Malta's sand beaches are mainly to the north while the most suitable stretches of flat white rocks are along the western side of the island where the

major resort areas are. The eastern coastline consists mainly of sheer cliffs, although it is possible to swim in a modest manner at either **Wied-iz-Zurrieq** near Zurrieq or **Ghar Lapsi** near Siggiewi, both of which are popular with scuba-diving groups who explore the rugged coastline.

Both Malta and Gozo are small and it might appear as if everywhere is within walking distance. It is not – and certainly never in the heat of the day. Although bus routes are simple to master, getting around by car is easier, especially in reaching the beaches.

By exploring the shoreline it is possible occasionally to find a minuscule cove with just a few yards of sand. In winter the rough seas sometimes move the sands; on the major beaches it has often been known for the sand to partially disappear, only to return again in full glory after the next storm. Fortunately the elements seem to know the rules and the sand is always back in place for the summer season, although it may also bring with it the odd boulder or

Preceding pages: off Golden Bay; the sands of Ramla; sunbathing. Left, Sunday t Golden Bay. Right, pride of ownership.

two that present a toe-stubbing threat as they lie hidden in the golden carpet.

Malta's most popular sandy beaches are the neighbouring beaches of Ghajn Tuffieha and Golden Bay. Both are in a superb, dramatic setting surrounded by flat-topped, golden-and-brown rocky cliffs and both have excellent stretches of fine sand. It is a rare occurrence, but should a red flag be flying from the old knights' watchtower at the tip of the promontory that separates the beaches, take heed when swimming. The flag signifies undercurrents out in the bay.

Golden Bay is the more accessible of the two, with an attendant-run car park close to the sand. There is a hotel to one side, the Golden Sands Hotel, and there are beach facilities with cold drinks and snacks as well as the opportunity to rent a windsurf board, pedalo or canoe. The beach is raked daily.

Ghajn Tuffieha, (pronounced: *eye-n-toof-ee-ha*), is the prettier of the two, having a less spoiled setting, and was, until recently, only accessible by a long staggered staircase down the side of the steep hill to the sands. The exhausting climb made the beach less crowded than its neighbour. However, in recent years the retaining gate has been broken and, unless it is repaired, cars will continue to drive down a narrow sweeping track that ends close to the beach, gradually expanding the parking area.

The open track has brought change to what was once a natural hillside planted with struggling tamarisk and acacia where for centuries goatherds have brought their small flocks. But it is nonetheless a delightful place. Model airplane enthusiasts fly their remote-control machines from the heights. At the far end in a sheltered corner below the table-top hill, well away from the beach bar, families flout the law by swimming and sunbathing nude.

At the far end, too, is a high and treacherous, narrow grey clay ridge; below it, on the far side, is a tempting, smooth, cream rock promontory. It is a difficult, if not a dangerous, matter scaling this crumbling vertical ridge to get there, but people do. Others walk from **On the sands of Ghadira.**

266

Gnejna on the other side. Mostly male bathers gather here.

Between Ghajn Tuffieha and Golden Bay is a tourist complex, the **Hal Ferh Tourist Village**, which was converted simply from a military rest camp used by service families in the days when the British garrison was stationed here. Nearby is the bus terminal for the 47A route to the Valletta terminus. It's a friendly, crowded and inexpensive route but its timetable must be constantly checked as it changes according to whim and season.

Gnejna (pronounced *j-nay-na*) is approached through the village of Mgarr with its surrounding fields in which, whatever the season, farmers seem to be working. Behind the silver-domed parish church dedicated to the Virgin Mary, the crooked road leads to a steep hill, then down, minutes away, to the beach. The car park touches the sands. (The 46 bus route goes only as far as Mgarr; the walk is about 15 minutes, and hitching is acceptable.)

Gnejna's sand is mixed with shingle with, to the right, a short stretch of smooth white rock. On the left of the bay are boathouses cut into the rock. Beach facilities – in this instance, only cold drinks and packet snacks – are sold from mobile kiosks or vans.

The most northerly village on Malta is **Mellieha**, a 10-minute car journey from the Gozo ferry jetty at **Cirkewwa**. Perched on a high ridge with its parish church on a spur, it has some good restaurants and shops catering to both residents of the village and the luxury estates as well as to visitors, many of whom self-cater in nearby apartments. Because cars can easily block the road that threads through Mellieha, it is continuously patrolled by policemen who issue parking tickets.

Down the long winding hill below the village is **Ghadira**, the longest sandy beach on Malta. Sometimes called Mellieha Bay, Ghadira, (pronounced *aa-dee-ra*), is highly popular and gregarious with facilities that improve each year. There are cafés, beach establishments and all the facilities for renting

Windsurfing in Mellieha Bay.

windsurfing equipment, canoes, waterskiing and parascending services. It is very crowded at weekends when families arrive early to select the best positions for their umbrellas. To one side is the Mellieha Bay Hotel, a favourite with tour groups.

A bus service, route 44, has its terminus by the sands. As Ghadira is quite a distance from the village and the hectic main road to Mellieha has no pavements, visitors without cars are well advised to use the bus connection.

Further to the north of Ghadira is **Marfa Ridge**, the tall ridge of land that on the map looks like the tail of Malta's fishlike shape. It is from Cirkewwa at the westerly tip of this craggy ground that the car ferries sail to Mgarr in Gozo. It is also the pick-up point for small boats belonging to the hotel on Comino.

It is an attractive ridge with rocky outcrops, fertile fields, forestry plantations of acacia and some pleasant beaches. There are two beach hotels.

The small, attractive **Ramla Bay** is dominated by its large hotel well-known for its beach and sports facilities (the hotel is open to non-residents using the restaurant or café). Alongside is a small, free stretch of sand suitable for family picnics.

Paradise Bay is also attractive, though possibly less so than Ramla, with a pleasant, crowded beach reached by narrow steps. It is usually sandy but in some years there is much shingle. It is very popular with Maltese villagers for their coach outings and can be particularly crowded at weekends. Kiosks serve simple refreshments.

Armier and **Little Armier** are small, flat, unsophisticated sandy bays facing towards Comino – not "smart" beaches but nonetheless popular. They have inexpensive beach cafés and simple facilities, and are good for parties with lots of young children.

Slug Bay, further along the rough road leading to the eastern tip of Marfa Ridge, faces Mellieha rather than the Gozo channel. To clamber down to it, there is a winding footpath whose small entrance is concealed in a car park and

Marsaxlokk, Sunday morning market.

picnic area among the acacia and eucalyptus. The wise park their cars where they can be seen from the main track, no matter how tempting it is to leave the car in the cool shade of a tree on a hot day. Cars are often broken into here.

The shore is starkly pretty with room for just a few people on the patch of sand in its tiny bay. Many prefer to swim off the flat rocks around the entrance, although most are sharp and it is not too easy getting out of the water. It is a remote and private place and, because of its ruggedness, never crowded.

Nearer Ghadira on the approach road down from Mellieha is a sign-posted turning to **Anchor Bay**, a curious name that sounds interesting, but offers little. The name comes from days long ago when a number of anchors were to be found on the beach. The film set of the Sweethaven village seen in the 1980 film *Popeye* is here and can be visited.

Close to the southernmost point of Malta is **Pretty Bay, Birzebbuga**. A modest small town, Birzebbuga was for many years the home of British services families. The inappropriately named sandy stretch runs alongside the road and hardly qualifies as a beach any longer. Birzebbuga is in **Marsaxlokk Bay**, not far from the picturesque fishing village of Marsaxlokk but closer to the fast-developing Freeport with its working jetties and containerisation.

On Gozo is one of the Maltese islands' best sand beaches and one of their most charming. **Ramla**, the best, is reached via the village of **Nadur** (on bus route 31 from Victoria). Its name translates as sand and here the sand forms a long red expanse bordered by ideal sea on one side and lush vegetation on the other. It is a popular spot for picnics all through the year. In the summer season the sand is raked daily and kept to a high standard; mobile kiosks offer snacks and cold drinks.

Facing the sea, on the hillside to the left (north) is **Calypso's Cave**, reputed to be, like so many other caves, where Odysseus lived for seven years with the enchantress Calypso before returning to his ever-faithful wife Penelope as she sat forever weaving. Below the cave are

the remains of a Roman villa and, touching the water, a redoubt. In the middle of the red sand is a simple statue of Gozo's favourite saint, Santa Marija.

San Blas is a picturesque jewel, a charming miniature beach in a secluded cove ringed with terraced fields and lush greenery. From Nadur, to get to the bay, the narrow road winds down finally reaching a steep hill that is accessible only for a short distance by car. But it is a superb walk the rest of the way downhill through a valley abundant with fruit and with several fields edged with tall bamboo fences to protect the crops from the sea winds rising from below. There is not much space on the beach and it is probably not best suited to families with young children.

Comino is the sun-baked island measuring only one square mile (2.6 sq. km) midway between Malta and Gozo. It is a rugged rock with a few small terraced fields, a flourishing hotel complex, a pig farm and, joining it to a rocky outcrop island known as Cominotto, the **Blue Lagoon**. To get to the Blue La-

goon, there are day trips from Sliema's Strand or Bugibba. To enjoy the hotel and the sand beaches of Santa Marija and San Niklaw, launches from the Comino Hotel collect guests by arrangement. Guests, in this instance, include non-residents who arrange to use their catering facilities as well as their sports amenities (tel: 529821/9).

As for the famous Blue Lagoon, boat cruises leave Sliema's Strand daily all through the year and in the height of summer from the resort of Bugibba and the harbour of Mgarr. This means that the turquoise waters are inclined to be crowded with boats in August as each one attempts to offer better and, regrettably, louder, entertainment than its neighbour. Private yachts and cruisers are inclined to make early evening visits after the day boats have sailed.

As for rock beaches, these are all around the islands. Some are well-known and popular, others fairly secret. As a rule, if a place is popular, with locals crowding the white rocks, it is because that is where the swimming is good, the rocks are kindest, and the getting in and out easy. In many places steps are cut into the rock; in others there are iron ladders. If in doubt, it's worth asking the locals for recommendations because they'll explain where not to swim – perhaps because of the shallows or the risk of *rizzi* (sea urchins) that might be trodden on (not dangerous, but uncomfortable).

All the resort towns are situated where the swimming is good: from Sliema to St George's Bay in Malta, for example, or from the majestic Sun Crest Hotel at Qawra around the coastline to Bugibba. But areas away from the hotels also have good beaches. At the southern end of the island, for example, there are the superb bays of **Delimara**, **St Peter's Pool** and **Island Bay**, although these are now under threat of pollution from the new electricity generating station sited close by.

In **Gozo**, the favourites are **Marsalforn**, **Dahlet Qorrot**, **Hondoq-ir-Rummien** and the **Fungus Rock** inlet near the **Inland Sea** at **Dwejra**.

Left, fishermen start young. Right, sailing in Marsamxett.

270

UNDER SAIL

With nearly 1,000 sheltered berths on offer, all close to the capital Valletta, Malta is now making its mark as an attractive international yachting centre: planes connect Malta International Airport to all the major European cities.

The first phase of the new Msida Marina Yachting Centre, set up to provide year-round service, began operating in 1989 with 274 berths on a floating pontoon system. Since then its capacity has reached around 1,000, including neighbouring creeks. Full information about the marina's constantly changing berth availability can be obtained from the Secretary, Yachting Centres Management Committee, Yachting Centre, Manoel Island, Malta. (tel: 330975. Radio Malta Marina Channel 37. International Channels 08 and 09)

The main island has an indented coastline of some 200 km of clear water. Many bays and coves provide secure anchorage for the night. In the calm delight of the warm months yachts anchor in secluded bays where water is still and translucent. Comino's Blue Lagoon, so called because of its brilliant turquoise water, is, however, so popular that it is now in danger of being overcrowded, so accessible has it become to commercial boat cruises. But

before the onset of the holiday season it is one of the islands' most delightful spots.

The Gozo Marina has now been inaugurated with quay and pontoon berths available.

The highlights of the sailing calendar are the two big races, Syracuse-Malta and Rimini-Malta-Rimini. (Windsurfers have their own event too in the world's longest single-stage race, Sicily to Malta. The record stands at 5 hours 56 mins.) The Valletta Yacht Club on Manoel Island (tel: 621839) organises regattas while an annual event is the single-handed, round-Malta race.

In the winter months the winds are usually northeasterly (in Maltese: *grigal*) which cause surges and can reach storm conditions that last an average three days. The worst are in January. The prevailing wind, however, is the northwesterly (*majjistral*: the French *mistral*) and can blow up to force 9. Spring and autumn winds are mostly southerly and humid (*xlokk*: sirocco).

Malta is a good wintering base. Berths are sheltered from rough seas and it is possible to live on board even in the cruellest weather. There are excellent repair and haulage facilities on Manoel Island for yachts up to 500 tons where boats can be stored on dry land and maintained throughout the winter. There are also several yacht agencies and general chandlers operating in the vicinity. Both areas are situated on the main bus routes to Valletta and Sliema.

A mail collection service does away with the need for a *post restante* arrangement. The General Post Office gathers all mail addressed to yachts and delivers it to the Yachting Centre Office which holds onto it until it is collected.

Crew members on non-luxury boats can freely use shower and toilet facilities by the administration block. Rates are competitive.

Water and electricity charges vary according to class of vessel, whether berthed alongside a quay or a pontoon. When berthed alongside a pontoon, the berthing fees usually include water and electricity charges. Quay berths are metre charged for water and electricity but smaller vessels are often allowed a weekly discount of 7c per metre.

Electricity, in 240V and 120V single phase, is available for a Lm40 refundable deposit.

Current rates can always be obtained by contacting the Malta Maritime Authority (tel: 250317/8, fax: 250320).

Yachts arriving from outside territorial waters must fly a "Q" flag and must make straight for Marsamxett Harbour, immediately north of the Grand Harbour and Valletta. After calling Valletta Port Control on VHF Channel 9 for berthing information, they should proceed to the indicated visitor's berth. The yacht's registration book and passports of everyone on board must be presented to Customs and Immigration.

Before final departure a passenger and crew list must be drawn up on the appropriate form and presented to Customs and Immigration. Duty-free stores may be taken out but they are loaded on to the yacht and sealed under supervision. They may not be used within territorial waters. ∎

GOZO

Tradition has it that Gozo is Homer's Ogygia, the island where the nymph Calypso held the Greek hero Odysseus captive for seven years. There are other contenders for the honour but, as long ago as the 3rd century BC, the great Greek scholar Callimachus said that the nymph lived here – and in this part of the world what Callimachus said goes. There is certainly a strange enchantment about the place. It feels untouched by the modern world, but things work: the water in the taps is drinkable, and it is as easy to buy a bottle of French champagne as it is delicious vegetables fresh from the soil.

A third of the size of its sister, Malta, it is greener and more rural (and very much cleaner and tidier). It is a land of farmers and fishermen and the solid values of those who live by the elements. It has an area of only 26 sq. miles (67 sq. km) and a population of 25,000, yet it is possible to stroll along Gozo's country lanes and goat tracks for an hour or more and see only a young boy herding his goats and sheep or a farmer hoeing his fields.

Edward Lear, of the *Nonsense Rhymes*, was so carried away by the scenery that he called it "pomskizillious and gromphiberous, being as no words can describe its magnificence". Flat-topped hills rise out of valley floors, drystone walls contour every gradient and church domes crest the skyline. The outcrops of limestone range in colour from imperious grey through glowing russet to gold as rich as whipped butter.

In spring it is a gaudy patchwork. Tiny fields of lush green wheat and barley jostle chrome-yellow daisies and spreads of crimson-flowered lucerne. Carpets of miniature wild flowers sprout from apparently solid rock, thyme and wild fennel scent the air and, as far distant as one can see, there is the cobalt sea and sky. In summer, when the hot sun bakes any ground that is not devoutly worked and watered, it is impossible to imagine all this bounty.

The island then sheds more layers than the average tourist and presents its beautiful skeleton to the world. The vistas become biblical, the shadows purple. As with most strip-teases, the ultimate revelation pleases some viewers more than others.

Name changes: The island's turbulent past is reflected in the shifts and changes that have gone into establishing its name. According to a local historian, Father Joseph Bezzina, it was called *Gwl* by the Phoenicians, most probably because its shape resembled their round ships of that name. The Greeks knew it as Gaulos (their word for *gwls*) and the Romans as Gaulus. Under the Byzantines it became Gaudes, which the Arabs phonetically transcribed as *Ghawdex* and medieval ecclesiastics Latinised into Gaudisium – which to them also meant joy.

When the Spanish took their turn to rule, they translated joy into Castilian and came up with Gozo. By this time the local population had retired from the game. Way back, they had taken a fancy

to *Ghawdex* (pronounced *Ow-desh*), to which they have remained steadfastly loyal ever since.

The island's tightly packed hilltop villages and the little fortress farmhouses that dot the countryside are a legacy of crueller invaders: the marauding Turks and those feared "sea-wolves of the Mediterranean" who sailed these waters, the Barbary pirates.

In 1546, infuriated by years of piecemeal plundering, the Gozitans burned the body of a captured corsair on the bastions of their Citadel. The charred remains belonged to the brother of the most dangerous pirate of them all, Dragut, and in 1551 Dragut himself, backed by the fleet of the Turkish General Sinan Pasha, arrived to exact revenge. He devastated the island, stormed the Citadel and carried off almost the entire population of 5,000 into slavery.

A few hundred resourceful Gozitans disappeared into the countryside where they hid before they could be loaded on to the enemy ships, and a few more eventually found their way back from captivity. Within a hundred years the population was back to half strength. Dragut met his come-uppance on Malta 14 years later, during the Great Siege.

Resilient people: No matter what history has thrown at them, the Gozitans appear to have adapted just enough to make life pleasant again and then proceed to carry on much as before.

They are a strong, resilient people who have long had the disconcerting habit of walking away with the nation's top jobs. Indeed, there have been more Gozitan presidents, archbishops and chief justices than the Maltese would care to count.

Surprisingly, although proud now to be their own masters, they seem actively to like foreigners. Tourists, the new invaders, are made wonderfully welcome – in a very Gozitan way. Concessions are made to accommodate their different tastes and needs, then they are gently absorbed into island life and island ways. It can be a very pleasurable experience.

Looking west towards Gozo's lighthouse.

VICTORIA

Gozo's bustling little capital, **Victoria**, is in all ways the hub of the island. It sits in the middle and from it radiate the main roads to everywhere. It is at its liveliest in the mornings and late afternoons and on warm summer Sunday evenings.

Queen Victoria gave her name to the town and elevated it to city status to mark her Golden Jubilee in 1887. The Gozitans politely installed a fountain and commemorative plaque in the Cathedral Square, then continued to use the ancient name of *Rabat*, which means a suburb. Like Malta's Rabat, which sprawls outside the fortress walls of Mdina, Gozo's suburb nestles beneath the protective bastions of its Citadel, a romantic mass of sheer rock faces, curtain walls, ravelins and bell towers that dominates the skyline from almost every approach road.

Origins: The ridge on which the heart of the town still stands has been inhabited at least since the Bronze Age. The Carthaginians left behind a Punic inscription thanking the *pᵉl whds 'm gwl* (the people of Gozo) for helping to restore three temples. A quick tally of Victoria's churches today indicates that it was work much to local taste. Under the Romans the town was fortified. One of the present-day crossroads, Triq Putirjal (Main Gate Street), and three elegant stone crosses mark the limits of the old walls.

The Arabs appear to have spurned the town and established themselves on the more easily defended heights of the hill. In the Middle Ages both suburb and Citadel were thriving, close-packed communities. Few of the medieval houses have survived, but the narrow twisting lanes and alleys remain.

Triq ir-Repubblika (Republic Street, formerly Racecourse Street) is the main thoroughfare, a pleasant mixture of shops and balconied houses which slices through the town from east to west. It accommodates all the main facilities: tourist information office, banks, police station, post office, two opera houses and the Bishop of Gozo's 19th-century palace. On high days and holidays it still lives up to its old name. On the Feasts of the Assumption (15 August, known locally as Santa Marija) and of St George (the third weekend in July) half the island turns out to cheer a medley of thoroughbred trotting ponies, gasping hacks and galloping donkeys as they pelt uphill towards a lavish carrot – a stupendous array of silver cups and salvers.

Gnien Rundle (Rundle Gardens), at the bottom of the hill, are taken over for "Santa Marija" by a jolly agricultural and industrial show, which is just as much fun for people watchers as sheep and onion fanciers. Next door is the island's oldest hotel (1881), the Duke of Edinburgh (named after Queen Victoria's son, though the present Duke and his wife, the then Princess Elizabeth, have stopped by for tea). The hotel is currently closed for extensive upgrading and renovation.

The fact that Victoria has two opera

houses is wonderfully Gozitan. Given a little rivalry, the native genius for dreaming improbably ambitious dreams – and finding the money to fund them – bears astonishing fruit. The whole thing began modestly enough a hundred years ago, with the founding of band clubs to provide music for the Saint's Day processions of Victoria's two main churches. Then, in the 1960s, St George's club, the **Astra**, built a theatre. The cathedral club, the **Aurora**, moved premises so that it could do the same. Since then there has been a tit-for-tat rivalry over facades, discos and, of course, opera productions. Since even the Gozitans haven't found a way of financing operas often, the theatres also double as cinemas.

Victoria's main square is **Pjazza Independenza** – although it is going to be a long time before this name catches on. Surrounded by tall, clipped ficus trees and busy little shops and bars, it has been known locally as *It-Tokk* for as long as the Gozitans have been saying *Ghawdex*. It means a meeting place and this is exactly what the square has been throughout its many incarnations.

It is graced, on the right, by the **Banca Giuratale**, a charming semicircular baroque confection built in 1733 as the council chambers of Gozo's governing Jurats. It now houses various government departments. On the left, the small church of **St James the Apostle** (1740) which has been rebuilt following the collapse of its foundations in the 1980s. The vigorous use of the bells of St James to drown out political meetings in the square is said to have contributed to the delay in the issuing of a restoration permit. An earlier church on the site was razed by Dragut in 1551.

Pjazza San Gorg, which lies immediately behind the main square, is dominated by the impressive **St George's Basilica**. The present building dates from 1678, though it has been much extended and the facade was rebuilt in 1818. The stunning interior decoration is proof that the skills of the baroque period were still alive and well in Gozo in the 1960s.

Waiting for customers.

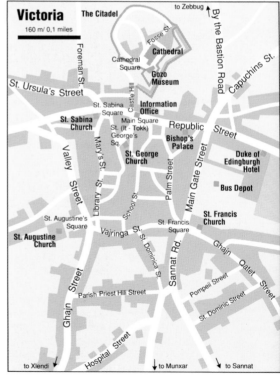

The paintings on the lavishly gilded ceiling and dome were completed between 1949 and 1964. The striking bronze altar canopy (1967) is a copy of Bernini's in St Peter's, Rome. Even amongst this competition, the main altar-piece shines out: a glowing St George, foot triumphantly poised on the dragon's head, white charger by his side, painted by Mattia Preti (1613–99) of Valletta cathedral fame.

Spreading out behind St George's is the old part of the town (**Il Borgo**), a maze of little streets and alleys designed to baffle invaders and deflect the flight of arrows and shot. Old stone balconies and religious niches are the things to look for here. Most of the shops go unannounced. Bakers can be tracked down by the aroma of hot loaves (if Maltese bread is the best in the world, then Gozitan bread can only be described as celestial), and the cobbler dangles cowboy boots above his door.

On the town's two big feast days (*festi*) the whole area seethes with life, a crush of humanity in its festive best:

tiny girls in organdie, glittering with dowry gold, well-corsetted matrons in brocade, and farmers without their customary flat caps, revealing astonishingly white bald heads. Bright blue nougat stands ("Genuine Nourishing Food"), topped with gleaming brass scales, line the main square. Statues and banners spread down Triq ir-Repubblika, and an extravaganza of fireworks bursts in the night sky.

The lively rivalry between St George's and the cathedral, which produced the two opera houses and, to some extent, the splendour of the basilica, ensures that these are bumper occasions. At Easter a truce is called: cathedral and basilica hold their Good Friday processions on alternate years. During Carnival days before Lent, costumed dancing competitions are held in Pjazza Independenza and intentionally grotesque floats parade the main streets.

The Citadel: The massive bastions, which rise golden above the town, date from the first years of the 17th century. It is thought that Francesco Laparelli,

Daily shopping in Rabat.

papal engineer, architect of Valletta and one-time assistant to Michelangelo, drew up the plans for them in 1567, two years after the Great Siege, but it was another 32 years before building commenced. King Philip II of Spain gave 40,000 scudi towards their cost and the Gozitans provided the rest by way of donations and taxes on wine, oil and agricultural exports.

The effectiveness of these splendid fortifications was never tested. By the time they were finished Suleiman the Magnificent, the knights' enemy, was dead and the Ottoman Turks had been driven out of the Western Mediterranean. For a few more years the upper town retained its importance because, by law, every Gozitan was bound to sleep there. When this restriction was lifted in 1637, the population began to drift away to more convenient houses in Victoria and the countryside. In 1693 an earthquake reduced many of the abandoned buildings to rubble.

Today, the knights' impressive bastions are being restored with the help of UNESCO and what remains of the old town is being revived. It takes some imagination to picture it in its medieval heyday, with its small palaces, chapels and warren of crowded alleys, but it is still worth a visit. The old entrance, which bore the drawbridge, is the small covered gateway at the end of the approach road. The more obvious, vast open arch was sliced out in 1956, to provide freedom of passage for the bands, dignitaries and shoulder-borne statues of the feast-day processions.

The government minister who sanctioned this gash was Miss Agatha Barbara (later President of Malta), which led the local wags to refurbish an old Roman witticism: *Quod non fecerunt barbari, fecit Barbara* (What the barbarians failed to do, was done by Barbara). Most Gozitans, however, find the breach totally acceptable, and it has opened up a fine view of the cathedral and its mighty apron of steps.

Built at the turn of the 17th century on the site of two or three earlier churches, a Roman temple to Juno and a possible **Religious artefacts for sale.**

Punic temple to Astarte, the **cathedral** is the work of the Maltese architect Lorenzo Gafa', who also designed Mdina cathedral. It has his usual lightness and grace, though the dome he intended for it was never completed. This deficiency has been turned into an asset by a *trompe l'oeil* substitute, painted by Antonio Manuele of Messina in 1739. From the nave this artful sham soars skywards in perfect symmetry; viewed from near the altar steps, it shoots off at an alarming angle. The cathedral floor is paved with the colourful tombstones of bishops and priests; a fine display of marble ecclesiastical hats, coats of arms and the grinning, skeletal figure of Death.

Pjazza Katidral, viewed from the great entrance arch, has on the left the early 17th-century Palace of the Governors of Gozo, with the "fat" mouldings that distinguished Maltese architecture in the previous century. It is now part of the adjoining **Law Courts**. On the right are the old **Bishop's Palace** and the **Chapter Hall**, built in 1899. The huddle of dwellings that once filled the square was demolished in the 1860s.

All of the island's small, delightfully undaunting museums are clustered here in the upper town, in buildings which form part of the display. The **Archaeological Museum** is housed in the fortress's last surviving private palace. The design of the sumptuously ornate balcony was reconstructed from the shattered remnants of the original. Among the exhibits from Neolithic times to the Middle Ages, the 12th-century tombstone of a young Muslim girl, Majmuna, is particularly touching.

The three houses that form the **Folklore Museum** date from around 1500. As a group they are architecturally unique in the Maltese islands, admired for the simple delicacy of the stonework and their "Norman" windows. Don't be deterred by the folklore label: the whole place is a delight.

High on a wall opposite and a little further up the hill is an inscription marking the house of the Sicilian soldier, Bernardo DeOpuo (*Audacis Militi*), hero of the 1551 siege. Preferring death to slavery, he killed his wife and two daughters, then dispatched several Turks before he himself was felled.

The **Natural History Museum** forms part of a cluster of 16th-century houses, while lances, cannon balls and things military are across the alleyway in the **Amoury**, a 17th-century hall that served as a British army barrack during the 19th century and again during World War II. The lack of wood available for ceiling beams resulted in its ingeniously buttressed arches.

The **Cathedral Museum**, in part of the cathedral's vestry, has Ionic columns (1st century BC) from the temple of Juno, a bishop's landau from the late 1860s, church silver and much more. Attractive little shops selling local crafts line the land leading to former storehouses and restrooms of the knights (1614), later the island's prison. This is now a **Crafts Centre**.

The view from the **ramparts** is splendid: a panorama of rolling valleys, strange, decapitated hills, with Malta in the distance across a flash of sea.

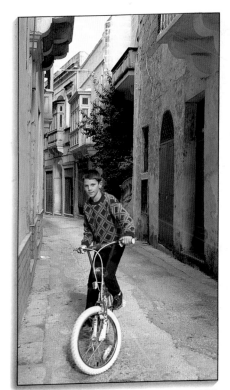

Biking through the narrow streets.

AROUND GOZO

A helicopter service whirls passengers between Malta and Gozo, but most visitors still arrive by boat, a 25-minute trip by car ferry from Cirkewwa at the northern end of Malta, or a longer sail from Sa Maison, near Valletta. In the summer, a small hovercraft also nips to and fro. En route, no matter what the vessel, it is bound to pass **Comino**, the third largest of the Maltese islands (*see page 309*).

This apparently bare rock has a fine fort (constructed in 1618), a gun battery, a hotel, the most magnificent bathing in the whole archipelago (in the limpidly turquoise **Blue Lagoon**), and four resident voters on the electoral roll. The battery is so attractive that it is often confused with the hotel, which is not visible from the ferries.

Thanks to the Italian blockbuster novelist Umberto Eco, the island now has another claim to fame; Abraham Ben Samuel Abulafia lived here. This troublesome cabbalist, who features large in Eco's novel *Foucault's Pendulum*, fled to Comino in the 13th century after escaping papal wrath in Rome and irate Jews in Sicily. He spent his time on the rock writing prophesies.

Sailing into Gozo's only port, **Mgarr**, gives a concentrated view of all that makes the island special; chapel, church spire and fort line the horizon, little flat-topped houses, tiny fields and greenery rise to meet them and at the water's edge bob gaily painted fishing boats with Christian shrines amidships and the pagan eye of Osiris on their bows. Only the mock-Gothic architecture on the skyline is out of character.

The cathedral-inspired church was started in 1924, delayed for lack of funds, then finished at a gallop in the 1970s after the priest in charge won the National Lottery.

Fort Chambray, which dominates the scene, was also built with prize money, the loot accumulated by the last great admiral of the Order of St John, Knight Grand Cross Jacques de Chambray. Having retired from active service in 1749, disgusted by the Order's peacetime lack of vigour, the old sea dog became Governor of Gozo and spent his last years refortifying Mgarr harbour at his own expense.

Fifty years on, when Napoleon's troops arrived on the island, the old warrior's ramparts, manned by knights and Gozitans, gave the French force a good deal more trouble than they had bargained for. Since then, the fort has been both a British garrison and a mental hospital. It now awaits luxury hotel development.

The main road from Mgarr to Victoria passes through **Ghajnsielem** (The Spring of Peace), a straggling, newish village which contains the church with the spire and, at its furthest limits inland, 1½ miles (2.4 km) from the port, a fine old farmhouse labelled **Gozo Heritage**. This provides a trot through more than 5,000 years of the island's history, accompanied by models and disembodied voices.

Around the next bend in the road the

Preceding pages: across the fields towards Comino and Malta; collecting salt at Qbajjar. Left, in the cool of the evening, Qbajjar. Right, five's company.

great round church of **Xewkija** rises across the fields to the left. The island's fourth largest community, Xewkija has disjointed the noses of every other parish by building by far the biggest church. The amazing dome is said to be the third largest in Europe. What is more important, if this is true (and one would be a fool to enter the controversy), then it is vaster than Mosta's dome in Malta. Based on the design of Santa Maria della Salute in Venice, the church was begun in 1952 and a bell tower was added later.

The whole of this great enterprise was financed by a population of under 3,000 and donations from Xewkijans abroad and built by willing local labour. Part of the early 17th-century church, which the **Rotunda** replaced, has been retained as a side chapel. The spectacular stone carving here is thought to be the work of two renegade Sicilians who sought sanctuary in the church from the laws of their own country.

High on a hill a couple of miles (3 km) due north stands the ancient village of **Xaghra**, home of an earlier and even more massive monument, the Stone Age temple complex of **Ggantija**. Constructed between 3600–3000 BC, this is the oldest free-standing stone building known to man, beating Egypt's pyramids and Britain's Stonehenge by several hundred years.

Of all Malta's unique Neolithic remains, this is the largest and the best preserved. The two temples cover a quarter of an acre (1,000 sq. metres), their astonishing rear wall still rises to nearly 20 ft (6 metres) and contains megaliths weighing in at 40–50 tons, the most gigantic blocks used in any of these herculean structures. As with all the Maltese temple sites, the position is pretty spectacular too.

Xerri's Grotto and **Ninu's Cave**, in narrow streets off Xaghra's attractive main square, display nature's wonders: weird stalactites and stalagmites in caverns beneath family homes. Entrance is through the householders' front doors.

Ta' Kola Windmill, just off the road to Victoria, is one of the few windmills

Repairing lobster pots.

still with its sails and original wooden machinery intact. Built in 1725 and well restored, it contains a forge, ancient tools and living quarters decorated with old country furniture and local fabrics.

Calypso's Cave, set high in the cliff face at the northeast corner of the Xaghra plateau, is reputed to be a labyrinth, reaching down to sea level in some places. Following a rock fall, it can no longer be explored but, from the viewing platform above, there is a fine vista of the fair nymph's domain: tumbling rocks, a wide, fertile valley and the red-gold sweep of **Ramla Bay**. It is here, if we are to believe local legend and Homer and Callimachus, that the wily Greek hero Odysseus (Ulysses to the Romans) was washed ashore and into the arms of the golden-haired temptress on his epic return from Troy.

A lucky Roman once had a villa in the dunes behind the bay. Since then it has been a no-go area for the building trade. Except for a few bamboo huts, serving drinks and snacks in summer, it is as uncommercialised as it was when Ca-lypso ruled the land. However, nymphlike nudity is not appreciated nowadays. There used to be notices advising swimmers to put on a raincoat when they left Gozo's beaches. These have been replaced by placards which *would* read "NO TOPLESS BATHING" if young jokers did not delight in erasing the negative.

Marsalforn, further westward along the north coast, is the larger of the island's two seaside resorts, a cheerful place, pulsing with life in the summer and just as much a playground for the Gozitans and Maltese as for the tourist. On Sunday evenings in July and August family groups stroll like a tide, back and forth, around the bay. There is one largish hotel, the **Calypso**, with a dance floor on the roof and an air-conditioned night club down below, several smaller hostelries, wall-to-wall restaurants and snack-bars, along with souvenir shops piled high with hand-knitted sweaters, which have ousted lace as the favoured local craft. The bay has a tiny fishing harbour tucked under one of its arms

Storing fishing gear.

and a choice of rock, shingle and sand for swimmers.

Salt pans, in use since Roman times, are dotted all along this stretch of coast: glittering little troughs and reservoirs cut into ledges of golden rock. The most impressive are just past Qbajjar on the Marsalforn road that leads up to the village of Zebbug. Not only are they highly photogenic, they also produce tons of prime sea salt a year.

Across the island on the southwest coast is the smaller resort of **Xlendi**, a grey-cliffed mini-fjord with protective tower at its entrance and colourful fishing boats anchored off the small sandy strip of beach.

On the way down from Victoria the road passes a cavernous 17th-century public wash-house, used more often now by young men grooming their saloon cars than ladies doing their family washing, and on the right, a spring-fed valley planted up by the knights for use as their private game reserve. On the last stretch down to the sea is the great meeting-place of the summer, **La Grotta**, an open-air disco set out like a lordly garden: flower-banked walks, discreet terraces and floodlit bamboo in the gorge below.

Xlendi itself has been much built up in recent years, mainly with banks of holiday apartments, but it still has charm. Tamarisks and pastel-painted buildings line the small promenade and again there is an abundance of restaurants, bars and souvenir sellers. The one seafront hotel, **St Patrick's**, is a stylish phoenix arisen from the rubble of an old louche hostelry. At night, the last sober man tends the bar. Throughout the summer every town and village takes it in turn to celebrate its *festa*. Xlendi includes the novel attraction of a greasy pole competition.

Going west: Gozo has been advertised as the island where time stands still. In the west it has nodded off. The landscape is gentler and the clusters of houses smaller and more sparsely spread. It makes a fitting backdrop for Malta's national shrine, **Ta' Pinu**. This sanctuary stands on a plateau off the

Lunzjata Valley, the island's green heart.

road between Victoria and Gharb and the name originates with one Pinu Gauci, who tended a small chapel on the site in the 17th century.

It was near here in 1883 that a local peasant woman, Karmela Grima, returning from her fields, heard a voice calling to her. A friend, Frangisk Portelli, confided that he too had heard the voice and together they prayed for Portelli's sick mother, who recovered. From then on miracle cures multiplied and the little chapel became a place of pilgrimage and supplication, though since the 1920s it has had a huge neo-Romanesque church attached to it. To the side of the main altar a small corridor contains poignant relics, such as crutches and trusses that bear witness to the cures effected by the devotion here.

Gharb (which fittingly means West) ends Gozo's church tour with a splendid fanfare: a riot of uniquely flamboyant late 17th-century baroque, based on a work by Francesco Borromini, the man who gave the style its name. The original stands in Rome's Piazza Navona.

The village also has some fine old carved stone balconies and a delightful **Folklore Museum** in a rambling old house on the village square. An old printing press, carriages, costumes and a mass of intriguing items are charmingly displayed.

By backtracking to the main road and heading for **San Lawrenz**, visitors soon reach the **Ta' Dbiegi Craft Village**, where knitwear, lace, leather-work, pottery, glass and stone carvings are on sale in a small former British army camp – more reminiscent of *Beau Geste* than Salisbury Plain. From San Lawrenz's church square, a road to the south dips down to **Dwejra** and some strange geological features.

Fungus Rock, to the left, guarding the entrance to **Dwejra Bay**, was much prized by the knights for the odd red plant that grows on top. Because of its colour they used it to treat blood diseases and to staunch wounds, and its phallic shape encouraged them to apply it to other parts too. They made the rock a knightly preserve, shaved down its

Sheer rock cliffs of Ta'Cenc.

sides to deter poachers, placed a sentry on the rope-and-pulley bridge and sent small samples of the fungus as princely gifts to the monarchs of Europe.

Sadly, the plant has not only proved to have no medicinal properties, but it isn't a fungus at all. It's a parasite which attaches itself to other plants' roots and only comes up for air during its short flowering season.

To the right of the road, the stunning **Azure Window**, a natural rock arch, stands with one foot in the sea but would look equally at home in a megalithic temple. Behind it, the **Inland Sea** is a pebbly-floored crater into which the sea flows through a cavernous fissure in the cliffs – an excellent suntrap in windy weather. Little boats ply through the gap for sightseeing trips around the other two features.

Sannat (due south of Victoria) has wonderfully wild cliffs, a 500-ft (152-metre) sheer drop to the sea, the home of nesting birds and rare plants as well as Stone Age remains and the most unostentatiously luxurious hotel on any of the islands, **Ta' Cenc**. On the ridge to the left and rear of the hotel is a **Neolithic necropolis**, which stared Ggantija in the eye across the valley before the Xewkija Rotunda came between them. Only one dolmen remains intact, but many more are abandoned. Samples of Malta's mysterious cart tracks are here too, though they tend to be elusive.

Seaside specials: On the northeast coast, approached through Nadur, **San Blas** has a pretty sandy beach, backed by tamarisks and a hillside of citrus groves. You have to be fit to contemplate the precipitous hike back to the road. **Hondoq ir-Rummien** (the Valley of the Pomegranates) is approached through Qala. The sea here rivals that of Comino 's Blue Lagoon, which shimmers opposite across the straits.

Getting around Gozo by car presents few problems. The signposting is excellent and the whole island can be crossed in 20 minutes. Calypso's isle tends to reveal the full potency of its magic to those who wander on foot.

Natural wonder at sea, the Azure Window.

COMINO

"Once a pirate's haven, this little island is now inhabited by snorklers, sun worshippers and the occasional mermaid. No cars – just one Swiss-owned cosmopolitan holiday complex consisting of two hotels dedicated to favoured guests, all refugees from cold European cities in search of sun and warm clear waters. Comino is an exclusive 'get away from it all' island with some of the best swimming in the Mediterranean and a range of water sports almost without equal. The island is for the discerning who wish to indulge in a few water sports activities in between lazy mornings, afternoon siestas and evening barbecues by moonlight."

So runs the text on Comino in the brochure of a leading holiday company in London, but it is a fairly apt description of modern Comino. Or rather, of present-day Comino: the word "modern" could be misleading as it might easily conjure up visions of high-rise hotels with glass atria and external lifts whizzing up and down the floors.

There is nothing like this on Comino. No such refinements have yet been installed in the low hotels which seem to retain a laid-back approach to the so-called benefits of high-tech tourism. Here, the ambience and the decor remain distinctly swinging 1960s.

True, the ceiling fans in the guest rooms are about to give way to the now *de rigueur* air conditioning units. It is also rumoured that the main hotel is to be pulled down, to be replaced by a modern Maltese village holiday complex. Presumably it will be something with more character; but, clearly, the accent will be on the modern. Be that as it may, conservationists in Malta have caught wind of it and started to protest. So far so good.

But what about the mermaids, you ask? First, seek out the playful dolphins, many of them female, which bob up and down in the deep sea channels between the islands. Clearly they like it here. Malta brags about having some of the cleanest waters in the Mediterranean, and in and around Comino the Mediterranean becomes see-through clear.

The colours are breathtaking: deepwater indigo and navy; sky and turquoise in the sandy bays peaking to the azure and emerald of the famous **Blue Lagoon**. Here in the **Fliegu Channel**, lying between Comino and its satellite sister island Cominotto, the sparkling waters of the lagoon are of a spectacular brilliance. This is the Mediterranean at its best; as it used to be, as it should be.

Hordes of trippers: In 1960 the World Underwater Fishing Championships were held in Comino. Then, because of the relative calm and absence of noisy pleasure craft, fish both large and small ogled curiously at point-blank range. Now things have changed. The new landing stage in the Blue Lagoon attracts hordes of day trippers on pleasure cruisers. Fast open day-boats piled high with tourists dart in and out of the pretty coves and inlets like landing craft about to disgorge invading marines. Little wonder the fish are now decidedly more

Preceding pages: Fungus Rock, treasured by the knights; repairing fishing tackle. Left, moored off Comino. Right, boat decoration.

cautious. Things just ain't what they used to be.

But all is not lost. The island is too minute for it to attract any serious large-scale development. Lying mid-way between Malta and Gozo, Comino is all of 1 sq. mile (2.5 sq. km) in size. It is likely to remain what it has always been: a barren rocky wilderness with a charming variegated coastline of jagged cliffs interspersed by two small sandy beaches, lots of pretty coves and creeks, arches, stacks and rock tunnels and with the gorgeous lagoon.

The nearest point to Comino is the picturesque fishing village and harbour of Mgarr in Gozo, 2 miles (3 km) away. The Gozitans have always affectionately regarded Comino as their own. The Maltese, who think they own Gozo anyway, have never raised any serious objections to this happy state of affairs.

In ancient times Ptolemy referred to the island as Cosyra but the name that stuck is Comino, from the spice cummin which used to be grown in vast quantities. Cummin still grows wild in clumps all over the island. However, it is pink and mauve wild flowering thyme that hits the eye and scents the air, especially in spring when the bees start buzzing to produce what is arguably the region's best honey.

Game reserve: It is said that when the Knights of St John arrived in the 16th century, the island was teeming with wild boar and hares. The sparse vegetation also attracted pelicans and visiting quail. Successive Grand Masters kept Comino as a private game reserve.

They were very serious about it, too. In 1695, Adrien de Wignacourt, nephew of Alof, issued an edict which stated in no uncertain terms: "Admission is strictly forbidden in future to subjects of any class or condition, armed with gun, dog, ferret, net or any device intended for game; under penalty of the galley for three years without pay, if the trespasser is an ordinary person; or a fine of forty ounces of gold, if a cleric or a member of the learned professions; and if a minor, of banishment from the dominions of the Prince

Comino: blue waters, tiny island, one hotel.

during His Highness's pleasure." Clearly, he meant business.

Long before the knights, one Abraham Ben Samuel Abulafia set himself up on Comino as the Messiah. Born in 1240 at Saragossa in Spain, Abulafia became a well-known figure and philosopher in medieval Jewish circles. On reaching the age of 18, he embarked on his search for the River Samation and the Ten Lost Tribes in Palestine. Three years later he was back in Spain, preaching and writing. His main ambition and pet project was to bring about the unification of Jews with Christians, and both with Muslims. In 1280 he even set out to convert Pope Nicholas III to Judaism but was promptly condemned by the Italians to be burnt at the stake.

It was only the sudden death of the Pope from an apoplectic stroke that saved the messianic Jew. He then headed south, hotly pursued by his enemies. In 1285, he finally sought and found shelter in the barrenness of Comino. Here he lived in great hardship, writing prophetic and cabbalistic literature that included his best-known work, *Sefer ha-ot* (Book of the Sign).

Throughout the Middle Ages, both Malta and Gozo were constantly attacked by Saracen pirates who used Comino as a base. The Maltese islands' security system was always primitive, based on sudden mass evacuation as everyone fled into the fortified citadels of Mdina in Malta and Rabat in Gozo. Those who were waylaid ended up as slaves, never to be seen again. It was also not uncommon for the pirates to launch sudden attacks on Gozitan ships crossing back and forth to Malta.

In 1416, the Maltese petitioned the Viceroy of Sicily to improve their defences. Two years later, a tax on wine was introduced to raise the money with which to finance the building of a fortified tower on Comino; but the Maltese were swindled by King Alfonso V of Spain, who used the money for his many adventures elsewhere. Comino remained unprotected and towerless for the next 200 years.

The Knights of St John were obvi-

ously more committed to defending the islands against the Turks and other marauding parties who roamed the Mediterranean. As early as 1532, a Florentine engineer, Piccino, was instructed to draw up plans for the improvement of the islands' fortifications, including a castle on Comino that would protect the Gozo Channel. However, precedence had to be given to the more imperative defensive systems in and around the Grand Harbour.

Valletta was the first link of an ever-expanding chain of defences that would embrace the whole island of Malta with supplementary systems for Gozo and Comino. It was not until the 17th century, however, that attention was finally drawn to the maritime defences of the smaller islands. The first tower built to protect the Channel was sited on Gozo, not Comino. This was erected in 1605 at Mgarr, due to the generosity of the recently deceased Grand Master Garzes, who made provision for it in his will.

In 1618, Alof de Wignacourt, feeling the need to protect the Channel more efficiently, arranged the erection of a complementary tower on Comino – again at his personal expense. Indeed, it was due to this Grand Master's benevolence that a number of coastal towers were built in certain bays accessible to invaders in Malta, like St Lucian's Tower in Marsaxlokk and St Thomas's in the bay of the same name. Probably designed by the Maltese architect Vittorio Cassar, the Wignacourt forts were square, with scarped curtain walls. At each corner, a vertical tower projected from the walls. **St Mary's Tower** on Comino was the most expensive; it cost 18,628 scudi, fully armed, and was equipped and manned by 30 soldiers.

In a review of the coastal defences in 1715, a more ambitious scheme for the fortification of Gozo and Comino included the construction of a battery on the southeast corner of Comino to guard the Channel, as well as a redoubt at **St Mary's Bay**. In 1722, in preparation for an expected attack, **St Mary's Battery**, also know as Perellos Battery, was complete and ready for action. As no Turk-

Sailing to the turquoise waters of the Blue Lagoon.

ish forces appeared, the fortifications were never seriously tested.

The impressive tower which dominates the island of Comino as it rises sheer and high above the jagged cliffs must have its secrets. Many an errant knight involved in disgrace or scandal in Malta was banished to it. With the tower in place, a small agricultural community of about 200 persons eked out a living for a time, growing cummin, cotton and producing honey. But it was an impoverished existence and the population declined.

In World War I, the British built an isolation hospital here for serious cases of infection. This military-style compound of stone buildings around a central square can still be seen. **Liberty Square**, as it was called, acted as a kind of village centre with a grocery shop, post-office box and even a bar. Two well-trodden paths named **Battery Street** and **Congreve Street** lead to it.

Not far, at **St Mary's Bay**, is the only **chapel** on the island. It is said to be of great antiquity, predating the fort. Over the altar is a picture of the Virgin Mary fleeing to Egypt. In 1667, it was badly desecrated and it was not until 1716 that the little chapel was reconsecrated.

Comino's luck changed with the tourist boom which followed Malta's independence in 1964. When the two hotels got their act together and were functioning properly, this little island was at last ready to carve out a name for itself within the upper echelons of Europe's tourist markets. With the arrival of Swiss management came considerable improvements and additional amenities and services. The expanded water sports centre now includes a surf centre with qualified instructors, a first-rate diving base and a diving school, also manned by qualified people. The tennis centre has six Covasco sand courts, three of which are floodlit.

Regular services operated by the hotels' cutters connect Comino to its sister islands. There is a general air of efficiency throughout and when this is combined with the other natural ingredients – unspoilt terrain, near-perfect swimming conditions and a superb climate – the result is very much the island paradise hailed by the advertisements as the last jewel of the Mediterranean.

The Maltese like Comino, too. Sheltering in the warm clear waters of St Mary's Bay and St Nicholas, an armada of luxury yachts and power boats belonging to the burgeoning new and affluent middle class of post-independence Malta has finally replaced that of the marauding Corsairs of yesteryear. Comino is the offshore playground and weekend retreat of the Maltese businessman and his chic entourage. Under the noonday sun on hot summer Sundays, popping corks disturb the stillness of the bays and the wine flows freely. It was not always like this.

After the day trippers have gone home and the snorklers are out of sight, there is a sudden magic in the night air. To the song of the nightingale, the mermaids swim the secret shimmering silver waters of the lagoon. Moonstruck, the island enters a midsummer night's dream until dawn. It is a special kind of peace and tranquillity that prevails.

All the family go to sea.

GOING TO SEA

The Maltese are understandably proud of their surrounding sea. In contrast with the waters of most other countries that border the Mediterranean, from Gibraltar to Greece, the waters around Malta, Gozo and Comino are clear, blue and unpolluted. In the Blue Lagoon, you don't need a snorkel and mask to watch a coin sink to 30 metres.

Sometimes there may be a jellyfish or two, but there is never the kind of grim pollution that is annually condemned by the European Union for failing to meet EC health standards. So it is little wonder that so much of life revolves around the sea and sport, both above and below its shimmering surface.

Visitors in search of boat trips are well catered for in Malta. Things have progressed remarkably since the heady, romantic days when the only way to have a day out was by finding, and bargaining with, a willing fisherman with a *luzzu*.

Gozo ferry: The simplest way to reach Gozo's harbour of Mgarr is by one of the old car ferries that depart from Cirkewwa on Malta's northernmost tip. Services run constantly each way throughout the day and, in summer, into the night. (To check seasonal timetables, tel: 571884.) And, once a day, the same company, the Gozo Channel Company, runs a much larger boat to and from Sa Maison, at Pieta outside Valletta. Most heavy trucks delivering cold drinks or collecting famous-brand jeans (made in Gozo) use this route.

The fare is the same on either route but travellers with cars should try to get to the boarding quays early in the day. This is an over-crowded route, high season or not.

To get across to Comino from either Cirkewwa or Mgarr, call the Comino Hotel, tel: 529821/9, to check arrangements and facilities available. The hotel runs its own private service.

Day cruises: The biggest choice of "Boat Cruises" can be found at Sliema's Strand. A number of companies offer a variety of tours using motor launches, some big, some very big, which set out daily. There are simple trips that take a morning or an afternoon, setting off with English-speaking guides around Marsamxett Harbour, with Valletta as its backdrop, to see Manoel Island and the Msida Yacht Marina before heading out to sea and turning through the breakwaters into the Grand Harbour. This is undoubtedly the best way to see Valletta, the Three Cities and Fort St Angelo as, for centuries, seafarers have done. History has never been more fascinating. Deep within the harbour itself there are also the modern dockyards and commercial enterprises.

Then, to make the most of a day in the sun, there are cruises whose ticket price includes a buffet lunch with local wine, constant refreshment, entertainment, the chance of a swim and, should it be required, door-to-door service by minibus. The largest company is Captain Morgan (tel: 343373/331961) with an ever-growing fleet of distinctive red-and-white boats. This company's selec-

tion includes a Round Malta cruise (leaving Sliema at 9.15am and returning at 5.30pm), the Round the Islands cruise (8.45am–6.30pm) and the Round Gozo cruise (8.45am–6pm). For the more adventurous, a small purpose-built submarine offers an opportunity for underwater exploration.

All the cruise companies run boats to the most popular destination for visitors, the Blue Lagoon on Comino, setting off at around 9am and returning about 5.30pm In the evenings it can seem as if there is a race in progress as, from St Paul's Bay to Sliema, the sea swarms with motor cruisers heading home, their engines at full throttle. Because of its popularity, this can mean that the Blue Lagoon seems overcrowded and short on the tranquil, turquoise charm that it once had.

Depending on the time of year, similar cruises set off from Bugibba, which is also the embarkation point for a glass-bottomed boat. Providing a simple way to while away the time, the boat motors around St Paul's Bay and takes in a view of the golden statue of Christ, placed on the sea-bed in May 1990 to commemorate the visit of Pope John Paul II who came by on a high-speed catamaran especially to bless it.

Blue Grotto: A boat outing on a smaller scale is a visit to Malta's delightful Blue Grotto just outside the rocky inlet of Wied iz-Zurrieq, the fisherman's hamlet near Zurrieq. A smaller grotto than the famous one on the island of Capri, it is nonetheless a cool and charming way to while away the time. It is best early in the morning. On a quiet day some boatmen will dawdle to allow passengers a swim.

In Gozo too there is a simple boat trip organised by fishermen. From Dwejra, small boats set out from the **Inland Sea** through the narrow fissure in the cliff's rock wall and into the deep, navy blue sea beyond to tour the **Azure Window** and **Fungus Rock**. It is a surprisingly exciting, small-scale adventure. Perfect for children.

In both these instances it is wise to bargain first about the price of the boat

Cruising the harbours in style.

trip, the number of passengers to be carried and the duration of the trip.

Going abroad: More functional are the car ferries that sail, as it were internationally, from the Grand Harbour to Syracuse and Catania in Sicily and to Reggio Calabria at the toe of Italy. This is the service used by travellers from Europe with cars. The journey from Syracuse to Malta takes about six hours; Reggio to Malta, 13 hours. Once a week the service sails as far as Naples. The route is becoming steadily more popular with European visitors and as a result the car ferry service is constantly being improved.

A fast catamaran, passenger-only service run by Virtu Rapid Ferries (tel: 318854) also makes a three-hour run to Catania three times a week (departure 5.30am) and to Pozzallo on Sicily's southernmost tip twice a week (departure 7am) in 90 minutes. For anyone wanting a holiday within a holiday but not wanting to go it alone in a typical Sicilian port, there is the company's additional tour, a coach trip to Syracuse to enjoy both the historic sights and some shopping. The Norwegian-built catamarans are designed for tough sea-going conditions.

Virtu Rapid Ferries have also inaugurated a seasonal, once-a-week passenger service to Kelibia in Tunisia. The catamaran's speed means that the journey only takes five hours.

Passport control: Passports are required when leaving Malta's territorial waters. Unfortunately, unlike Luqa International Airport where the customs and emigration procedures are simple, customs formalities on entering Malta by sea are long and laborious – even for day trippers. Expect long delays, frayed tempers and all baggage to be inspected. Presents for anyone Maltese are liable for duty; personal shopping is not. The engine and chassis numbers of arriving cars are recorded to ensure the same parts leave with the car (which is permitted to stay a maximum of three months). Don't worry about locating these numbers: customs officials know where to find them.

Traditional *luzzu* **converted for passengers. Following** page: *ghaqaq ta' l-ghasel,* **sweet treacle ring.**

INSIGHT GUIDES
Travel Tips

Let your message travel with Insight Guides

With 200 titles covering the world, Insight Guides can convey your advertisement to sophisticated international travellers.

HÖFER MEDIA PTE LTD

Singapore: 38, Joo Koon Road, Singapore 628990
Tel: (65)-865-1629/30 Fax: (65)-862-0694

London: PO Box 7910, London SE11 8LL, United Kingdom
Tel: (44 171)-620-0008, Fax: (44 171)-620-1074
e-mail: insight@apaguide.demon.co.uk

INSIGHT GUIDES

Getting Acquainted

Area: *Malta*: 320 sq. km/124 sq. miles. *Gozo*: 67 sq. km/26 sq. miles. *Comino*: 2.5 sq. km/1 sq. mile
Capital: Valletta
Population: 360,000
Language: Maltese and English
Religion: Roman Catholic
Time Zone: GMT + 1 hour. From 31 March until the last Sunday in September, clocks are a further hour ahead of GMT.
Currency: Maltese Lira
Weights and Measures: Metric
Electricity: 220/240-volt and 110 for shavers. Electricity is expensive. Visitors from the UK may use their normal three-pin plug items. Visitors from elsewhere may need an adaptor.
International dialling code: 356

The Geography

The Maltese archipelago consists of three populated and two unpopulated islands. Situated at the strategic crossroads of the Mediterranean, Malta is just 95 km (60 miles) from Sicily and 320 km (220 miles) from the North African coast. The largest island, from which the country takes its name, is **Malta**, which is about 320 sq. km (124 sq. miles): 27 km (17 miles) long and 14 km (9 miles) wide. There are no rivers or mountains, but there are undulating hills inland and rocky creeks and inlets around the coast. There are few sandy beaches. The total population of the islands is around 360,000.

To the northwest of Malta is **Gozo**, characterised by a more lush and dramatic landscape. Only 67 sq. km (26 sq. miles) in size, with 30,000 inhabitants, it is far less industrialised than Malta, an idyllic patchwork of cultivated terraces climbing up to meet scrubby slopes. It is the place most Maltese wish they could be, and the demand for traditional Gozitan farmhouses far outnumbers supply. In spring, Gozo bursts into colour – narcissus and daisy grow wild and give the island a vibrancy Malta lacks.

Comino, midway between Malta and Gozo, is a tiny stopping-off point for watersports enthusiasts. There is a flourishing sporty hotel and a thriving pig farm. No car or bus disturbs the calm of this tiny paradise. Close by is the uninhabited speck of Cominotto.

To the southwest of Malta is Filfla, a protected bird sanctuary, accessible only with special permission from the Ministry of Education.

The Climate

The climate of Malta has been its fortune. Even in winter the temperature rarely drops below 12°C (54°F). Snows or frosts are unknown and rain is likely to fall only between November and February. During the summer months it can top 43°C (109°F) although 29°C (mid-80°s F) is more usual. Between April and September, there is virtually non-stop sunshine and soaring temperatures.

Temperature

The Celsius grade is used for temperatures. For an equivalent Fahrenheit reading, see below:

0°C	=	32°F
10°C	=	50°F
15°C	=	60°F
20°C	=	68°F
25°C	=	75°F
30°C	=	86°F

The People

Malta appears at first sight to be a country made up entirely of other nations, the architecture and the cuisine owing something to Italy, North Africa, Spain or Portugal. And in this Roman Catholic country it is quite disconcerting to hear a language so like Arabic, yet written in the Latin alphabet. God is called "Allah".

Beyond this, the colonial traces have imparted a knowledge of and affection for the British which was confirmed during the World War II and is enduring still for the many British who visit. Ultimately one realises that all these flashes and glimpses of other cultures no longer conjure visions of elsewhere: this is the kaleidoscopic result of Malta's very own identity.

The Maltese themselves have given the islands a warmth and genuine honesty that is quite unexpected. There is no formality, faking or ceremony designed to con the visitor, and, although the pace of life suggests a healthy respect for the *mañana* mentality, things do get done, road signs lead more or less to where they say they will, and someone in difficulty will always be helped.

The family unit is very strong and children rarely, if ever, leave home before they marry. Although youth culture is very much alive, it is not an excessively permissive society and visitors are respectfully asked not to offend certain standards; when visiting churches, women must not arrive in a bikini top and thigh-skimming shorts. Sometimes they may be handed a scarf to cover bare shoulders or politely refused entrance. Topless and nude bathing is (officially) against the law and is punishable by fines; both are customary on certain secluded beaches.

The Economy

Tourism accounts for over one-fifth of Malta's gross national product. Other main sources of income are agriculture, the dockyards (the second largest employer), and manufacturing, particularly of textiles, electronic components and computer software. One of its most successful agricultural exports is to Holland: potatoes.

The creamy-toned buildings that give the islands their soft, dreamy appearance are made from local quarried stone. All other raw materials have to be imported. To augment the islands' financial muscle, legislation has been introduced to encourage Malta to become an attractive offshore centre. A stock exchange was established in 1992 and today has 54 listed securities and 77,000 registered stockholders.

The Government

After a history dominated by the presence of other nations, the Maltese islands became a truly independent state in September 1964. They had been under Britain's protection since 1800.

The Malta Independence Constitution established that the islands would be within the Commonwealth as a liberal parliamentary democracy that guarded the fundamental rights of the citizens and guaranteed the separation of the executive, judicial and legislative powers. Elections would therefore continue to be held on universal suffrage, the government elected by proportional representation.

Until 1974 the islands were a Constitutional Monarchy with Queen Elizabeth II as Queen of Malta, represented by a resident Governor-General. The executive power, however, lay with the Prime Minister and Cabinet. In that year Parliament voted by a two-thirds majority to make the islands a Republic with the Head of State, henceforth Maltese, the President. (In 1979, as the last of the naval garrison set sail, Britain's presence, which had been negotiated by Defence Agreement, was terminated by mutual consent.)

The role of the President is largely nominal and has not created a Presidential system of government. While the President assents to bills and prorogues and dissolves Parliament, he acts only in accordance with the Prime Minister.

In the present Parliament are 65 members, excluding the Speaker. Thirty-five sit on Government benches. The Speaker may be appointed from within or from outside the House. In 1987, an amendment to the Constitution was agreed in order to ensure that the party polling an absolute majority of the popular vote would govern, if necessary through added seats. In a two-party nation of Nationalists and Socialists (known as the Labour Party), this had not always been the case in previous elections when boundaries of electoral divisions were creatively redrawn.

It was also agreed Malta would follow a policy of neutrality and non-alignment. The islands, is was further agreed, would neither participate in military alliance, nor permit foreign military bases to be established on their territory nor allow foreign interference in Maltese elections.

Planning the Trip

What to Bring

In summer, bring only loose cotton clothing, or other natural fibres, avoiding synthetics. Sunglasses and a hat with a brim are essential. A shawl is useful for evenings. Between October and May, always bring a rainjacket or umbrella; during winter months, add a heavy sweater and strong shoes. Men will need to take a jacket for some restaurants.

Maps

Banks and hotels often provide free basic maps for orientation and to help get around the islands. The Mid-Med Bank's map, for example, gives a clear street plan of Valletta with all important locations listed (including their branches for exchanging money) and a simple orientation map that not only identifies the main towns and villages on Malta and Gozo but also the beaches and other places of interest.

To make the most of a stay, a car is a considerable asset and, for drivers who need clearer instructions, there is *Hildebrand's Travel Map*, published locally by Progress Press. Many new fast, regional roads have been built in recent years and this map has many of them.

When to Visit

April and May are delightful, although the sea is not warm enough for swimming. Flowers are in full bloom, temperatures are balmy, and the crowds have not yet arrived. September and October are also great: although the flowers are not as abundant, the warm seas more than compensate. December is also pleasant; after the short rainy season, buttercups and mustard plants form a yellow carpet over much of the island. Avoid July and August when the islands are overcrowded.

Entry Regulations

EU and Commonwealth visitors to Malta require a valid passport or a visitors passport to entitle them to a maximum stay of three months as a tourist. Also entitled are visitors from British dependencies, Japan and the US. Should you wish to extend your stay beyond three months, perhaps to take up temporary residence, apply to the Immigration Police at Police Headquarters, Calcedonius Street, Floriana, tel: 224002. Most other nationals require visas.

Malta is represented by an ambassador, high commissioner or consulate in most major cities throughout the world, with offices where information or advice on passport and visa queries can be obtained. Where Air Malta is represented, its offices can offer assistance too.

In Britain the Malta High Commission is at 36–38 Piccadilly, London W1V 9OA, tel: 0171 292 4800.

Animal Quarantine

Malta is free of rabies, so no animal may be imported from any country where rabies is endemic. Cats and dogs may be brought from the United Kingdom but have to undergo a 3-week quarantine period. From elsewhere, the quarantine period is 6 months.

A formal application to import any animal should be made before arrival to: The Director of Agriculture, Department of Agriculture, 14 Mickel Anton Vassallo Street, Valletta, Malta, tel: 224941.

Customs

Personal effects intended for one's own use are not subject to any duty. You may bring into Malta, 200 cigarettes or 250g of other tobacco products, of which not more than 50g in loose tobacco. In addition, you may bring in 0.75 litre (1 bottle) each of spirits and wine. Perfume and toilet water may be imported in a reasonable quantity. Gifts for locals are taxed.

Health

For visitors arriving from the US, Canada, Australia and Europe, no inoculations are required, though it's always a good idea to check when you last had a tetanus booster.

The Maltese islands are bathed in sunshine virtually year round. In the summer don't underestimate the intensity of the sun. Take precautions; the wearing of a hat in the middle of the day is recommended for the elderly and the very young. As far as sunbathing is concerned, going for the "burn" is dangerous and painful. Begin with a high SPF factor suncream or total sunblock until you have acclimatised your skin to the sun's rays. Change to a lower SPF suncream to build up a healthy tan. All popular sun tanning creams are readily available in shops and pharmacies.

As with any Mediterranean country, the usual troupe of gnats, mosquitoes and cockroaches may be resident. Insect repellent creams and sprays are readily available. Malta has a few snakes but happily they are not poisonous. Sometimes the odd jellyfish lurks in the island's clear waters.

Drinking water: The process of reverse osmosis has ensured that tap water is quite safe to drink, though fountain water must be avoided as it may not come directly from the mains supply.

Currency

The Maltese currency is the Lira (Liri), sometimes referred to as Maltese pounds (written as Lm). Each lira is divided into 100 cents, each cent in turn divided into 10 mils. Denominations are: *Notes:* Lm2, Lm5, Lm10, Lm20, Lm50. *Coins:* 1c, 2c, 5c, 10c, 25c, 50c, Lm1.

Commission is not charged when changing travellers cheques but remember to take your passport for identification. Hotels accept travellers cheques but shops and restaurants will take only cash or credit cards.

You find a better rate of exchange at the banks than at the hotels. When visiting Malta, the maximum amount of Maltese currency you are allowed to bring with you is Lm50. On departure, you may take out no more than Lm25 worth. To change Liri back to foreign currency you will need all exchange receipts to prove foreign currency was brought in initially.

Credit cards are widely accepted, even by the women who sell their net bags at the village waterfront. You should have no problem paying with Visa or MasterCard; American Express is not always accepted. American Express Card members needing assistance may call at the representatives offices at 14 Zachary Street, Valletta, tel: 232141.

Banks have different opening hours in winter and summer. The main banks are the Bank of Valletta, the Mid-Med Bank, Lombard Bank and the APS Bank.

Opening hours: *In winter:* 1 October–14 June, Monday–Friday 8.30am–12.30pm, Friday afternoon 4.30–6pm, Saturday 8.30am–noon. *In summer:* 15 June–30 September, Monday–Friday 8am–noon, Friday afternoon 2.30–4pm, Saturday 8–11.30am.

There is a 24-hour, seven days a week service available at the Bank of Valletta and the Mid-Med Bank at Luqa International Airport. Certain foreign exchange bureaux are open after normal banking hours while others are closed in winter. Both the Bank of Valletta and the Mid-Med Bank publish maps of Malta with complete lists of their branches and opening times. They are available from the banks and from the Tourist Information centres throughout the islands. ATMs are available at most localities and accept major credit cards.

Public Holidays

Religion is the cornerstone for the Maltese people. Papal fever gripped the nation long before Pope John Paul II kissed the tarmac at Luqa airport in May 1990, and there are countless public holidays commemorating patron saints' feast days. Every parish celebrates its own as well as those that are national. On these days, shops, businesses and schools are closed though restaurants and bars will most likely remain open.

Below is a guide to the public holidays. On New Year's Day and Christmas Day, buses stop between noon–3pm to allow everyone time with their families.

1 January:	New Year's Day.
10 February:	St Paul's Shipwreck.
19 March:	Feast of St Joseph.
31 March:	Freedom Day.
1 May:	St Joseph the Worker.
7 June:	Commemoration of 7 June 1919.
29 June:	Feast of St Peter and St Paul. *Mnarja* (harvest festival).
15 August:	Feast of the Assumption, Gozo.
8 September:	Feast of Our Lady of the Victories.
21 September:	Independence Day.
8 December:	Feast of the Immaculate Conception.
13 December:	Republic Day.
25 December:	Christmas Day.

The harvest festival of *Mnarja* takes place on the night of 29 June at Buskett Gardens near Rabat and Mdina, and continues into the next day. Folkloric celebration and an all-night picnic are followed the next morning by horse and donkey races through the streets below Rabat.

The weekend before Lent is Carnival. Floats, dancing and masked parades fill the streets of Valletta with the islands' biggest show while merrymaking in Nadur is worth experiencing too. Village *festi* are held throughout the summer months and combine religious celebration with fireworks, band parades and crowds.

A full calendar of religious and secular events throughout Malta and Gozo is available from Tourist Information centres.

Special Facilities
Children

Although there aren't many specific attractions for children, many are thrilled to visit the film set of *Popeye* at Anchor Bay. Sandy (rather than the rocky) beaches are ideal places for youngsters to use up energy. There are no lifeguards, so keep a watchful eye. Older children might like to go snorkelling. Folk festivals provide a colourful spectacle.

Students

NSTS, the Student and Youth Travel organisation in Malta is located at 220 St Paul's Street, Valletta, tel: 244983/246628. The Gozo office is at 45 St Francis Square, Victoria. They'll provide you with an invaluable little booklet, the *Student Saver Discount Scheme*, which lists shops, exhibitions, restaurants and transport, offering reductions of between 15 and 40 percent on prices to those with ISIC

(International Student/Scholar Identity Card). Entrance to museums is free.

Disabled

Malta is not the ideal country for the disabled. The hilly streets, particularly of Valletta and Victoria, mean getting around can be difficult. Many pavements are hazardous. However, the hotels on Malta have done a great deal to accommodate disabled persons. Exhibitions like *The Malta Experience*, cater for disabled groups. The natural willingness of Maltese people can be counted upon to help if needed.

For further information regarding handicapped facilities contact the Health Education Unit, tel: 224071 or the National Commission for the Handicapped, tel: 487789. Tourist information centres advise on the accessibility of sites and museums.

Gays

There is no helpline or contact magazine for the gay community. The age of consent is 18. Cases of Aids have been registered.

Getting There
By Air

There is one airport on Malta, none on Gozo or Comino. There is a new heliport terminal in Gozo to service private planes as well as the regular 20-seater helicopter service that flies between Gozo and Malta. Environmentalists are against further innovation.

All schedule and charter flights arrive at Malta International Airport; the schedule flights in daylight hours, the charter flights at night. The airport is constantly being updated and a new terminal has been constructed. There is a bus service (nos. 8 or 39) from the airport to either the neighbouring village of Luqa or the capital, Valletta. For visitors making their way independently, there are (white) taxis, usually diesel Mercedes. It is wise to agree prices for the journey before entering the taxi.

Malta's national airline, Air Malta, operates from many European cities and some North African ones. In Britain, for enquiries, tel: 0171 292 4949. Air Malta flies from Heathrow Terminal 4, Gatwick and Manchester airports in Britain. In Europe, it flies from Athens, Frankfurt, Paris, Rome,

Catania, Munich, Geneva and Copenhagen.

Charter flights are available usually from Belfast, Birmingham, Bristol, Cardiff, Edinburgh, East Midlands, Glasgow, Leeds/Bradford, Gatwick, Luton, Manchester, Newcastle and Stansted. Flying time from Britain is about 3 hrs 15 mins.

Air Malta has offices in Paris, France, tel: 1-44 86 08 40; Frankfurt, Germany, tel: 239076/9 and Rome, Italy, tel: 6-488 3106.

Other airlines operating schedules services to Malta are Aeroflot, Alitalia, Austrian Airlines, Balkan Bulgarian Airlines, British Airways (GB Airways), Egypt Air, Interflug, JAT, KLM, Lufthansa, Monarch, Swissair, Tunisavia and UTA.

TRANSIT/TRANSFER

If your final destination is not Malta, but the nearby islands of Gozo or Comino, the Tourist Information office within the airport concourse will be able to advise you of your best onward journey.

Taxis from the airport or, in the daylight hours, the bus service from Valletta will be able to take you on to the port of Cirkewwa for the ferry to Gozo. For transfers to Comino, contact the Comino Hotel which runs a ferry service from Cirkewwa to the island, tel: 529822.

By Sea

Many cruise ships call in at the Grand Harbour with tourists on day visits. But, for independent travellers, the only means of getting to the islands by sea is by car ferry from Sicily or Italy, or by a new fast catamaran passenger-only service from Sicily that runs in good weather. The services run once a week to and from Naples (car ferry); three times a week from Reggio Calabria, Catania and Syracuse (by both car ferry and catamaran). There is also a regular ferry service from Tripoli, Libya.

The car ferry service is run by a specially set up Maltese-Italian shipping consortium. The ship leaves Naples on Friday evening with boisterous Italians heading south to Reggio and to Sicily where the ship arrives the following morning. It has good cabins and a simple, self-service restaurant. The journey from Naples takes 24 hours. With this ferry the Catania–Malta and

Syracuse–Malta trips take 8 hours and 5 hours respectively.

Also on the Catania route in the summer months is the car ferry *Ghawdex,* run by the Gozo Channel Company (tel: 571884) and used mostly by Maltese on a day out, shopping in Catania. This means considerable delays at Customs on return to Malta while duty is levied by Customs officials who are notoriously severe on their own nationals.

The fast catamaran service is Malta-run by Virtu Rapid Ferries with five regular crossings a week, rough sea permitting. This passenger-only service goes to Pozzallo, the southernmost tip of Sicily, in 1 hr 30 mins, and to Catania in three hours. Once a week the company also run a service to Kelibia in Tunisia, sailing time five hours. They are also subject to Customs delays. A good, if long, day trip on the catamaran includes a coach trip to Catania and Mount Etna, Lm35.

Cabins for the Naples–Malta–Naples service should be booked early. Cabins are unnecessary for the shorter routes.

In Malta most travel agents can arrange bookings for the fast catamaran service or information and bookings from the Virtu Rapid Ferries office, 3 Princess Elizabeth Terrace, Ta'Xbiex, Malta, tel: 318854/5/6.

By Car

Arriving with a car does not require a permit, but the car must have "Green Card" insurance specific to Malta. Cars may be imported to the islands for a period of up to three months (the maximum permitted stay for a tourist); any longer will require special police permission.

On arrival the car's engine and chassis numbers are logged by customs officers. This is to ensure that the same items reappear for departure and are not sold as spare parts or exchanged on the local market. (Armed with torches, the officers know where to locate the numbers.) The same officials examine the cars for goods on which duty is payable.

National Tourism Organisation of Malta can be contacted in the following countries:

Belgium: Avisales International, Boulevard Maurice Lemmonier 131–6, B-1000 Brussels, tel: 2513 6528.

Eire: Domino Marketing Services, Charlemont Place, Dublin 2, tel: 478 1544.

France: Office National de Tourisme de Malte, 9 Cite de Trevise, 75009 Paris, tel: 48 00 03 79.

Holland: Nationaal Verkeersbureau Malta, Geelvinck Building, 4th Floor, Singel 540, 1017 AZ Amsterdam, tel: (20) 620 7223.

Italy: Ente Nazionale per il Turismo di Malta, Via Gonzaga 7, 20123 Milano, tel: (2) 867359.

United Kingdom: Malta National Tourist Office, Malta House, 36–38 Piccadilly, London W1V OPP, tel: (0171) 292 4900.

United States: Malta National Tourist Office, Empire State Building, 350 Fifth Avenue, Suite 4412, NY 10118, tel: (212) 695 9520.

West Germany and Switzerland: Fremdenverkehrsamt Malta, Schilerstrasse 30–40, Frankfurt am Main 1, D-6000, tel: (69) 285890/20788.

Practical Tips

Business Hours

Malta opens early for business and the working day is usually 8.30am–5pm. In the summer months work will start and finish even earlier. Shops are generally open 9.30am–7pm, with a long siesta-like lunch break between 12.30pm and 3 or 4pm.

Tipping

It is a refreshing experience to come across people so genuinely willing to be of assistance. If you wish to show your appreciation, here's a rough guide: at the airport, 50c; 10 percent for a waiter or hairdresser; 50c (per week) for a hotel chambermaid. Tipping taxi drivers is not entirely necessary (taxis are quite expensive).

Religious Services

Malta is a Roman Catholic country but all religions are tolerated and services are held in various languages for foreign visitors (on Sunday). For Catholics there are as many churches for mass as there are days of the year.

In English:
Rabat – St Dominic's, St Dominic's Square, 11.15am.
St Paul's Bay – Parish Church, St Paul's Street, 11am.
Sliema – St Patrick's, St John Bosco Street, 7.30, 9, 10am 6.30 and 7.30pm.
Valletta – St Barbara's, Republic Street, noon.

In Italian:
Valletta – St Catherine of Italy, Victory Square, 11am.

In French:
Valletta – St Barbara's, Republic Street, 10am.

In German:
Valletta – St Barbara's, Republic Street, 11am.

There are two **Anglican churches** in Malta.

Valletta – **St Paul's Anglican Cathedral**. Enquiries: tel: 225714.
Sliema – **Holy Trinity**, Rudolph Street, tel: 330575.

Union Church of Scotland and **Methodist**: St Andrew's, South Street, Valletta, tel: 222643.
Greek Orthodox: The Greek Orthodox Church is at 83 Merchants Street, Valletta, tel: 221600.
Synagogue: Spur Street, Valletta. Secretary of Jewish Community, tel: 625717.

Media

Newspapers

Most European daily newspapers arrive in Malta on the same day of publication and newsagents stock everything from Le Monde, Die Welt, La Repubblica, London's Times and Sun to the International Herald Tribune. (On Gozo, newspapers arrive the following morning.) An up-to-date supply of international **magazines** and **journals** is also widely available.

There is one English language daily, The Times, which gives an interesting insight into the politics and priorities of the country. Also take a look at the two English-language weekend papers: The Malta Independent and the Sunday Times.

Radio & TV

L.P.B.S. Malta is the national broadcasting organisation. All programmes are in Maltese. Radio Malta 1 on 999khz medium wave is a music and general news station. Radio Malta 2 on 93.7 VHF/FM broadcasts popular music. There are also 11 commercial radio stations, three of them broadcasting in English. The programmes are mainly pop music. It is possible to pick up the BBC World Service and Deutsche Welle on short-wave, though the reception is variable.

There are three local TV stations showing Maltese programmes plus the familiar roster of British, American and Australian soaps during its evening broadcasts. In addition, both satellite and cable TV are widely available and very popular.

Post & Telecommunications

Post

Post Offices are found in most towns and villages. Hours of business are Monday–Saturday 7.45am–2pm. The Main Post Office in Valletta is open until 6pm. Stamps are obtainable from post offices, hotels, newsagents and some souvenir shops in tourist areas. You'll find letter boxes look like the red British ones or are built into walls.

For the main post offices go to:
Malta: The General Post Office, Auberge d'Italie, Merchants Street, Valletta.
Gozo: Main Post Office, 129 Republic Street, Victoria.

A poste restante service is available. Write in advance to The Postmaster General at the General Post Office address listed above. A passport is necessary as identification when collecting post.

Telephone

The telephone system has been highly upgraded in recent years to include the Internet, e-Mail, etc.

For internal enquiries: tel: 190. International calls to the countries listed below should prove no problem; other connections will require the overseas operators' help. For operator assistance in Malta: tel: 194. In Gozo: tel: 894. For faults on the line: tel: 133.

Call boxes are like the old red British ones and almost exclusively take phonecards which are on sale from numerous outlets.

International codes from Malta:
France: 0033.
Germany: 0049.
Italy: 0039.
United Kingdom: 0044.
United States: 001.

Fax/Telex

Faxes and telexes may be sent from Telemalta offices located at:
Luqa International Airport, tel: 225861. Open: 7am–7pm daily.
South Street, Valletta, tel: 241409 or 224131. Open: 7am–7pm daily.
St George's Road, St Julians, tel: 338221. Open: 24-hours.
St Paul's Street, St Paul's Bay, tel: 577288.
Fliegu Street, Qawra, tel: 576603.
Racecourse Street, Victoria, Gozo, tel: 556690.
Bisazza Street, Sliema, tel: 333952.

Tourist Offices

The main tourist office is situated in the city centre – **National Tourism Organisation**, 280 Republic Street, Valletta, tel: 225048/9.

Tourist information centres are located at:
Malta: 1 City Gate, Valletta, tel: 237747.
Arrivals Lounge, Luqa Airport, tel: 2496 6073.
Bugibba, Bay Square, tel: 577332.
Sliema, Bisazza Street, tel: 313409.
Gozo: 1 Palm Street, Victoria, Gozo, tel: 558106.
Mgarr Harbour, Gozo, tel: 553343.

Embassies

American Embassy: Development House, St Anne Street, Floriana, tel: 235960/5, fax: 246917.
Australian High Commission: Ta'Xbiex Terrace, Ta'Xbiex, tel: 338201/5, fax: 344059.
British High Commission: 7 St Anne Street, Floriana, tel: 233134/7, fax: 292001.

French Embassy: Villa Seminia, 12 Sir Temi Zammit Street, Ta'Xbiex, tel: 331107/335856.
German Embassy: Il-Piazzetta, Entrance B, Tower Road, Sliema, tel: 336531, fax: 333976.
Italian Embassy: 1 Vilhena Street, Floriana, tel: 233157/8 or 230265.
Spanish Embassy: 145/10, Tower Road, Sliema, tel 314164/5.

Emergencies
Security & Crime

The islands are still a comparatively safe place for a holiday. A woman needn't feel threatened when out on her own at night, but common sense should always prevail. Don't make yourself into an obvious target for bag snatchers or pickpockets. Should you be the victim of a crime, notify the police immediately and, if necessary, seek assistance from your embassy or consulate. Contact them too for advice should you happen to be detained by the police. The police are quite approachable, although rarely in evidence on the streets. Parking fines are imposed if you leave your car blocking an exit or in a restricted zone. The narrow streets of Valletta in particular are well worth avoiding.

There is a police station in each town or village. **Police General Headquarters** are at Calcedonius Street, Floriana, tel: 224001. This building also houses the Immigration Department, Licensing Office, Traffic Department and Criminal Investigation Department.

Gozo's General Police Headquarters are at 113 Republic Street, Victoria, tel: 556342.

Medical

Ambulance/Emergency Service, tel: 196.
St Luke's Hospital, Gwardamanga, near Valletta, tel: 241251/234101. Malta's main hospital
Craig Hospital, Ghin Qatet Street, Victoria, tel: 561600. The only hospital on Gozo.

DENTISTS

For dentists, call directory enquiries, tel: 190 (tel: 890 from Gozo).

Malta follows the World Health Organisation's recommendations for health safety. Pharmacists and chemists have quite wide prescribing powers and most well-known prescribed drugs are available here. Visitors with specific requirements must ensure they have an adequate supply of medication, or bring a prescription to present to the pharmacist or doctor.

Britons who fall ill are able to take advantage of a reciprocal free medical care agreement between the two countries. This entitles treatment for a period of up to one month. Health agreements also exist with Belgium, Czechoslovakia, Yugoslavia, Australia, Poland and Italy. Visitors from elsewhere should buy adequate medical insurance. All doctors on Malta and Gozo speak English and, probably, Italian.

Alternatively, there are several Polyclinics, where you may go for medical assistance – **Floriana**: Frangisk Saver, Fenech Street. (24-hour service), tel: 243314. **Rabat**: Parish Square, tel: 459082. **Mosta**: Mosta Square, tel: 433256.

Pharmacies

There are numerous pharmacies and chemists throughout the islands, though they have no recognisable symbol by which to identify them. They keep normal shop opening times, from 8.30 or 9am until 1pm and then 3.30–7pm. A roster of pharmacies open over the weekend is listed in the weekend newspapers. The qualified staff can dispense many products without a doctor's prescription.

Doing Business

Business transactions can take time and require patience. In the Latin manner, there is a considerable amount of formality involved and one or two Maltese businessmen are known to be especially sharp in their practice. It is always advisable for any newcomer to the local business scene to undertake thorough research and to take advice, legal or political. But, this being a small society with much intermarrying, recommendations may often suggest a brother, cousin or other relative. As is any other country, this may or may not be an advantage.

Many deals may require intricate dealings with what seems an endless bureaucracy and this can be frustrating. On the plus side, after agreements have been reached, it is usually plain sailing. Successful, long-established companies working in or with Malta and Gozo are proof of this.

The economy: In the most recent figures Malta's gross domestic product totalled US$2.5 billion – that is, US$7,000 per person. This represents a growth rate of 6.7 percent. In the 1990s the economy continued to expand following the etablishment of a Stock Exchange, financial services and tourism. Three times the total population of the islands now visit as tourists. The government policy is to encourage numbers of tourists and hope for an upgrade in quality.

Setting up business: The Government has introduced many attractive incentives for companies considering manufacturing on the islands. These include considerable tax-free concessions, soft loans, training grants and a choice of ready-made factories at subsidised rental on industrial estates close to areas with a large workforce. Contact: Malta Development Corporation, Mriehel, PO Box 571, Valletta, tel: 448963, fax: 449244.

Malta Freeport: This is Malta's new customs-free zone, located in Marsaxlokk Harbour. Dedicated to being an effective distribution centre within the Mediterranean, the Freeport helps reduce the costs of handling cargo and delivery time. A government-owned company, within its perimeter are container and bulk-break terminals, a mineral oil terminal and extensive storage facilities. The Freeport is free of customs and excise duties, income tax, exchange control and other duties. Benefits are guaranteed by law for 15 years. Information: Malta Freeport Corporation Ltd, Freeport Centre, Marsaxlokk, tel: 650200, fax: 684814.

To promote Malta as an international financial and trading centre, the government has enacted legislation to transform the island into an offshore centre. Contact the Malta Financial Service Centre, Ahard, Tel: 441155, fax: 441188.

Conference Centre: The Maltese government has studied the potential of the incentive travel and business conference market and is actively encour-

aging larger hotels to participate by fully developing their facilities to encourage this kind of visitor. As a result many hotels are proficient indeed and offer excellent facilities. These include the Holiday Inn, Phoenicia, New Dolmen Hotel Corinthia, Dragonara Palace and Suncrest.

The government's own centre, the Mediterranean Conference Centre in Valletta, has come into its own too. Originally the hospital of the knights of the Order of St John, the building has seen many uses and during World War II was badly damaged by bombing. Now it has been wonderfully restored and is excellently equipped with halls that can accommodate between 70 and 1,400 delegates in theatre style. The restaurant, La Vallette, is available for banquets of up to 1,000 or for theme nights, their most successful being a recreation of a Maltese village *festa* complete with fireworks on the city's bastions outside. The Great Ward is now the longest exhibition hall in Europe. Contact Mediterranean Conference Centre, Valletta, tel: 243840, fax: 24590.

Film facilities: Many important films and television series have had their action sequences filmed on the islands. As long ago as the early 1950s film crews could be seen setting up on the remoter spots of the islands and since then film credits have included, amongst many others, *The Bedford Incident*, *Casino Royale*, *Sinbad*, *Orca the Killer Whale*, *Midnight Express*, *Popeye* and *Cut-throat Island*.

Special studio facilities include two water tanks on the southern coast, tanks that face out to sea and, because of the ingenious way in which they are sited, have the sea as their natural horizon. The sky is always their backdrop. The surface tank is large enough for a full-size ship to be built; the underwater tank perfectly designed for even the most elaborate underwater sequences. Professional crew are on hand. Contact: Mediterranean Film Studios Ltd, Fort St Rocco, Kalkara, Malta, tel: 245466/245467/242289.

Getting Around

On Arrival

Luqa International Airport is no more than 15 minutes drive from the capital, Valletta. There are taxis available at the airport as well as car hire companies. If you decide to take a taxi, make sure the meter is on, or at least agree a price before setting off as taxis can be expensive. Buses number 8 and 39 run through Luqa village to Valletta.

Public Transport

Water Transport

The **ferry** systems between Malta, Gozo and Comino serves the population for pleasure and work. The Gozo Channel Co. operates a car ferry and passenger service between Cirkewwa on Malta and Mgarr harbour on Gozo, offering 12 return crossings daily from 6am (7am from Cirkewwa). Journey time is about 20 minutes. During the summer, services continue into the night. Another less frequent service operates between Sa Maison (at Pieta Creek near Floriana) and Mgarr (check with the ferry operator for variable times).

In addition there is a rapid, passenger only, **catamaran** service between Mgarr and Marsalforn on Gozo and Sliema and Bugibba on Malta.

For more detailed information on timetables contact the Gozo Channel Co.:

Mgarr (Gozo), tel: 556114 or 556743.
Cirkewwa (Malta), tel: 571884 or 573732.
Sa Maison (Malta), tel: 243964.
For recorded information: tel: 522467.

If your destination is Comino, it means you must be staying at the Comino Hotel at San Niklaw Bay. But even if you're just visiting for the day, the hotel runs a ferry service to Cirkewwa throughout the year departing Comino 6.50am, 9.05am, 11.10am, 2.50pm and 4.45pm. Sailings from Cirkewwa commence

7.30am, 9.35am, 11.40am, 3.30pm, and 5.25pm. To confirm details: contact the Comino Hotel, tel: 529822.

Helicopter

A 20-seater helicopter service flies from Luqa Airport to Xewkija, Gozo. Lm17 for a day return. It's an excellent way to see the islands.

Buses

Books have been published and posters printed to the glory of Malta's buses in the past. Sharp fendered 1950s-style charabancs, they used to be brightly painted in the colours of the village – that way, even at a distance you would know its route. Now, however, they have all been painted bright yellow and, though many of the true boneshakers are still more than roadworthy, coaches are being introduced. As so many people depend upon the buses, the system is reliable and inexpensive.

On Malta, the main bus station is just outside the city gates of Valletta. Fares are zonal (1, 2, or 3), depending on the length of journey. Services begin at about 6am and stop at about 10pm weekdays, 11pm weekends. Check the time of the last bus you require as they do vary. For bus information on Malta: tel: 225916.

Gozo's main bus station is on Maingate Street, tel: 556011. Around Gozo, the buses are a little less frequent and finish earlier. A flat fare of 10c will take you anywhere on the island.

Malta bus routes: Check timings of service at terminus. Last bus varies route to route, and seasonally. The services are gregarious and crowded, slow and hot in summer.

Gozo bus routes: Most routes are now circular, doing away with the previous trend of having many different numbers. On most of the routes the maximum journeys made each way in one day is four. Also, route numbers can be changed with alarming regularity so check locally on the current services. The first bus may be at 5.30am or 6 a.m; last bus from 6.30pm to 9pm depending on direction and season. Do check first.

The terminus at Victoria/Rabat is where most routes start and finish. In fact, most buses either start at, or go via, the terminal.

Taxis

Taxis are white. They have red number plates with a "Y" preceding the registration number (registrations are presently being changed), a sign saying "TAXI" and more often than not, are Mercedes. Pick one up at the various ranks around town, at the airport, harbours and outside hotels. Street hailing is not normal, though on a Saturday night, passing cabbies may hoot to let you know they're available for hire.

Insist that either the meter be switched on, or make sure you agree a price before you start your journey. All garages run chauffeur-driven cars as taxis too.

Carriages

Karrozzin are today more of a tourist attraction than a practical means of getting from A to B. But a jaunt in a Maltese "surrey with a fringe" *gharry* is a charming way of taking in the sights of Valletta, St Julians, Sliema or Mdina. Your driver will halt every now and then to tell you a little about each view or monument. The average tour costs about Lm5 and usually includes a chance to be photographed at the reins.

Private Transport

Driving

Ask any Maltese about driving conditions on their islands and they'll laugh and warn you to go carefully. Driving is indeed an education, but not such a difficult one. The most important thing to remember is that, though they may drive on the left (like the British), the mentality on the roads is pure Mediterranean. Overtaking on the inside, reversing into main roads and cutting up is the norm. There are some traffic lights, and a great series of roundabouts which seem to enlarge as the traffic grows heavier.

The best way to drive safely is to look out for what the other person is doing. It really is worth mastering the open road here, for then you have the freedom to tour as fast or slowly as you wish.

All current driving licences and International driving licences are recognised. Visitors arriving by car may use their own driving licences (the car should also be covered by Green Card

with insurance extension to cover Malta).

Fuel is comparatively inexpensive and a full tank of petrol should last you a whole week. Petrol stations are open daily 7am–6pm but are closed on Sundays and public holidays.

All the familiar European firms have car rental services and there are innumerable small garages that will hire you cars at even more attractive rates. Make sure the car is equally as attractive. Check insurance cover and liability. Rates are from about LM6.50 per day for six days and prices are subject to increase during the holiday season, so book well in advance if visiting in the summer. Payment by credit card is fine for large companies; smaller hire firms will prefer cash. The minimum age for hiring is generally 25 years of age and you will need to produce a valid driving licence or international driver's permit. The speed limits are 64 kph on highways and 40 kph in built-up areas.

Car Hire Firms

Inter Rent Europcar: Luqa International Airport and, through their licencee, John's Garage, at 38 Villambrosa Street, Hamrun, tel: 238745.

Avis Rent-a-Car: 59 Msida Seafront, tel: 225986.

Wembley's Rent-a-Car: 50 St George's Road, St Julians, tel: 345353, 332074, 345454; St Andrew's Road, St Andrew's, tel: 335436.

Hertz Rent-a-Car: Sliema, tel: 314636/7, 319939.

Gozo United Rent-a-Car: 5 Xaghra Road, Victoria, Gozo, tel: 553736.

Chauffeur-driven cars are quite popular with tourists and most car hire companies also offer this service.

Cycles & Motorbikes

Cycling is a delightful though somewhat strenuous way of seeing the islands: they are more hilly than is at first apparent. It's best to hit the road before or after the hottest part of the day. Bicycles and motorbikes are available for hire throughout the islands. A few shops are listed below:

Cycle Store: 135 Eucharistic Congress Street, Mosta, tel: 432890. (Bicycles only).

Victor Sultana: New Building, Main Gate Street, Victoria, Gozo, tel: 556414.

Motorbikes only:

L'Aronde: Frank Galea, Upper Gardens, St Julians, tel: 370765.

Peter's Scooter Shop: 175A D'Argens Road, Msida, tel: 335244.

Albert's Scooter Shop: 216/6 Rue D'Argens, Gzira, tel: 340149.

Rush Hour

The roads into the commercial and industrial areas such as Sliema, St Julians, Valletta, Zejtun and Marsa are busiest between 7–8am and 4.30–5pm. Saturday night in the Paceville, St Julians and Spinola Bay areas is one long rush hour. Being able to park is a matter of luck. Police are quick with parking tickets in Valletta and Victoria. Good weather also brings out the cars, with families heading for beaches, the coast roads and countryside beauty spots.

On Foot

Malta and Gozo are favourite places for ramblers to stride out, especially in spring when the landscape is carpeted green with wild flowers and trees in full bloom. Reaching the top of any hill gives you a breathtaking view over a remarkable landscape and out to sea. On a clear day it's possible to see Sicily from Gozo.

Some of the best walks are those suggested in the excellent Sunflower Countryside Guide, *Landscapes of Malta,* available in Britain and also in Malta at Sapienza, 26 Republic Street, Valletta, tel: 233621. The Bartholomew Clyde *Leisure Map of Malta and Gozo* also makes some picturesque recommendations. Should fatigue take over, it is safe to thumb a lift back to base.

Where to Stay

Hotels

Malta

The hotels on Malta, Gozo and Comino were reclassified in 1989 by the Hotels and Catering Establishments Board of the Ministry of Tourism. In order to meet the standards required by the guidelines set out for international compatibility by the World Tourism Organization, many undertook substantial renovation programmes, raising standards considerably. All hotels are now classified from 1–5 stars.

☆☆☆☆☆: Superior standard. Fully air-conditioned. All rooms with private bath and shower, radio, television, telephone. 24-hour room service. Bar, restaurant, coffee shop, pool, sports facilities. Laundry, pressing, dry cleaning. Shops, hairdresser.

☆☆☆☆: High standard. Air-conditioned. All rooms with private bath or shower, radio, telephone. Room service breakfast to midnight. Bar, restaurant, pool or beach facility. Laundry, pressing, dry cleaning. Lounge. Shops, hairdresser.

☆☆☆: Good accommodation. All rooms with private bath or shower. Bar and restaurant. Lounge. Front office 24 hours. Laundry, pressing and dry cleaning. Around Lm15 B&B.

☆☆: Modest accommodation. At least 20 percent rooms with private bath or shower. Breakfast facilities. Telephone or service bell in rooms. Front office during day; porter at night. Around Lm12 B&B.

☆: Small hotel. Common bath or shower. All rooms with wash-hand basin. Breakfast facilities. Office service during day; porter at night. Around Lm10 B&B.

Tourist complexes and aparthotels are from Lm4.50 to Lm9 bed only, depending on star-rating. Guest houses, from Lm5.0 to Lm10.0.

☆☆☆☆☆

Corinthia Palace: de Paule Avenue, Attard, tel: 440301. Redecorated with grand style. In the centre of the island, near San Anton Palace. Indoor and outdoor (heated) pool. Restaurants. Transport provided to Valletta and to San Gorg Lido, part of Corinthia Group's new, well-appointed and elegant beach resort at St George's Bay.

Corinthia San Gorg: St George's Bay, St Julians, tel: 374114/6. Opened in 1995, this is one of the Corinthia Group's flagship hotels. Good location and with excellent facilities that includes a wide choice of restaurants on its own beach resort and a well-appointed lido. Business centre and executive suites.

Holiday Inn Crowne Plaza: Tigne Street, Sliema, tel: 341173. In quiet residential area, within walking distance of main shopping area. Excellent family pool (heated). Beach, tennis, sauna, gym. Malta's international top hairdresser, Maurice Saliba, has a salon here. Four restaurants. Conference facilities.

The Malta Hilton is presently closed for rebuilding and scheduled to reopen alongside new man-made marina and conference halls in 1999.

Phoenicia: The Mall, Floriana, tel: 225241. Long established as Malta's prestige hotel, outside the gates of the city of Valletta. Pool (heated). Secretarial services available. Conference facilities.

Westin Dragonara, Dragonara Road, St Julian's, tel: 381000; fax: 378877. Opened in spring 1997. Stylish, comfortable and modern, set in landscaped gardens that also house Malta's only casino and the Reef Club beach lido where Malta's smart set gather. Good conference facilities and shops.

☆☆☆☆

Cavalieri: Spinola Road, St Julians, tel: 336255. Quiet spot on edge of the harbour facing Sliema. Just minutes away from resort area, cafés and restaurants. Indoor and outdoor pool, gym, sauna, water sports. Popular for families.

Eden Beach: St George's Bay, St Julians, tel: 341191. Young family orientated. Disco. Indoor and outdoor pools. Tennis, gym, sauna.

Fortina: Tigne Sea Front, Sliema, tel:

343380. On waterfront, minutes from shopping streets. Comfortable family hotel, facing across harbour towards Valletta. Excellent pool and gym. Tennis. Also owns Turkish restaurant nearby.

The Forum: St Andrew's Road, St Andrew's, tel: 370483. Pool, sauna, gym, tennis. A 10-minute walk to St Julians or the nearest rock beach.

Grand Hotel les Lapins: Ta'Xbiex Sea Front, Ta'Xbiex, tel: 342551. New hotel. Not by the sea but alongside the thriving Msida yacht marina deep within the harbour area. Pool. Tennis.

Grand Hotel Verdala: Inguanez Street, Rabat, tel: 451700. Centre of the island. Once a prestige hotel, it is being refurbished as a business and conference centre. On high ridge edge of Rabat. Panoramic views.

Jerma Palace: Marsascala, tel: 823222. The only major hotel on the south side of the island. Pools, water sports, tennis, gym, sauna.

New Dolmen: Qawra, tel: 581510. Popular, large family hotel midway between sleepy Qawra and bustling Bugibba. Facing into Bay. Pools, water sports, tennis, gym.

Paradise Bay: Cirkewwa, tel: 573981. Isolated setting, near ferry jetty to Gozo and popular Paradise Bay. Heated indoor and outdoor pools. Good man-made beach with full amenities. Tennis, squash. Nightclub disco.

Preluna Towers: Tower Road, Sliema, tel: 334001. On Sliema's promenade, minutes from main shopping area and cafés. Ever expanding. Small heated pool but good beach facilities during long summer season. Water sports, gym, tennis, sauna. Nightclub.

Ramla Bay: Ramla Bay, Marfa, tel: 573522. Faces Comino in excellent location. Good water sport facilities, waterskiing, canoeing, etc. Qualified instruction for sailing or windsurfing. Tennis. Nightly entertainment. Apartments. Terrace dining in summer. Theme nights.

Salita: Main Street, Mellieha, tel: 520923. In centre of village main thoroughfare. Roof pool.

Selmun Palace: Selmun, outside Mellieha, tel: 521040. In isolated location, large modern hotel attached to small knights tower. Pools, water sports, beach nearby. Tennis.

Suncrest: Qawra, tel: 577101. New and growing into Malta's largest hotel.

Go-ahead management. Well appointed. On waterfront with own beach, pools, restaurants. Water sports amenities. Apartments. Conference facilities.

☆☆☆

A rapidly growing number of hotels are in this category. Among them:

Castille: Castille Square, Valletta, tel: 243677/8. Just within the city walls, alongside Auberge de Castile, the prime minister's offices. Good location. Rooftop restaurant with views.

Eden Rock: Tower Road, Sliema, tel: 335575. Family hotel on Sliema's promenade with its wide selection of rock beaches, restaurants and shops.

Golden Sands: Golden Bay, Ghajn Tuffieha, tel: 573961. Above one of Malta's best sandy beaches. Attractive location. Good for young families. Pools, tennis.

Imperial: Rudolph Street, Sliema, tel: 344093. In central residential Sliema. Unpretentious, sedate clientele. Large pool.

Mellieha Bay: Ghadira, Mellieha, tel: 573844. Facing into Mellieha Bay, minutes from the long stretch of Ghadira sand beach. Popular with groups. Pools, watersports, tennis.

Milano Due: The Strand, Gzira, tel: 345040/1. Very near Sliema. All the rooms are air-conditioned and with television.

Plevna: Qui-Si-Sana, Sliema, tel: 331031. A quiet friendly hotel in quiet residential section close to shops, cafés and rock beaches. Own beach facilities with pool.

Tigne Court: Qui-Si-Sana, Sliema, tel: 332001. Facing sea on residential waterfront. Cafés and shops nearby. Own beach facilities.

Tower Palace: Tower Road, Sliema, tel: 337271. Currently closed. Scheduled to reopen spring 1999. On seafront promenade close to shopping centre. Roof restaurant and bar. Smooth rock beach across the road popular with Sliema residents.

Victoria, Gorg Borg Olivier Street, Sliema, tel: 334711. Smart, small town hotel in the middle of residential Sliema, opened 1997. Good restaurant. Within a minute's walk of all amenities and beach.

Gozo

☆☆☆☆☆

L'Imgarr: Mgarr, tel: 560455, fax: 557589. Spectacular position overlooking the habour. 74 rooms, the majority with comfortable sitting rooms, all with balconies, air-conditioning, ceiling fans, mini-bars and satellite TV. Several with impressively large terraces. Good restaurant, two pools, sauna, gym and conference facilities. A hit with those who usually find the Mediterranean short on curtains, carpets and wood panelling.

Ta' Cenc: Sannat, tel: 556830, fax: 558199. Regularly featured as one of world's top hotels. Quiet, in tranquil location. Superbly and elegantly understated, single-storey, some chalets and bungalows. Pool. Access to rock beach and sea nearby. Floodlit tennis.

☆☆☆☆

Andar: Xlendi, tel: 560736/7, fax: 560737. Perched on a peaceful, rural hillside a few minutes from the bustle of Xlendi Bay. 34 rooms, most with balconies, all with air-conditioning, mini-bars and satellite TV. Dining terrace overlooks the valley, pool and diving school.

Cornucopia: Gnien Imrek Street, Xaghra, tel: 556486, fax: 552910. Pretty hotel on hill outside village a distance from resort area of Marsalforn. Good pool and restaurant.

The Grand, St Anthony Street, Mgarr, tel: 556183; fax: 559744. Stylish new hotel with stunning views over Mgarr Harbour and the Gozo Channel to Malta. Good-sized rooftop pool, sauna, fitness and games rooms. Roof garden restaurant and conference hall.

St Patrick's: Xlendi, tel: 562951, fax: 556598. Seafront hotel at the head of a pretty but over-built Bay seething with life in summer. Refurbished in 1993. Air-conditioning, ceiling fans, mini-bars and satellite TV in all 49 rooms. A few have Jacuzzi baths and extra-large balconies. Attractive restaurant and water's-edge terrace, roof garden and plunge pool.

☆☆☆

Calypso: Marsalforn, tel: 562000, fax: 562012. Large hotel. On popular, noisy waterfront. Beaches close by. Simple restaurant. Apartments.

Comino

☆☆☆☆
Comino: Tel: 529821/9. Peaceful, simple hotel. Excellent water sports facilities. Boat services to mainland Malta and Gozo. A favourite with honeymooners. Tennis, gym.

Holiday Flats

There are a number of holiday complexes, tourist villages and aparthotels.
Mistra Village: Xemxija Hill, St Paul's Bay, tel: 580481. Set on the hill above the village. Pool, restaurants and tennis.
Bugibba Holiday Complex: Tourists St Bugibba, tel: 580861. Set in central Bugibba with many amenities.

Timeshare

Many people are attracted by the idea of buying into a timeshare complex or exchanging their option to Malta. There are two organisations to contact should you wish to find out more:
RCI, Kettering Parkway, Kettering, Northants, NN15 6EY, tel: 01536-310 111.
Interval International, 4 Citadel Place, Tinworth Street, London SE11 5EG, tel: 0171 820 1515.

Youth Hostels

There are several youth hostels in Malta, one on Gozo. Average cost is Lm3.00 for a bed and locker.

Malta

Sliema: Hibernia House, Depiro Street, tel: 333859.
Marsaxlokk: Zejtun Road, tel: 871709.
Bugibba: Trafalgar, 100 Triq ic-Centurjun, tel: 460412.
Paceville: Paceville, Triq Wilga, tel: 339261.

Gozo

Myha Ghajnsielem: Triq Cordina, Ghajnsielem, tel: 569361.

Eating Out

What to Eat

Eating out on either of the main islands can be a pleasure but, as many will vouchsafe, it can often be a disappointment. It is best not to expect too much from restaurants that for many years catered to the unsophisticated palates of British servicemen partial to chips and brown sauce served with everything, or to the tastes of British package tourists. Until recently the Maltese themselves rarely ate out, knowing that nothing could beat home cooking.

As lifestyles change with increasing wealth, and with the arrival of a much broader selection of European visitors, so new cafés and restaurants have blossomed, ready to cater both for the much-travelled Maltese (whose presence is not seasonal) and the discriminating tourists, many of whom are well-heeled. However, even the most constant of good restaurants can have its off days, particularly so here on islands where crops and chef's contracts have short seasons.

There are exceptions. In Valletta, for example, there is **Giannini**; in Sliema, **Barracuda**. In St Julians there are **La Dolce Vita** and **San Giuliano**. In Gozo, the restaurant at the incomparable **Ta' Cenc Hotel**.

What might be termed authentic Maltese cooking is hard to find although dishes that are part Maltese, part Italian, are on most menus. Fish is often delicious and many restaurants reputations hinge on their skill with it. During the winter months few fishermen dare venture into the rough seas in the hope of a catch; most fish served will have been frozen.

Rabbit (*fenek*) is a favourite dish with the Maltese though it rarely appears on a menu. A *fenkata*, an evening at an inexpensive village café where fried or stewed rabbit is served with lots of red wine, is a popular casual event for a crowd of friends. But go with a Maltese host; these meals

need to be booked and a successful evening can depend on knowing the café's owner. Favourite places are at Wied-iz-Zurrieq, around Bugibba and at the tiny village of Mgarr (Malta) where two village bars with long-standing fans are **il-Barri** (tel: 573235) and **Sunny Bar** (tel: 573705); both face on to the church square.

A government levy of 10 percent is added to all restaurant bills. This is not a service charge.

Where to Eat
Malta

The city is silent by night. As the shops close around 7pm, so the city empties. This is not the place for nightlife; that centres around Sliema, St Julians, Bugibba and Mellieha.

Valletta

British Hotel, 276 St Ursula Street, tel: 224730. A 2-star hotel in prime position on bastion walls facing into Grand Harbour. Its long restaurant has six tables on the balcony in summer. Cooking, like the hotel, is friendly and unassuming. Finish with riccotta and almond gâteau called *ta'Rubino* after the man who makes it. Or with *gbejniet*, the local goat's cheese, which, here, is peppered and pickled. Casual and inexpensive.
Bologna, 58 Republic Street, tel: 246149. A few steps from the Palace of the Grand Masters on the main thoroughfare to Fort St Elmo. Maltese-Italian food well regarded at lunch by bankers, lawyers, businessmen. Visa and MasterCard.
The Carriage, Valletta Buildings, South Street, tel: 247828. Do not be put off by the building, this is an elegant rooftop restaurant with pretty decor and imaginative cooking of consistently high standards. The dishes are original, blended into Maltese style. Dashing young owners, smart clientele, spectacular view. "Specials" of the day are invariably delicious. Known for its vegetarian dishes too. Lunch Monday-Friday. Dinner Friday and Saturday only. Booking essential. Major credit cards.
Castille Hotel, Castille Square, tel: 243677/8. A favourite of many, this small hotel has a roof restaurant with fine views of inland Malta, particularly by night when the island is lit. International dishes. Major credit cards.

Caffe Cordina, 244 Republic Street, tel: 234385. The city's most prestigious café, known for the superb quality of its confectionery. Typically Italian in its outlook, from the spelling of *caffe* to the long centre counter where regulars stand (having first paid for and collected a receipt at the cash desk for their order). There are small tables for waiter service inside and a number on Queen's Square outside. A meeting place where, mid-morning, everyone orders espresso or cappuccino with two *riccotta pastizzi* (hot, savoury cheesecakes). All traditional seasonal cakes to be had here as well as ice cream, gâteaux and pastries. In the Caffe Cordina wrapping, these make welcome presents when invited into Maltese homes. Light lunches daily. Closes around 8pm.

Giannini, St Michael's Bastion (off Windmill Street), tel: 237121/ 236575. One of the island's top restaurants and consistently good. In a patrician house overlooking Marsamxett Harbour with Manoel Island and Sliema across the water, the bar is on the groundfloor, the restaurant, via elevator, on the top. Panoramic views enhance its understated elegance. Pasta, fish and roasts in the Maltese manner are excellent. So is the welcome and the service. A restaurant for power lunching as well as romantic interludes. Lunch served daily (except Sunday); dinner Friday and Saturday. Booking essential. Major credit cards.

Pappagall, 174 Melita Street, tel: 236195. Charming (air-conditioned) basement restaurant. In narrow street behind Auberge de Castile. Menu Italian. Very much favoured for business lunches but also serves dinner. Major credit cards.

Phoenicia Hotel, The Mall, Floriana, tel: 225241/221211. Just outside the city gate, by Valletta's teeming bus terminus, this hotel has long been a base for visiting dignitaries, businessmen and travellers more interested in Malta's heritage than its sunshine. Excellent verandah setting. Small band for dancing in the evenings. Maltese enjoy lunch or dinner here when celebrating a special event – it has that kind of atmosphere. International cuisine and wines. Formal – that is, no beach clothes; jackets for men in the evenings. Booking recommended. Major credit cards.

Da Pippo, 136 Melita Street, tel: 241975. Different menu of traditional Maltese food daily, according to the chef's preferences. Restricted covers, quick service. Good wholesome Maltese food. Casual atmosphere but very popular with businessmen. Lunches only. Booking essential.

Pizzeria Bologna, 58 Republic Street, tel: 238014. Situated on the ground floor of the Bologna restaurant but under different management. Excellent pizza. A family favourite.

Sicilia, 1 St John Street, tel: 240569. The tiniest restaurant, seating for 14 indoors, but outside on a small piazza with views of Grand Harbour, a large number of tables are used when the weather allows. Popular with locals and tourists particularly for pasta and fish. Inexpensive. Lunch weekdays only.

Trattoria Palazz, 43 Old Theatre Street, tel: 226611. Underground (steep stairs) but air conditioned, in the ancient foundation of the *Biblioteca*. Small popular trattoria with welcoming atmosphere. Excellent pasta dishes and fresh fish. Crowded after events at the Manoel Theatre. Closed Sunday. Book in advance.

Sliema

Barracuda, 195 Main Street, tel: 331817. Smartly decorated restaurant overlooking Balluta Bay and St Julians. Pricey, but often highly recommended by regulars, most of them businessmen.

Christopher's, Ta'Xbiex seafront, Ta'Xbiex, tel: 337101. Considered by many to be the best restaurant on the islands. Costly, except for business lunches. Located by Msida's Marina. Booking essential at weekends. Casual but smart and impressive clientele.

Galeone, 35 Tigne Sea Front, tel: 316420. Sliema's most popular casual restaurant with Victor Bezzina cooking in the kitchen where regulars visit him. His recommendations are worth following. Fish, steaks and, as a starter, *spaghetti alla rabbiata* (a maddeningly hot sauce) invariably excellent. Small; booking recommended. Major credit cards.

Mangal, 84 Tigne Sea Front, tel: 343380. As tourism expands, so hoteliers become more adventurous. Long ago the islanders fought the Otto-

man Turks until the Great Siege defeated the scourge of Christianity; and now the Fortina Hotel has opened the island's only Turkish restaurant. With a Turkish team responsible for menu and kitchens, the result is declared by regulars as authentic.

Piccolo Padre, 195 Main Street, tel: 344875. A fun pizzeria beneath the Barracuda restaurant. An excellent, rowdy place popular with families and children. Some tables with views over harbour and sea. No bookings taken. Queueing at weekends.

Ponte Vecchio, Tower Road, tel: 314591. On the corner of Stella Maris Street, close to **La Gelateria**, Sliema's excellent ice cream shop. A Maltese restaurant with international menu. Tables on pavement during summer. Major credit cards.

St Julians/Paceville

With Paceville at the top of the hill, this burgeoning resort area has a wide selection of pizza houses, cafés and Chinese restaurants. The following are favoured by the Maltese.

Caffe Raffael, Spinola Road, St Julians Bay, tel: 319988. Café with large terrace under same management as San Giuliano restaurant. Pretty location.

Il Brigante, Ball Street. Maltese/Italian cuisine in the heart of Paceville. Renowned for its decor and service.

La Dolce Vita, 155 St George's Road, tel: 337836. Favoured by the young, trendy, noisy crowd. Always busy. In summer rooftop restaurant is open. Looks on to Bay. Specialities pasta and fish. Booking recommended. Major credit cards.

Peppino's, 30 St George's Road, tel: 373200. Considered the in-place by many locals. Terrace and air-conditioned restaurant. Groundfloor bar (serves lunches) and is a late-night meeting place. Crowded.

Pizza Hut, St George's Road, tel: 376600. A pretty setting, popular with young families. Visa, MasterCard.

Saddles, 132 Main Street, tel: 339993. At the hub of St Julians Bay, this is the meeting place of the beer, wine and hamburger set. Fast sports cars and motorbikes keep the regulars in constant motion.

San Giuliano, Spinola Road, tel: 332000. Sometimes considered the smartest meeting place; with an international clientele where visiting television stars are given star treatment. Much table-hopping. Good-looking restaurant with good view over St Julians waterfront. Cooking erratic; fish sometimes good. Booking recommended. Major credit cards.

Sumatra, 139 Spinola Road, tel: 310991. Popular with locals looking for a change from Maltese and Italian cooking. Specialises in Malaysian, Singaporean and Indonesian cooking. Maintains good standards.

Bugibba

Big Foot, Borodino Street, tel: 581141. Excellent tradition in rabbit dishes, fried or stewed. A very rustic, "rough and ready" outlet.

Mellieha

The Arches, 113 Main Street, tel: 573436. In central Mellieha, a large and brightly lit place, with bustling service and large portions. Roof open in summer. Crowded. Varied menu. Booking advisable. Visa, MasterCard.
Giuseppi's, 8 St Helen's Street, tel: 574882. On two floors, Giuseppi's is considered a fine example of a truly Maltese restaurant, both in its decor and in its cooking. Menu changes daily and depends on what is available in local market. Very popular. Moderately priced. Dinner booking essential.
Il Mulino, 45 Main Street, tel: 520404. Set in a windmill style arrangement, excellent for baked dishes and fish.

Attard

Rickshaw (set in the Corinthia Palace Hotel), tel: 440301. Oriental restaurant with Chinese, Malaysian and Vietnamese dishes.

Marsascala

Fisherman's Rest, St Thomas's Bay, tel: 822049. On the edge of the ramshackle buildings at the water's edge, a highly informal fish restaurant. Simple cooking, friendly casual service. Modestly priced.
Grabiel, Marsascala Bay, tel: 684194. A modern family-run restaurant that has built up a serious local following of diners who drive across the island for the sea-date and clam starters to be followed by octopus stew or a prawn platter. Good standards. Can be costly. Booking recommended.
La Favorita, Gardiel Street, tel:

684113. On the narrow roads to St Thomas's Bay an informal, noisy restaurant known for its constant standard of fish which is unpretentiously served in a manner Maltese rather than Italian. Moderately priced. Crowded at weekends when booking imperative.
Zonqor Point, tel: 822540. Named after the promontory on which it and the National Waterpolo Pitch are sited. Terrace. Steadily working towards reputation for good fish. Visa, MasterCard.

Marsaxlokk

Hunter's Tower, Wilga Street, tel: 871792. On waterfront facing into the pretty Bay but flanked by new power station. Its fortunes fluctuate.
Rizzu, The Waterfront, tel: 871569. Renowned for its fresh fish dishes. Booking is a must. Outdoor roof terrace in summer.
Skuna 2, 4 Duncan Street, tel: 873317. Set on the waterfront the speciality is naturally fish in this picturesque fishing village.

Mdina

Bacchus, Inguanez Street, tel: 454981. Originally with a Roman theme, has now applied itself to entertaining large parties. Major credit cards.
Il-Hakem, Villegaignon Street, tel: 456301. Set in the very heart of Mdina, this is an unpretentious and cheerful choice.
Medina, 7 Holy Cross Street, tel: 674004. A pretty courtyard restaurant complete with tall oleander tree. A romantic setting. Unadventurous international cooking with British overtones. Faithful clientele. Major credit cards.

Qawra

The coastline of Qawra and Bugibba (leading to St Paul's Bay) is burgeoning with new cafés and restaurants catering for the package holidaymaker. There are many inexpensive places to choose from.
Gran Laguna, Ta' Xtut Street, tel: 571146. Ambitious Italian cooking of a surprisingly high quality. Known for its pasta and fresh fish.
Luzzu, Qawra Road, tel: 573925. This was the first lido on this stretch of the coast. Somewhat dwarfed by new hotels. Known for its fish, its casual and relaxed atmosphere with friendly serv-

ice. Tuscan-born owner Andrea Latughi offers excellent Italian regional dishes.
Savini, Qawra Road, tel: 576927. On the outskirts of Bugibba, this is a converted farmhouse complete with open-air terraces for dining in the summer months. Rich Italian cooking served with what was once known as silver service. Regarded by some as one of the island's top restaurants.
Suncrest Hotel, Qawra Road, tel: 576927. Giant new hotel with self-catering apartments. Restaurants open to non-residents. Its **It-Tokk** restaurant serves only Maltese dishes.

St Paul's Bay

Gillieru, Church Street, tel: 573480. For many decades a tiny restaurant catering for Maltese who would travel miles for their fresh fish, the Gillieru prides itself in the variety of fish always available. Jutting out into the sea – with an open terrace in summer – it is now a large restaurant. Grilled fish can be excellent; check which is fresh, which frozen. Unsophisticated and friendly. Visa.
Da Rosi, 44 Church Street, tel: 571411. Small, friendly family-run restaurant with a fine range of fresh fish. Booking a must during weekends.

Gozo

Gharb

Jeffrey's, 10 Gharb Road, tel: 561006. Closed Sunday and mid-January to mid-March. Excellent little trattoria hung with local artwork. Courtyard dining in summer. Local and vegetarian specialities with ingredients fresh from the cook's own farm. Good value.
Salvina's, 21 Triq il-Blata, tel: 552505. Closed Sundays. Pretty little restaurant in village house on narrow village street. Local and international cuisine. The food doesn't always live up to the decor.

Marsalforn

I-Kartell, Bakery Street, tel: 556918. At the water's edge. Downstairs trattoria, friendly atmosphere, good fish and local dishes, including pasta and pizzas. Very reasonably priced. Upstairs, charcoal grill and flambés.
Auberge Ta' Frenc, Marsalforn Road, tel: 553888. Dinners only. Stylishly converted farmhouse. Wide range of international dishes elegantly pre-

sented. Spacious, peaceful atmosphere.

The Republic, 18 Triq ix-Xatt, tel: 556800. Closed Mondays. Trattoria with pleasant beach-side terrace.

Mgarr

Il-Kcina tal-Barrakka, 28 Manuel de Vilhena Street, tel: 556543. Small pretty restaurant at harbour's edge, with excellent, imaginative menu. Slightly cramped but very reasonable prices. Open summer only. Wise to book.

Sea View, Shore Street, tel: 553985. At harbour's edge. Excellent fish, including fresh mussels and clams. Sensibly limited menu and a little more expensive than most. Owner-chef strums a guitar as the evening wears on.

Xaghra

Gesther, 8th September Avenue, tel: 556621. Lunches only. Run by two jolly sisters, Gemma and Esther, hence the name. Authentic local food and atmosphere.

Oleander, Victory Square, tel: 557230. Owned by Gemma and Esther's nephew, who has added a few refinements to his aunts' cuisine. Excellent local dishes, fish and steaks, reasonably priced, and a view of the bustling heart of the village.

Xlendi

Il-Cima, St Simon Street, tel: 558407. Away from the crowds near the mouth of the bay, with a restful terrace. Good local fare and a winning way with fish.

Paradise, Mount Carmel Street, tel: 556878. Fondly known by aficionados as the Elvis Presley Memorial Bar – pictures of "the King" all over. Basic as far as comfort is concerned but excellent simple cooking, fresh fish and jumbo prawns. Exceptionally good value.

The Village Inn, Xlendi Road, tel: 558181. Air conditioned. Pleasant, not very imaginative food, reasonably priced.

The local privately produced Maltese and Gozitan wines are quite potent. Marsovin Special Reserve, Green Label and Citadella are the most well-known locally produced wines but they are not to everyone's taste. Try the locals beers – Cisk lager, for example. Bars and cafés are open 9am–1am and there is no lower age limit although children are not usually brought into bars. Hotel bars may close between 1pm and 4pm.

Culture

There is something to appeal to the culture buff, sports enthusiast, sunshine seeker and night owl in Malta. Valletta may take several days to see in its entirety, but other towns and villages are no more than a sedate half-day excursion. Museums and temple sites on Malta are government-run and follow the same hours. In winter (1 October–15 June): 8.30am–4.30pm all week although some times may vary due to government overtime. Most entrance fees have been raised to Lm1.00. They are closed on public holidays.

Malta
Valletta

Named after the victorious French Grand Master, Jean Parisot de la Valette, who led the besieged during the Great Siege of 1565, the capital city of Malta is laid out on a grid system but is riven with little alleyways and beckoning pedestrian walkways. One of the nicest times to stroll through the capital is by night or on a Sunday. Another good time is off-season, when it is quiet and the cafés are open but not crowded and you have the opportunity to notice the remarkable mix of architectural styles – the baroque auberges, tightly packed shops, apartments with their green wood-shuttered balconies and the grand scale of the squares dotted with neatly cropped trees and ornate lampposts.

MUSEUMS & MONUMENTS

The Armoury: In the Palace of the Grand Masters, Republic Street, tel: 225577. Over 5,700 pieces including shields, guns and cannons as well as some stunning ceremonial suits of armour and paintings.

The Auberges: Each different *langue* within the Order of the St John had its own residence typifying the splendour of the knights. Of the original eight, only five auberges now remain, some of them museums, others government offices. They are: **Auberge de Provence** (National Museum of Archaeology), Republic Street. **Auberge de Castile et Leon** (Prime Minister's Office), Castile Place. **Auberge d'Aragon** (Government Offices), Independence Square. **Auberge d'Italie** (Main Post Office), Merchants Street. **Auberge d'Angleterre et de Baverie** (Government Offices), West Street.

Malta Library: Republic Square, tel: 232691. A majestic baroque building, the National Library or *Biblioteca* contains priceless manuscripts dating back to the 11th century and documents tracing the history of the Order of St John. Entrance is free but carry some form of identification such as passport. Visit the library Monday–Friday, 8.30am–5.45pm, Saturday 8.30am–1pm.

Manoel Theatre: Old Theatre Street. For booking enquiries: Tel: 246389. One of the oldest theatres still in use in Europe, it was built by Grand Master Manoel de Vilhena in 1731. The tiered gilded boxes reach almost up to the ceiling of the auditorium and make it a jewel of a theatre to visit or in which to perform. Tours of the theatre take place on Monday–Friday 10.45am and 11.30am only, summer and winter. Entrance fee charged.

National Museum of Archaeology: Republic Street, tel: 237730. Housed in the Auberge de Provence, built in 1571, is an enthralling collection of megalithic pottery, sculpture, personal adornments brought from Malta's temples and prehistoric sites.

National Museum of Fine Arts: South Street, tel: 225769. A beautiful white building, this palazzo, once a home to the knights, houses works by Italian masters such as Perugino and Tintoretto as well as the work of eminent Maltese artists.

National War Museum: Fort St Elmo at the far end of Republic Street, tel: 222430. A very personal museum of items dating back to before World War II, including uniforms and kits, weaponry, aircraft and marine equipment.

Palace of the Grand Masters: Republic Street, tel: 221221. Completed in 1574, and the original Magisterial Palace of the knights, this building is now the office of the President and also contains the House of Representatives. Savour the silence of Neptune's Courtyard; visit the former council chamber and the Halls of St Michael, St George and the Ambassadors displaying some excellent frescoes and paintings.

Palazzo Parisio: Merchants Street. Closed to visitors, it is now home to the Ministry of Foreign Affairs. This was where Napoleon briefly stayed.

CHURCHES

St John's Co-Cathedral: St John's Square, between Republic and Merchants Streets. A feast of baroque exuberancy, the cathedral was designed by Maltese architect Gerolamo Cassar in 1577 for the Order of St John and contains frescoes by Calabrian artist Mattia Preti, intricate marble burial tombs, Caravaggio's *The Beheading of St John*, and a series of Flemish tapestries (on view only during June or special state occasions). Its museum is open Monday–Saturday 9.30am–1pm and 3–5pm. Entrance: fee charged.

Other churches worth visiting while in Valletta, include:
The **Carmelite Church** with its 138-ft (42-metre) high dome, Old Theatre Street; **St Paul Shipwrecked**, St Paul Street; **Church of St Roque**, St Ursula Street; **Gesu**, Merchants Street; **St Paul's Anglican Cathedral**, West Street; **The Church of Our Lady of the Victories** and **St Catherine**, both in Ordnance Street.

OTHER PLACES OF INTEREST

Fort St Elmo: The Armed Forces of Malta trains its new recruits here now, but this immense fortification is worth visiting to admire the sheer proportions. Within the fort is housed the War Museum. At Valletta's furthermost tip facing the sea.

Hastings Gardens: On the west side of Valletta overlooking Marsamxett Harbour, these gardens are more spread out than the Barrakka Gardens and lead to St Michael's Bastion.

The Mediterranean Conference Centre: North end of Merchants Street, tel: 243840. Built as a hospital for the Order of St John, its Great Ward (now an exhibition hall), was one of the longest in Europe. The Mizzi Hall is the venue for *The Malta Experience*, a 40-minute audio-visual show recounting 5,000 years of Maltese history, from the prehistoric communities to the arrival of the knights of St John and the Great Siege, up to the present day. Shows are as follows: Monday–Friday 11am, noon, 1pm, 2pm, 3pm, 4pm. Saturday 11am and noon.

Open-Air Markets: A daily market held in Merchant's Street by St John's Square until noon. On Sunday a larger market is held just outside City Gate, by the bus station, in St James' Ditch. Here you'll find everything from inexpensive audio tapes to jeans, confectionery to lace tablecloths.

Upper Barrakka Gardens: A pretty planted area with benches, colonnades, *Sciortino* sculpture and a marvellous view high up over the Grand Harbour, from Fort St Elmo, on the left, to the quays of Marsa, right. Off Castile Place.

Mdina

The beautiful medieval capital of Malta is a fortified enclave inland to the southwest of Malta. Try to visit early or, indeed late in the day to appreciate the hush of the narrow streets (Mdina is known as the "Silent City"). Explore the narrow streets with their tiny cream-stoned churches cast in shadow, and wrought-iron or painted balconies overhung with flowers.

MUSEUMS & CHURCHES

Mdina Cathedral and Museum: St Paul's Square, tel: 674697. Behind the baroque facade, the creation of Lorenzo Gafa', is a wealth of paintings, sculpture and marble mosaic work. The museum to the right of the Cathedral houses a collection of historical vestments, grand illuminated tomes, a vast coin collection and paintings and engravings by Rembrandt, Piranesi, Van Dyck and Durer. Open October–May Monday–Saturday 9am–1pm and 1.30–4.30pm; June–September Monday–Saturday 9am–1pm and 1.30pm–5pm.

National Museum of Natural History: Just inside the city gate, a few metres down on the right, tel: 6455951. A quaint, slightly tired collection of different species contained in the exquisite Vilhena Palace. Worth visiting just for the building, for the courtyard and lovely scrolled doorways.

Villegaignon Street: The city's main thoroughfare leading from the **Main Gate** to **Bastion Square** with its fine views over the countryside. The finest and grandest houses are along its length.

The first grand house is **Casa Inguanez**, still home of the oldest Maltese aristocratic family, the Inguanez. The Governorship of Malta was held by the head of this family until the arrival of the Order of St John in 1530. Part of the house dates back to 1350.

Opposite this house is the chapel of **St Peter** which forms a part of the **Nunnery of St Benedict**. The altar piece by Mattia Preti shows Madonna and Child with saints Benedict, Peter and Scolastica. Further along is **Palazzo Santa Sofia**, reputed to be the oldest house in Mdina. Or at least its ground floor is, having been built in 1233. The first-floor family conversion was added in the 1930s.

The **Carmelite Church** on the other side of the road was built in 1666 and attached to the monastery of the Carmelite Fathers. It was here, on 2 September 1798, that French troops entered in order to sell the church's treasure by auction to raise monies for Napoleon's campaign in Egypt. Seeing their church desecrated, the locals rioted. The French retreated and, as the church bells rang out, so the Maltese were alerted to rebellion. Within two years the French were forced to abandon Malta. It heralded the start of Britain's tenure of the islands.

A few steps away is the **Norman House**, also known as **Palazzo Falzon**. It takes its name from the double-arched windows on the first floor, added in the 16th century to an earlier house. A private house, it contains a museum of fine furniture, paintings, armour and carpets. Open Monday, Wednesday and Friday only 9.30am–1pm and 2pm–4pm, tel: 455951.

Rabat

Outside the walls of Mdina, Rabat (it means "suburb") also has some important historical sites.

MUSEUMS & CHURCHES

The Catacombs: There are two. The larger is dedicated to **St Paul**, the smaller to **St Agatha**. These labyrinthine burial chambers are macabre and fascinating, dating from AD 50.

Roman Villa and Museum: Museum Esplanade, tel: 454125. Remains of a classically proportioned villa with remarkable mosaic floors restored to their vivid ochre, blue, red and black plus some pottery and grand columns. From Roman era.

St Paul's Church and **Grotto:** The original parish church of Rabat believed to have been built originally in 1575 above one of the first Christian chapels in Malta. It was rebuilt in 1694, having been damaged in the earthquake that felled Mdina's cathedral. The Grotto is reputed to be where St Paul spent much time after his shipwreck in AD 60. The stone is said to be miraculous and the finest scrapings will cure the sick if kept by their beds.

TEMPLES & RUINS

Preserved in outstanding condition, the temples, scattered all over Malta and Gozo afford one of the best insights into prehistoric man's ritual way of life. That societies should have been ordered enough to support this kind of architectural project testifies to a very sophisticated culture. Museum curators are more than willing to explain the structure and use of the temples.

Borg in-Nadur: St George's Bay. A fortified village dating back to 1500 BC.

Ghar Dalam Cave: At Birzebbuga, tel: 824419. Found here, the fossilised remains of animals that roamed the area 100,000 BC when Malta was probably joined to Africa.

Hagar Qim and Mnajdra: South of the island, near Zurrieq Temples constructed in the early megalithic period facing the sea and the rock island of Filfla. Note the mushroom-shaped altars and the oracle hole at Hagar Qim. Mnajdra is similar in layout to Hagar Qim but structurally better preserved since it was built from sturdier corraline limestone, although it was badly damaged during storms in 1994–95.

The Hypogeum: Burial Street between Paola and Tarxien, tel: 825579. An underground network of passageways, cubicles and chambers 5,000 years old. Used as a burial chamber, on the ceilings are the faint sienna-coloured remains of primitive cave paintings.

Opening times are very specific to allow as little light as possible to reach the Hypogeum and are as follows:

Monday–Saturday 10–10.45am, 11.30am–12.15pm, 1–1.45pm, 2.30–3.15pm, 4–4.45pm; Sunday 8.30–9.15am, 10.30–10.45am, 11.30am–12.15pm, 1–1.45pm, 2.30–3.15pm.

Undergoing major preservation work.

Skorba: At Zebbiegh. The site of one of the oldest known and longest surviving prehistoric communities – experts believe for over 1,000 years. Here see remains of the village wall built some 4,000 years ago plus megalithic temples and Bronze Age pottery.

Tarxien Prehistoric Temples: Old Temples Street, Tarxien, tel: 225578. An odd approach via a normal front door in an average street. The intact remains of these pagan temples dating back 3 or 4 millennia BC, display well-preserved chambers, altars, libation holes and detailed carvings including a statue of the "Fat Lady" believed to relate to a fertility cult. (The original is in the National Museum of Archaeology, Valletta.)

Elsewhere in Malta

Buskett Gardens: Tel: 454021. The perfect place to spend an afternoon under the welcome shade of well manicured orange trees.

The Blue Grotto: Tel: 826947/826721. Boat trips around and through caves tinged pink and orange by the coral content and luminescent with the reflection of blue waters. Arrive at **Wied iz-Zurrieq** fisherman's hamlet. Weather permitting boat trips ply from the inlet. Agree tariff first.

Dingli Cliffs: The site of ancient cart tracks at Clapham Junction. These immense cliffs are 656 ft (220 metres) above sea level and drop almost vertically down to the sea. Fabulous views and country walks. The island of Filfla is visible from here.

Ghar Hasan: Large cave fronting immense cliffs on the south-east coast.

Ghar Lapsi: Fishing village, popular for subaqua diving and picnickers.

Golden Bay and **Ghajn Tuffieha:** Further round, on the southwest coast, there are good beach and boating facilities at Golden Bay, while less accessible Ghajn Tuffieha remains a secret retreat.

Marfa Ridge: Malta's "fish tale" has both rocky and sandy inlets. Ramla Bay in particular is well maintained. The ferry to Gozo sails from Cirkewwa.

Marsascala: Small and picturesque fishing village.

Marsaxlokk: The ideal sleepy fishing village. Bobbing *luzzus* in the harbour, lace tablecloths fluttering in the breeze and the daily ritual of mending nets.

Mellieha Bay: The largest Bay on Malta, with Ghadira, the longest sand beach. Unfortunately usually crowded.

Mosta Dome: Visible from all over the island, the Mosta Dome that is St Mary's Church is one of the largest unsupported domes in Europe. A bomb which fell during a service in 1942 without exploding or injuring anyone is displayed in the vestry.

St Paul's Bay: One of Malta's largest bays with the island where St Paul was shipwrecked in AD 60.

San Anton Palace and Gardens, Attard, tel: 442509. A profusion of shrubs and trees planted by Grand Master Antoine de Paule in the 17th century and still thriving today. The official residence of the President of Malta and closed to visitors. The gardens are open: September–February Monday–Friday 7am–5pm, Saturday and Sunday 8am–5pm; March Monday–Friday 7am–6pm, Saturday and Sunday 8am–6pm; April Monday–Friday 7am–7pm, Saturday and Sunday 8am–7pm; May–August 7am–8pm.

Senglea and **Cospicua:** Pitifully damaged during World War II, not much of the original remains, save for the view out over the Grand Harbour.

Sliema: The most populated and the smartest area of Malta. Find here international fashion shops, restaurants, and entertainment. The seafront which extends for about 2 miles (3 km) is alive with the buzz of cafés. Explore Tower Road, Bisazza Street and Manuel Dimech Street.

Verdala Castle: Close to Rabat, the castle, built by Gerolamo Cassar for the Grand Master de Verdalle in 1586, sits atop Buskett Gardens and provides visitors with a vast panoramic overview. Open Tuesday and Friday only 9am–noon and 2–5pm.

Vittoriosa: One of the Three Cities across the Grand Harbour facing Valletta. Visit the Inquisitors Palace and the Church of St Lawrence. At the tip of Vittoriosa is Fort St Angelo (closed to visitors).

Zabbar Sanctuary Museum: Tel: 821010 for an appointment. A small museum housing relics and paintings from the Order of St John.

Gozo

So near to Malta, yet a world away in pace, Gozo offers pastoral simplicity to the visitor. Once the visitors have disembarked at Mgarr harbour and gone their separate ways to tour the island, the seductive spell of the island is immediate. All modern pressures and preoccupations cease, the only noise is a diesel tractor spluttering round a bend or the patter of hooves as disgruntled goats are chaperoned to a new enclosure.

Gozo is where you'll come across some of the most noble views and glimpse a rustic way of life that gently but firmly seems to resist any attempt at change. The capital Victoria (known also by its original name, Rabat) is a cosy weave of little streets and squares. Outside Victoria, one finds many of the attractions from Malta, but in even closer proximity; temples, churches, beaches and rocky promontories.

MUSEUMS

Gozo's museums are generally open from 8.45am–3.15pm daily.

Folklore Museum: Tel: 556144. The craft and handwork of Gozitan life. The Citadel.

The Gozo Heritage: 20 Mgarr Road, Ghansielem, tel: 551475/553106. Gozitans are even more proud of their own history than Malta's. This exhibition, with models and disembodied commentary, traces the events and personalities that have shaped 7,000 years of Gozitan life. The Gozo Heritage is on the main road between Mgarr Harbour and Victoria. Open 10am–5pm daily.

Gozo National Museum: Situated at the former Bondi Palace, within the Citadel walls, housing a collection of artefacts from Roman, Phoenician and prehistoric times.

CHURCHES

The Cathedral and **Museum:** Just inside the Citadel gates. Museum – tel: 556144. Built by Lorenzo Gafa between 1697 and 1711, note the *trompe l'oeil* ceiling by Antonio Manuele, giving the effect of a dome. At the rear, the cathedral museum contains sacred objects and some paintings.

St George's Church: St George's Square. Contains sculpture by Azzopardi and paintings by Mattia Preti and Batista Conti.

Elsewhere in Gozo

CHURCHES

Ta' Pinu: Striking basilica and a place of pilgrimage. Tiny original chapel, remaining intact and decorated with antique ecclesiastical candles, is integrated at the very front of the 20th-century Romanesque style addition. Macabre corner with evidence of modern miracles granted.

Xaghra Church: Our Lady of Lourdes. Baroque flourishes adorn this 19th-century church in charming and peaceful village.

Xewkija Church: One of the largest unsupported cupolas in Europe.

TEMPLES

Xaghra: Tel: 553194. Ggantija Megalithic Temples. Perhaps the finest preserved temples within the whole of Malta. Well over 4,000 years old, these gargantuan pieces of coralline limestone give the closest approximation of how these temples really looked.

OTHER PLACES OF INTEREST

Azure Window: Reached by boat from the inland sea. A shimmering blue eye of sea fashioned over thousands of years as the sea has worn through the rock, creating the effect of a huge sea-filled window.

Calypso's Cave: Above the sandy beach of Ramla. Gozo is sometimes referred to as Calypso's Isle, recalling the legend of Ulysses, who spent seven years here as the nymph's "prisoner of love". The cave is now closed but an observation platform above offers panoramic views.

Fungus Rock: More legend here as the knights believed the "fungus Gaulitanus" growing on top of its knoll to be blessed with special healing powers. Near to Dwejra point on the south-west of Gozo.

Gharb: Almost locked in time, this idyllic village sums up the dreamy atmosphere of Gozo.

Il-Mithna ta'Kola: Triq-il-Bambina, Xaghra. Attractively renovated 18th century windmill, with original machinery, forge and living quarters.

Inland Sea: Near Dwejra. An inland sea of warm water for swimmers who can reach the sea via a tunnel through the cliff. The caves here offer excellent diving, while on dry land prehistoric fossils reveal some of the ancient marine life of Gozo.

Marsalforn: A lively (by Gozitan standards) seaside spot, popular with swimmers and holidaymakers.

Nadur: Gozo's second town, 100 ft (30 metres) above sea level.

Ninu's Cave and **Xerri's Cave:** Ninu's Cave, 17 January Street, tel: 556863. Open all day. Xerri's Cave, 31 Xerri's Grotto Street, tel: 557865. Open 9.30am–noon and 3.30–5.30pm. Both in Xaghra. These caves, in private houses, show eccentric stalagmite and stalactite alabaster rock formations.

Pomskizillious: (Toy Museum), Xaghra. A small treasure trove in a village house, with a wax-work on nonsense rhymer Edward Lear, inventor of the word that gives it its name.

Ramla Bay: Gozo's favourite beach is reached by travelling north of Nadur until you can go no further. Excellent safe swimming.

Sannat: En route to the superb Ta'Cenc Hotel. Take a pause to visit some of the lace shops you'll find here.

Ta'Cenc: Gozo's luxury hotel is here, built deliberately simply and highly acclaimed. Nearby are the sights of ancient prehistoric cart tracks.

Xlendi: A quiet, relaxed fishing village with a rather thin strip of sand that stretches the length of the main street – all of 500 yards. Stairs up the cliff to the right of the Bay offer a view out to sea; spot fish and crabs in the little rocky cove beyond. Visit before too many holiday apartments are built.

Concerts/Ballets/Opera

Malta and Gozo play host to many international as well as home-grown performing companies. The Ministry of Tourism publishes a full events calendar listing annual and one-off events.

The **Manoel Theatre** also publishes updated information regarding forthcoming performances. Malta's season is from October–May.

Annual events listed below:

At Christmas: Traditional Pantomime (Manoel Theatre).

During January: Folk Festival.

From end-April: Maltafest.

Mid-July: Cultural events spread over the island including ballet at St Francis Ravelin under the stars.

November: The Malta International Choir Festival.

Movies

The annual Film and Video Competition, organised by the Malta Amateur Cine Circle is held in June. In November the Golden Knight International Film and Video Festival takes place.

Excellent cinema facilities available at the Eden Century (six cinemas), Paceville.

Libraries

If you wish to borrow books from a lending library, contact the Public Library tel: 243473, near the police headquarters, Floriana. British library tickets are valid and you may borrow a book for three weeks.

Attractions
Boat Cruises

Two companies dominate pleasure cruising in Malta. Both offer tours to Comino and harbour cruises but Captain Morgan also has an underwater boat to reveal what's beneath the sea as well.

Jylland, tel: 343373/9.

Captain Morgan's Cruises, tel: 336981.

Nightlife

During the summer, discos thump on into the night in every resort area, particularly at St Julians and Paceville. There are open-air summer discos – keep an ear out for the venue as it changes – and on Gozo there's the disco that draws Maltese over by ferry, to party away the small hours. For a quieter night out, several restaurants on Malta can offer superb dining or there are the bars, too numerous to

mention, scattered to every corner.

Discotheques available on the Islands are located at:

Axis, St George's Road, St Julians, tel: 344742

Euphoria Disco, St George's Bay, tel: 341191.

La Grotta, Xlendi Road, Xlendi, Gozo, tel: 551149. The prettiest nightclub in the Maltese islands, a latter-day hanging gardens of Babylon. Open-air terraces, a vast cave (from which it gets its name), and flower-decked walks, suspended above floodlit ravine, Xlendi and the sea.

Gambling

Gambling is a local passion, evidenced by the numerous Lotto booths on both islands. There is a weekly Lotto where the smallest stake is 10 cents and the National Lottery which twice a year offers major prizes.

At Marsa, there's the racetrack but for an evening of traditional Black Jack or roulette, the **Casino** at the Dragonara Palace (tel: 312888) in Paceville has all the familiar atmosphere of the international scene.

The Gay Scene

Certain clubs and bars are favoured at different times, but the patronage shifts and therefore is difficult to pinpoint. The age of consent is 18.

Outdoor Activities

Malta advertises itself as a haven for subaqua fans and indeed, the waters around the Malta, Gozo and Comino must surely be some of the cleanest and bluest in the world. The outdoor life is almost year round and, whatever sport you favour, there's sure to be an association for it.

Participant
Diving

A network of associations ensure that Malta has first-rate diving instructors and excursion leaders. There are numerous licensed schools and equipment can be hired for periods of a week or so. In the calm waters of the Maltese archipelago, there is a constant and flourishing marine and botanic population affording opportunities for some colourful close encounters and startling photography.

The caves, arches and grottos formed over thousands of years are home to grouper, squid, lobster, sting-ray and damsel fish, to name but a few. The government Tourist Organisation publishes a pamphlet detailing Malta's diving associations and schools, and information on diving sites.

If interested in exploring, always join a party with an experienced group leader to guide you. If you wish to take a diving course, you will need a medical certificate confirming your state of health. Some of the best areas for diving include: Ahrax Point (Cirkewwa), Anchor Bay, Qawra Point and Wied iz-Zurrieq on Malta; Ras ir-Qieqa and St Marija Caves on Comino and Reqqa Point, Dwerja Point and Mgarr Ix-Xini on Gozo. Should misfortune befall, there is a decompression chamber located at St Luke's Hospital at Gwardamanga. There is also a professional air and sea rescue service.

Diving Associations of Malta: FUAM (Federation of Underwater Activities in Malta), PO Box 29, Gzira, Malta; APDS

(Association of Professional Diving Schools), Msida Court, 61/2 Msida Sea Front, Msida, Malta. A updated list of licensed diving schools is available from Tourist Offices.

Nude Bathing

Nude bathing is prohibited. So is topless bathing for women. But both take place in secluded corners of some beaches where like-minded bathers (and peeping toms) gather. Both require utmost discretion; anyone taking offence may inform the police.

Horseriding

Centred around the Marsa racetrack are several equestrian schools. Some hotels may also arrange for riding facilities in the countryside.

Ten-Pin Bowling

Situated at the Eden Super Bowl. Open: every day from 10am to past midnight. St George's Bay, St Julians, tel: 341196/319888.

Spectator
Football

Soccer is a passion in Malta. League and international football matches are perfect occasions for fans to drive around town sitting on their horns, waving their teams colours from the window. The season is between September and May and the modern National Stadium is at Ta' Qali. Other pitches are at Marsa, Paola and Santa Lucia. For details of matches, contact the Football Association Headquarters in Valletta, tel: 222697.

Golf

Malta's par 68 golf course (currently being upgraded) is to be found at the Marsa Sports Club. The well-equipped complex also boasts 18 tennis courts, a polo field, badminton and five squash courts, an archery field plus football and cricket pitches. Many other sporting federations hold their events here. Weekly membership is available for tourists.

For further details, tel: 233851/243464. The Royal Malta Golf Club welcomes visitors, tel: 232842.

Horse Racing

Malta's only racetrack is at Marsa. From October every Sunday, ferries bring over horse-mad Gozitans to join the Maltese for an afternoon at the races. There is a bar, restaurant and betting facilities. Races continue through the winter, tel: 224800.

Water Polo

There are several pitches on the islands, with the National Pitch at Tal-Qnoqq. Team matches are played throughout the summer with fans getting as heated and argumentative as football fans. There is a waterpolo league championship.

Sporting Diary

A non-stop calendar of events fills the year. Listed below are some of the annual highlights.

February: Malta Marathon.
March: International Snooker Tournament.
April: International Archery Tournament, Marsa Sports Club.
May: Sicily to Malta Windsurf Race.
June: International Air Rally.
June/July: International Lawn Tennis Summer Open Tournament.
August: Rimini/Malta/Rimini Yacht Race.
September: Football season starts.
October: Autumn Series Yacht Races; Middle Sea yacht race.
November: Four-Wheel Drive Rally of Malta and Gozo.

Shopping
What to Buy

Malta's most traditional craft is lacemaking. Endless hours of nimble fingered work are poured into the creation of intricate tablecloths, napkins, place mats, collars, shawls and delicate blouses. Knitwear is popular – if you go for the heavy-duty styling and don't mind some unusual colour combinations. Glass in particular is a Maltese speciality. It's possible to visit the manufacturers and watch your souvenir being made, then purchase it.

Some crafts can be found in the local markets but the typical tourist souvenir shop is not the kind of place to go unless you want to find the ultimate in Malta kitsch.

Take back the best of Malta from the following:

Malta Crafts Centre: St John's Square, Valletta, tel: 221221.
Ta' Qali Crafts Village: Ta' Qali, Malta.
Ta' Dbiegi Crafts Village: Limits of St Lawrence, Gozo, tel: 556202.
Gozo Crafts Centre: The Citadel, Victoria, Gozo, tel: 556160.

Bookshops

It is possible to find books published in English, *Malti* and Italian without too much difficulty. For the best bookshops in:
Valletta: Sapienza, 26 Republic Street, tel: 233621.
Victoria: Rose Bookshop, Republic Street, tel: 555816; Swan Bookshop, Orienti Arcade, Republic Street, tel: 555811; C & S Bookshop, Main Gate Street, tel: 556609.

Complaints

The Maltese are very concerned to meet their visitors' standards and will do their utmost to put things right. If a formal complaint is the only feasible course of action, the National Tourist Organisation is the best place to start. Complaints to the police will normally be referred back to the Tourist Organisation unless they are clearly of a legal nature.

Further Reading
Fact to Fiction
Historical

The Crusades, by Antony Bridge, Granada.
Fortress Colony 1945–1964, by Joseph Pirotta. Studio Editions.
The Last Crusaders, by Roderick Cavaliero.

Malta, an Account and an Appreciation, by Sir Harry Luke. Corgi.

Malta Convoy, by Peter Shankland.

Malta: The Triumphant Years 1940–43, by George Hogan. Robert Hale.

Mediterranean: Portrait of a Sea, by Ernle Bradford. Penguin.

The Royal Navy at Malta, by Richard Ellis and Ben Watson.

The Shield and the Sword, by Ernle Bradford. Penguin.

The Siege of Malta, by Ernle Bradford. Penguin.

The Story of Malta, by Brian Blouet.

Autobiographical/Biographical

The Air Battle For Malta, by Lord Douglas-Hamilton MP. Mainstream, Edinburgh.

The Moon's a Balloon, by David Niven. Penguin.

Night Strike From Malta, by Kenneth Poolman. Jane's Publishing.

Specialist

Ancient Malta: A Study of its Antiquities, by Harrison Lewis.

Approaches to Medieval Malta, by Anthony T. Luttrell.

History of St Elmo, by Michael Ellul.

Malta, an Archaeological Guise, D. H. Trump.

Malta in British and French Caricatures 1798–1815, by Albert Ganado.

The Malta Railway, by B. L. Rigby. Oakwood Press.

St Paul's Catacombs, by Professor Sir Themistocoles Zammit.

Architectural

Fortress, by Quentin Hughes. Lund Humphries.

History of Maltese Architecture, by Leonard Mahoney.

Art

Antique Maltese Furniture, by Joe Galea Naudi.

Iconography of the Maltese Islands 1400–1900, by Mario Buhagiar.

International Dictionary of Artists who Painted Malta, by Nicholas de Piro.

Social

British Malta, by A. V. Laferla.

Malta Revisited, by Eric Gerada-Azzopardi.

Recipes from Malta, by Anne and Helen Caruana Galizia. Progress Press, Malta.

Saint and Fireworks, by Jeremy Boissevain. Holt, Rinehart & Winston, New York.

Studies in Maltese Folklore, by Joseph Cassar-Pullicino. Malta University Publications.

A Village in Malta, by Jeremy Boissevain. Holt, Rinehart & Winston, New York.

Photographic

Images of Malta, by Geoffrey Aquilina Ross. Miranda, Malta.

Malta 360°, by Geoffrey Aquilina Ross. Priuli & Verlucca, Italy.

Malta, an Island Republic, by Eric Gerada. Editions Delroisse.

Fiction

Earthly Powers, by Anthony Burgess. Hutchinson.

Foucault's Pendulum, by Umberto Eco. Secker & Warburg.

The Kappilan of Malta, by Nicholas Monsarrat. Cassell.

Other Insight Guides

Europe is comprehensively covered by the 400 books in Apa Publication's three series of guides to the world: *Insight Guides*, which provide a full cultural background and top quality photography; *Insight Compact Guides*, which combine portability with encyclopedic attention to detail; and Insight *Pocket Guides*, which highlight recommendations by a local host and include a full-size fold-out map.

A perfect companion, *Insight Pocket Guide: Malta* offers a series of tailor-made itineraries designed to help readers get the most out of Malta during a short stay.

Insight Compact Guide: Malta offers the reader an on-the-spot reference guide full of interesting facts and figures.

Insight Guide: Sicily explores Malta's nearest neighbour and closest historical companion.

Insight Guide: Italy offers the reader a fascinating insight into Italy's history, culture, cities and countryside. Informative text combines with captivating photography.

Index

A
B
C
D
E
F
G

I
J
a
b
c
d
e
f
g
h
i

k
l

The Insight Approach

The book you are holding is part of the world's largest range of guidebooks. Its purpose is to help you have the most valuable travel experience possible, and we try to achieve this by providing not only information about countries, regions and cities but also genuine insight into their history, culture, institutions and people.

Since the first Insight Guide – to Bali – was published in 1970, the series has been dedicated to the proposition that, with insight into a country's people and culture, visitors can both enhance their own experience and be accepted more easily by their hosts. Now, in a world where ethnic hostilities and nationalist conflicts are all too common, such attempts to increase understanding between peoples are more important than ever.

Insight Guides:
Essentials for understanding

Because a nation's past holds the key to its present, each Insight Guide kicks off with lively history chapters. These are followed by magazine-style essays on culture and daily life. This essential background information gives readers the necessary context for using the main Places section, with its comprehensive run-down on things worth seeing and doing. Finally, a listings section contains all the information you'll need on travel, hotels, restaurants and opening times.

As far as possible, we rely on local writers and specialists to ensure that the information is authoritative. The pictures, for which Insight Guides have become so celebrated, are just as important. Our photojournalistic approach aims not only to illustrate a destination but also to communicate visually and directly to readers life as it is lived by the locals.

Compact Guides
The "great little guides"

As invaluable as such background information is, it isn't always fun to carry an Insight Guide through a crowded souk or up a church tower. Could we, readers asked, distil the key reference material into a slim volume for on-the-spot use?

Our response was to design Compact Guides as an entirely new series, with original text carefully cross-referenced to detailed maps and more than 200 photographs. In essence, they're miniature encyclopedias, concise and comprehensive, displaying reliable and up-to-date information in an accessible way.

Pocket Guides:
A local host in book form

However wide-ranging the information in a book, human beings still value the personal touch. Our editors are often asked the same questions. Where do *you* go to eat? What do *you* think is the best beach? What would you recommend if I have only three days? We invited our local correspondents to act as "substitute hosts" by revealing their preferred walks and trips, listing the restaurants they go to and structuring a visit into a series of timed itineraries.

The result is our Pocket Guides, complete with full-size fold-out maps. These 100-plus titles help readers plan a trip precisely, particularly if their time is short.

Exploring with Insight:
A valuable travel experience

In conjunction with co-publishers all over the world, we print in up to 10 languages, from German to Chinese, from Danish to Russian. But our aim remains simple: to enhance your travel experience by combining our expertise in guidebook publishing with the on-the-spot knowledge of our correspondents.